Treating Families and Children in the Child Protective System

THE FAMILY THERAPY AND COUNSELING SERIES

Consulting Editor

Jon Carlson, Psy.D., Ed.D.

Ng	*Global Perspectives in Family Therapy: Development, Practice, Trends*
Erdman and Caffery	*Attachment and Family Systems: Conceptual, Empirical, and Therapeutic Relatedness*
Crenshaw	*Treating Families and Children in the Child Protective System*

Treating Families and Children in the Child Protective System

Strategies for Systemic Advocacy and Family Healing

Wes Crenshaw, Ph.D., ABPP

Brunner-Routledge
New York and Hove

Cover Art: Katie Vickers, Self Portrait (2002). The piece was begun as a collage of magazine page material and photographic images ripped by hand, giving it the fractured lines and dark edges. Extracted from this background is a self-portrait of the artist using Nevr-Dull wadding polish to lighten the areas by removing ink from the collage. Details were then added to the face and other areas of the piece with oil paint and china marker. The building and other background objects were then sketched with china marker and oil paints were used to add color to the piece. The entire process took 5 weeks, with an additional 6 to 8 weeks for refinement. When she created the piece, Ms. Vickers was a high school senior under the direction of Patricia Numchock, art instructor at Lawrence (Kansas) High School. At the time of publication Katie was studying on scholarship at Milwaukee Institute of Art and Design.

Published in 2004 by
Brunner-Routledge
29 West 35th Street
New York, NY 10001
www.brunner-routledge.com

Published in Great Britain by
Brunner-Routledge
27 Church Road
Hove, East Sussex
BN3 2FA
www.brunner-routledge.co.uk

Brunner-Routledge is an imprint of Taylor & Francis Group.
Printed in the United States of America on acid-free paper.
Design and typesetting: Jack Donner, BookType

10 9 8 7 6 5 4 3 2 1

Library of Congress Cataloging-in-Publication Data
Crenshaw, Wes.
Treating families and children in the child protective system / Wes Crenshaw.
p. cm. — (The family therapy and counseling series)
Includes bibliographical references and index.
ISBN 0-415-94870-3 (Hardback)
1. Child welfare. 2. Family counseling. 3. Family psychotherapy. 4. Abused children—Services for. 5. Family social work. I. Title. II. Series.
HV713.C72 2004
362.76—dc22 2003022219

Dedicated to my father Howard Crenshaw,
who lived his life humbly but fully in ministry to young people.

Contents

Series Editor's Foreword

> Families cannot find justice within their confines if the system around them is unjust, and a system cannot be just if it does more harm than good. This necessarily broadens what is meant to "do therapy" directing the therapist to address the complex hierarchy of needs of the child, family, and society and to integrate them into every aspect of this case.
>
> —Wes Crenshaw in *Treating Families and Children in the Child Protective System*

I met Wes Crenshaw at a Brief Therapy Conference in New York City. Somehow we ended up having dinner together with mutual friends. Wes talked about the multiple challenges and complexities of working with families around issues of justice. It seemed like the typical therapy bitch session that many clinicians take part in at professional meetings, but there was something different about Dr. Crenshaw. I couldn't put a finger on it and in time soon forgot. A few years later we reconnected at another professional conference and he was still talking (with great passion) about working with families who were in the child protection system. I am sure I made some comment about him being the energizer bunny of family justice. Most of us, you see, get burned out, overwhelmed, zapped, and angry beyond belief when we work in this area. Seeing children abused by both families of origin and then by the justice system leaves us feeling powerless and hurt.

Dr. Crenshaw, however, has a different explanatory model that allows for effective results with less damage to the therapist. As more and more of us are called upon to provide treatment to children in state custody and their families, the importance of this model emerges. When you complete your reading of *Treating Families and Children in the Child Protective System,* the strategies, concepts, attitudes needed to rethink how we are doing therapy, and the impact of the larger system will be yours. We all owe Dr. Crenshaw a big debt of professional gratitude.

—Jon Carlson, Psy.D., Ed.D., ABPP
Series Editor

Foreword

Treating Families and Children in the Child Protective System is an important book. It is on the cutting edge of a growing awareness by those in the counseling field that at the very core of all treatment are people with free will who are making choices based on moral and social values. Complementary to that fundamental principle is the notion that therapists are active agents in the helping process who conduct their work from their own belief systems. In the tradition of Viktor Frankl, the book treats clients, even those living under the most devastating conditions, with the dignity of their humanity, as people who enjoy the freedom to make choices that will lead them to better life solutions. It also holds therapists accountable for the values upon which they base their interventions. Both clients and therapists are viewed as something much more than objects and subjects of technical interventions. The essential dignity of our humanity is brought to front and center with the recognition of the critical role in counseling and therapy that our moral values play, even when viewed under the parlance of social justice.

What makes the book particularly interesting and challenging is that it addresses these concepts not in the comfortable and controlled context of the private psychotherapy office, but in the tough and complex context of children in state custody. It does so from the perspective of theory as well as that of practical application to intervention. It speaks to the treatment of these children in relation to their families, the courts, and social service agencies. *Treating Families and Children in the Child Protective System* links with clarity the principles of right and wrong to the methods therapists employ in their work with these neglected and abused children.

Where there has been the basest violation of these children in their families, there is severe damage to the essential relationships in the children's lives. Fundamental questions arise about the values and ideals that motivate change and repair, and about the responsibility of society to enable the human spirit to discern the "possible" and choose the "good" in the family.

Forgiveness and reparation receive special attention in this volume. The book will stimulate therapists with all belief systems to consider what moral and social values underlie their own ideas of healing.

My hope is that *Treating Families and Children in the Child Protective System* will inspire others to articulate and share with the rest of the professional community the values that form the foundation of their work so that the dialogue about moral and social values in our work will be more actively engaged in the fields of psychotherapy and social services.

—Harry J. Aponte
M.S.W., L.C.S.W.

Acknowledgments

We are each a culmination of the efforts of those who raised us personally and professionally throughout our lives, responsible to and for that social context. This book is, therefore, the work of many. I am most indebted to Cloé Madanes for her contribution to my thinking on families in general and family justice in particular. Her work has been an inspiration and challenge to me for 14 years. I would also like to thank Jeff Zeig and Jerome Price who have always encouraged me professionally, and Jon Carlson, George Zimmar, and the reviewers at Brunner-Routledge for believing in this project.

I cannot say enough about my colleagues at the Family Therapy Institute Midwest. Dave Barnum co-authored two chapters and co-developed the contrition model. Greg Tangari was integral in early publication of the model, and his film of Justin's case in chapter 5 remains its best illustration. Mary Lu Egidy has greatly informed my views on the strategic application of medication within a humanistic framework.

Just as important has been the experience and training afforded me by the young people and families I have served over the last 10 years, each of whom has affected my humanity and my practice. It has been a privilege to watch them grow up and to have them watch me.

I am also indebted to my wife Lucinda, who for reasons I cannot explain still puts up with me, and to my daughter Alyssa, who at 6 has proven a constant source of supervision and training experience.

Finally, I offer a special acknowledgment to Erica, who became my daughter at 15 and in doing so taught me a great deal more than I wanted to know, all of which has made me a better person, therapist, and father. Coming to us as she did, her contribution to my understanding of foster care has been immeasurable, particularly where spiritual pain is concerned. And for this poignancy, I am humble and appreciative.

In consideration of the offerings of these and many others over the years, I offer this book in the hopes that it will do a measure of justice to the part of me that is them.

Introduction

On first blush the notion of justice may seem an unlikely subject for family therapy intervention; the topic seems more in the domain of lawyers, judges, and philosophers than psychologists, social workers, and family therapists. Issues of boundaries, engagement, hierarchy, differentiation, triangulation, birth order, and circularity seem more appropriate targets for intervention than the abstract and often ambiguous realm of justice. Yet a significant failure in any of these domains may initiate a process of wrongfulness that ultimately leads to what we have come to call *family injustice.* For example, marriage ceremonies are designed to transfer the loyalties from the family of origin to the new spouse. Sometimes the family does not surrender that loyalty, violating the boundaries and hierarchy across generations, leading to a sense of injustice in the new couple and within the individual that can cause one spouse or the other to feel torn between past and future loyalties (Madanes, 2000). In blended families, a stepparent may reject or compete with a stepchild or vice versa, creating another sort of injustice with serious ramifications for family functioning. Another example involves implicit contracts in the family regarding who takes care of whom. Injustices occur when, for example, a child is expected to take on adult roles to the detriment of his or her own childhood. It is not difficult to generate a hundred more examples, varying from the simple and elegant to the most profound and tragic.

None of this is lost on our children. It is nearly universal among parents that we will eventually face our child's first attempt at the invocation of justice when they protest "Daddy, that's not fair!" My youngest daughter began this strategy shortly after her third birthday. Far from an annoyance, this should be seen as the beginning of the child's struggle with right and wrong, and her attempt to hold us to the same standard. In fact, I see families as being in a constant struggle to establish justice at home, and then to establish it in the world around them. And even if the understanding of right and wrong is not pre-programmed into us as a universal code, the need to understand and distinguish one from the other is. Thus, the thoughtful family therapist, always striving to understand complex systems of human interplay, cannot avoid dealing with themes of justice and injustice, even as they often try to.

When the wrongfulness of a family reaches a certain threshold, it may evoke response from a powerful external system of child protection, and with it the potential for either the restoration of justice or its further degradation. More often than not, the pendulum swing between an auspicious and tragic outcome is uncomfortably arbitrary and tied to contingencies far from the theory and rubric of that system. These are the ultimate cases of family injustice in which therapeutic intervention is virtually incomparable to anything else the therapist will encounter in common practice, and bringing the therapist face to face with myriad problems that do not fit neatly into traditional family psychology. Although much of this book is applicable to families facing less severe circumstances, it primarily addresses the unique treatment needs of children in state custody and their families. One requires only a few iterations of these cases, typically involving a multigenerational abusive or neglectful family, an inadequate and underfunded child protective system (CPS), the dubious involvement of courts and attorneys, and a flawed placement and reunification protocol to realize the inadequacy of traditional family therapy and theory. The approach described herein is intended to help therapists, officers of the court, and social service providers join together to respond efficiently and effectively in these cases to repair and reconcile even extreme family injustice. Not incidentally, an understanding of these cases also points the therapist toward interventions that work with less severe cases or those that have not been inducted into the social service system.

A critical theme runs throughout the theory and case studies in this text: Intervention at both the familial and larger-system levels is vital to success in these cases. Families cannot find justice within their confines if the system around them is unjust, and the system cannot be just if it does more harm than good. This necessarily broadens what it means to "do therapy," directing the therapist to address the complex hierarchy of needs of the child, family, and society and to integrate them into every aspect of the case. For September, a girl lost in the child protective system, therapy will begin in the traditional manner, building a relationship and mentoring her through a terrible time in her life. But it will quickly extend to facilitating her disclosure of sexual abuse and then, as a result of that disclosure, defending her against an encroaching and imprudent system. At one point it will involve the fight simply to keep her alive, which will in turn require reconciliation of her relationship with her offender. It will involve supporting her through an unjust internment in a detention home. And when she is at last free to make her own choices, it will require an ultimate test of the therapeutic relationship as her own volition takes her close to disaster and forces an emotional confrontation. In the end it will mean watching her release from custody at age 18, homeless and without any means of support and following her transition to young adulthood and final reconciliation of her abuse history. As this case will illustrate, ours is a comprehensive approach, designed to consistently intervene at every level of the client's experience over the course of her contact with the system. Anything less inclusive is ineffective at best. At worst it is quite tragic.

In addition to these overarching goals, the book is intended to:

- Teach the strategies, concepts, attitudes and, most important, the will to rethink what we are doing in therapy and in the larger system.
- Encourage flexibility, creativity, and conscientiousness among therapists and caseworkers in recognizing and confronting injustice in the family and larger system.
- Illustrate the feel of this approach, not only to teach it, but also to foster a sense of compassion and empathy for children and families struggling with the system.
- Identify and conceptualize the various components of the child protective, court, and mental health system to suggest the common language and conceptualization necessary for a seamless integration of services.

A good portion of this book is case study material collected in four different jurisdictions across the country, and these cases are used to illustrate the chapters on theory and technique that comprise the rest. Because issues of validity and generalizability are always at play in case study methodology, it is important to note that none of the cases were selected for their unusual content but rather for their relative ubiquity. Every component in September's case has appeared many times over in other cases, though rarely all within the same case. Moreover, her case and the others herein illustrate quite dramatically the obstacles we face and how we address them in dealing with family injustice. Each is a real story replete with the techniques, emotion, and humanity of both client and therapist in what is typically a very painful and complex therapy. Each case has been carefully disguised, though never to the detriment of content and process accuracy. Where I felt that disguise was thin in any way, specific publication releases were obtained. Likewise, all dialog was taken from transcripts and videotapes specifically released for education and training.[1]

Practicing this way will not guarantee an endless string of therapeutic victories, but our students have found that they are more confident than their peers when approaching these difficult cases, and typically they are more effective in helping children move beyond the child protective system. It is my hope that the approach discussed in this book will contribute to the restoration of justice both within client families and in the systems that are ultimately charged with serving them.

We owe these children no less.

NOTE

1. Methods of disguise and release were based on principal 4.07 of the 2003 revision of the APA Guidelines on Privacy and Confidentiality (American Psychological Association, 2003). Obtained releases in no way extend to other professionals who might believe they recognize a given case. They remain prohibited from disclosure by statue and/or ethical guidelines of their professional disciplines.

CHAPTER 1

Turning Points

> . . . [T]he perception of meaning, as I see it, more specifically boils down to becoming aware of a possibility against the background of reality or, to express it in plain words, to becoming aware of *what can be done* about a given situation.
>
> —Viktor Frankl, *Man's Search for Meaning* (1990)

September was in an awful state once again. I had seen her now for over a year, and the 15-year-old had never looked worse. She was just a week out of a 9-month stay at a distant psychiatric facility. I had pulled every string in the book to arrange a placement with Connie Dixon, a trusted therapeutic foster parent after child protective services (CPS)[1] couldn't or wouldn't pursue her release. Now, on a cold January evening, September sat in my office, plumped up on lithium, angry and sullen and ready to give up again.

I sat there stunned at her condition and thinking back to our first session over a year ago, so remarkable that I'd written it up on the speculation that it might someday be useful in training. At the time, her family was referred for reintegration and reunification after September had called CPS alleging that her father had hit her. The charge was confirmed, and CPS removed her that evening to the girls' shelter. I'd met the week before with her father, Tommy, and stepmother, Barbara, and on that evening I was getting to know September. Overburdened with difficult cases at the time, I had actually taken the referral because it appeared a simple and quick case—something I could feel successful at. In such cases, appearances are often deceiving.

The 14-year-old was nearly bubbling over in the waiting room that evening, not at all like the rebellious punk described by the referring CPS worker, Hanna Winthrow. She was pretty, with short jet-black hair and a gentle face. There was a light in her eyes that suggested a sense of depth and intellect. That could be good if you had a wonderful life to think about, and a disaster if you didn't. Bright and thoughtful kids are more efficient at figuring out how to destroy themselves, they face a deeper than average understanding of life's pain.

"Hi." She smiled.

"Your name is *September*?" My tone underscored the oddness of the name.

"Yeah . . . what about it?" she said sharply, catching the emphasis in my voice.

"Don't know," I smiled. "I've just never actually met anybody named September. I suppose you were born in September, huh?"

"Nope. May."

"Then why . . ."

"Ask my mom," she snapped. "She was probably drunk at the time."

"Hey, it's a good name," I said trying to recover quickly. "I like it."

"Whatever," she scoffed.

We entered my office, she picked out a chair, and we continued. She was clever and interesting, with a sort of wildness about her, born not of rebellion but of survival. Still, her success in foster care would depend on her setting aside the wildness and accepting the influence of authority long enough to get some therapy done. I would try to get her attention.

"I hear from Hanna that you've got all sorts of stories about your life."

"Yep, and if you're gonna see my family you need to know that I hate my stepmom . . . and I'm not too thrilled with mom either." September was a take-charge kid.

"Ya know, you're lucky to be able to see me," I said matching the bombastic tone she'd set for the interview.

Her eyes widened. "Oh yeah, and why's that?"

"I'm the director of this institute. I don't take many clients, and those I do I help a great deal. I only take people who want to be here. I hope you'll decide to be one of them."

She seemed quite taken. "You mean you're not a therapist . . . you're like above them?"

"Well, sort of," I said, hoping this would make her feel important.

"Wow, I must be really screwed up," she said with a surprising tinge of sadness. I quickly changed course.

"No, no, no," I said much more gently. "I *chose* your case. Hanna talked about it with me, and I thought we might do good work together. I thought you were an interesting young lady and that I could help you get things straightened out with your family. It has nothing to do with you being crazier than anyone else. However, if I'm gonna give you my time and energy—and I will give that to you if you want it—then I expect something in return."

"Okay, let me hear the deal," she said, taking charge once again.

"You will not run under any circumstances. You will follow the rules in your foster home. If there are problems, you and the foster family will bring those problems here and we'll work them out. I know Hanna personally, and I promise you that if you take off she'll snap you back so hard you won't know what hit you. And I'll help her."

She nodded.

"You'll not be running the streets . . ." I continued.

"Wait a minute—what's wrong with that? My brother used to do it. . . ."

"And what happened to him?" I bluffed, because I didn't know her brother.

She flashed a sheepish grin. "He's locked up."

"Gotcha," I laughed with her. "You do what I say, okay?"

"Okay, what else?" She was taking the pleasure that all teens feel in spite of themselves, when a competent adult takes charge of their lives, leaving them free not to.

"You will never lie to me in here. In return I will not tell anyone anything you say unless you tell me that someone is being abused or hurt or you're gonna hurt yourself."

"God, anything else?" she grinned, feigning overload by my list of demands.

"Yes . . . you need to trust me."

She became quite serious. "Now that'll be harder. After everything that's happened to me I don't exactly trust people, you know?"

"Yeah, I know. But that one *you'll* have to work on."

"I'll try," she said dutifully. "You really won't tell stuff I say to you? You won't tell anyone?"

"Except for those things I mentioned. No, I won't tell."

September sat silently for a moment, contemplating some unspoken decision. "You need to understand something. . . . There'll be things I can never tell you. If I did, it would get a lot of people in trouble."

"Well, we'll have to deal with that on another day," I said, restraining her first session disclosures, but at the same time encouraging them paradoxically.

"No," she replied quietly. "You don't understand. We'll *never* be able to deal with it."

The admission of things unsaid was an almost hypnotic command for me to continue to pursue her secrets, without any commitment to reveal them. She would be good at playing the mind games of disclosure. This, combined with her fear of getting someone in trouble, hinted at the familiar pall of silence maintained by an incestuous family.

"You'll be surprised what can be dealt with here, and how many ways there are to deal with things. By the way, what's this business of you talking about killing people all the time?" I had seen this in the referral notes from Hanna and found it rather disturbing.

"Oh, I wanted to kill my mom back when I was 12," she said in a matter-of-fact tone. "She was drunk all the time, she let me get sexually abused by her boyfriend, she was a complete bitch and I hated her. I'd have done it too." The coldness in her voice suggested that she was telling the truth.

"What happened when you were 12?"

"One day she says, 'Honey we need to go to a meeting,' and she takes me to the hospital. These two guys come in the waiting room and start to take me away. I had no idea what was going on, so you know I'm like hysterical and then. . . ." September's voice began to break, "they put me in handcuffs and drug me out of the room. I was screaming and crying . . . god." She bowed her head and fought hard to choke back tears. After a few moments and some effort, she pulled herself together. "I'm just so full of anger. It's like I'm two different people. On the outside you see this little innocent sweet girl. I don't drink or use drugs. I'm giggling and happy. But on the inside, I'm different. I could kill her . . . or my stepmom. Neither one cares about me at all."

"I understand," I said.

"No, you don't," she said, almost pleading with me. "You think I'm just kidding. I mean I'm capable of taking a shotgun and blowing her fucking head off."

I wasn't sure which woman she was talking about, but it didn't matter. I could imagine her going on a spree. "I know you're not kidding," I said emphatically. "I understand that completely and I'm taking you dead serious. But, you gotta know that if you pull it off you'd go to jail as an adult. Maybe for the rest of your life."

"No, it would be self-defense," she said. "I'd put a knife in her hand and say she came at me."

"For godsakes, September," I said with a touch of irritation to cover my concern. "You're not gonna pull that kinda shit off. It won't work, and you need to let it go. You'll throw away your life just to get back at someone who isn't worth the fight. Why would you want to do that?"

"It won't matter," she said sadly. "I'll be dead before I'm 16 anyhow."

"What the hell is that supposed to mean?" I asked, now worrying about her potential for suicide as well as homicide.

"The guy who molested me . . . he's up for parole. He's told everybody he's gonna find me and kill me."

"They all say that. They're all whacked out."

"He'll do it," she said with chilling certainty.

"Hm," I said gently so as to break the escalation. "Now I see why you're so angry and violent inside."

Her body visibly relaxed as if she now felt understood and a small part of a big load had been lifted. "Maybe I should just go and kill them and then put the gun to my head and pull the trigger." This child's pain was beyond my reckoning.

"And then the world would never know you," I said softly. "And that would be quite a loss."

"For who? I mean, who the hell would care?" It was a desperate plea to be argued with, to be reassured she was wrong. "Who *would* really care . . . you? Yeah, I'm sure." Her voice was sarcastic as she asked and answered her own questions before I could respond.

It was a difficult moment so early in our therapy, and I decided to be indirect.

"Hey, they don't pay me to like you . . . just to sit here." I paused only a moment to get her attention before finishing the part about choosing to like her, but she was too quick for me.

She raised her eyes and gazed at me with a look so sad that I will never forget it. "So that means you don't like me either?" There was no ego strength left in this poor girl. I had hurt her easily.

"My god, no," I said quickly and apologetically. "September, what I'm telling you is that I don't *have* to care about you to do my job. I care because I want to. I like you. I think you're a neat kid. That's why I'm taking your case." I really meant it.

She smiled a bit as she turned up her nose. "A neat kid? Neat?!"

"Sorry," I smirked. "How about 'really cool'?"

She grinned and nodded. "A little better."

"You can trust me when I say that this world would be worse off without you. Give me a chance, and I'll prove it to you." The genuineness and authority in my voice overrode the superficiality of the platitude.

"Have you ever read the book *The Giver?*" she asked.

"No, what's it about?"

"We're reading it in school. This old man is able to touch other people on the back and take away their thoughts and fears and ideas and stuff. They just go to him and he does it."[2]

"Really?" It was a very hopeful metaphor that September was sharing with her new therapist—the idea that someone could go to someone and get help for terrible problems. "I bet you'd very much like to meet that person, huh?"

"Yeah, I would."

"And I bet I know why."

"Oh yeah? Why?" she challenged.

"Because you'd like to have all the thoughts and feelings, about everything that has ever been done to you taken away."

"Yeah . . . that's right," she said with surprise. It was sucker bet, knowing her background, but my "mind-reading" seemed to touch her. "Sometimes I feel like all I am is skin and anger."

"Well, you know, that's sorta what we do here," I said. "You talk about the pain and the anger and I help you to make it go away—or at least make it smaller."

She nodded slowly as a few seconds passed. "Do you know why you're on this earth?"

Unprepared for this level of profundity, I tried to dodge. "September, you have to ask the philosophical questions early in the hour. That's another rule I forgot to tell you about."

"No, really," she insisted, glancing down. "I mean, I know we're supposed to be God's servants and everything, but do you know why *you're* here." She was not about to let up until I had answered, for in her question to me there was the question of her own existence. Was there any purpose in her life, anything worth living for? Could she allow herself to have hope? I could not fail this test. Everything seemed to rest on it.

I dug deeply for a fitting answer, and found in myself a therapeutic story that might suffice. It was reminiscent of Erickson's "my friend John" induction and it would fascinate the girl for years to come.

"I knew a girl once. She was a client of mine and she had been hurt just like you, sexually abused, physically abused, it was terrible. She was just your age in fact."

September listened intently.

"She told me that all of us are somehow connected . . . that as we go through our lives we meet the people that we really need and they help us, and we help them. And in doing so, we survive and grow and change because of those relationships."

"Really?" she said in a neutral tone.

"So maybe, for right now and right here, the reason I'm in this world is to help you. Do you suppose it could be?"

"To help me?" she said skeptically. "How? Like what? My guardian angel?" Her tone was again neither rejecting nor accepting of the premise.

"Well . . ." I paused, trying to get the cosmology just right, "I don't know myself so much about that, but actually that's what she used to call them . . . the people that helped her."

"Hmph," she offered thoughtfully.

"You know, that girl wrote a poem about it," I said rummaging around in my desk. "You wanna see it?"

"Sure," she said reaching for the typed copy I had pulled from the drawer. September read "Grounded Angel" silently as I looked on, trying to gauge her reaction.

> The grounded angel
> banned from the stars.
> Goes through the labyrinth of life.
> Finding only dead ends
> and deadbeats.
> No one to guide her.
> Confused and alone.

The lonesome angel wanders
through hate and turmoil.
Searching.
Searching for the stars,
the end of her quest.

Will the wandering angel find her dream?
Or will society take her dream, and wings,
so that she may never find the stars
and fly to her happiness?

"Wow." She was now genuinely moved. "You know, I write poems too."

"Really?" I had expected as much. It was one of those moments when technique, theory, humanity, and luck all come together to form the perfect intervention.

"Yeah, and stories. I've always wanted to write a book about my life . . . but all I can remember are the parts where my dad beat the hell out of me when I was three because I wouldn't get potty-trained, and when he threw me across the room. I don't remember anything that happened in between. I wouldn't want anyone else to read it . . . just me."

"I'd be happy to help you with that," I said with full awareness of the implicit dual meaning.

"Would you really?" she said,

"Well sure . . . of course. I'm always ready to help a young author . . . even if she's just writing for herself."

"I'll bring some stuff I wrote to our next session."

"I'll look forward to that. Does that mean you'll promise not to kill anyone or yourself til you give me a crack at this thing with your family?"

"Yeah . . . sure," she said, smiling. "Why not."

"And you'll try and trust me a little bit?"

She glanced at the floor and then raised her eyes to meet mine. "Obviously, I already do."

"Then I promise to do my best to live up to that."

I could not have imagined as September left the clinic that evening what it would take to keep that promise.

Sexual abuse in September's family was more than an educated guess. It was likely by process of elimination alone. I already knew that her father had been physically abusive to her and had a history of substance abuse. She easily admitted these facts, as had her father. She'd also admitted molestation by a man she'd later put in prison. She'd expressed the wish to kill her mother and stepmother and shared that she had been hospitalized by her drunken mother who had ultimately abandoned her to her father. With so much tragedy out in the open, there were precious few things this beleaguered girl could have left *never* to tell.

A lifetime had passed for September in the year since that session. In the first 90 days we had engaged in a weekly test of wills as she slowly disclosed that her father had molested her during a year in which Barbara was off finding herself, leaving September in charge of the house and her brothers, Billy and Bobby. Yet before she had been willing to acknowledge him as her offender, she'd made me promise to write a letter recommending "the person who did something" would get treatment rather than prison. I had agreed, but only if I found that person forthcoming and amenable, which I had. In fact, once confronted with her disclosure, Tommy had confessed to everything, first to me and later to the police. He had been so forthcoming that no one had even had to interview the girl. But despite this solid beginning the case had deteriorated rapidly. September had been mistakenly placed in a "therapeutic" group home that turned out not to be therapeutic at all. The 23-year-old foster mother encouraged her to disclose the abuse to me and pledged to help her through the therapy to address it. However, the minute September did disclose, the young woman became so symptomatic from her own history of incest that her husband made his wife withdraw from the sessions. Yet another adult had abandoned September, this time at the very moment she had renounced her father.

In response, she ran away from the group home, and called me to have her picked up by the police, ending the night back in the girls' shelter. The chaos of this poorly managed facility, including two resident uprisings, did little for her disposition. Three weeks into the placement, her mother, Mattie, made a rare visit on the day before September's 15th birthday, but the shelter wouldn't allow contact as she wasn't on the pass list. No one had expected Mattie to show up, and Hanna could not be reached by phone over the weekend to give authorization. As angry as she was with her mother, September would have preferred Mattie's birthday visit to none at all. Instead, she found herself like so many foster kids on special days of their lives—totally alone, except for those who do not matter.

The following Monday evening, dejected, lonely, and without hope of placement, September celebrated her 15th birthday with her therapist over a lukewarm pizza in a small undecorated corner office. There was no one else to invite. Neither of us was very hungry, and the hour went slowly. As she got up to leave, the girl did something very unusual for her—she came close to my chair, bent down, and gave me a little hug.

"Thanks," was all she said.

That night she stowed a bottle of bleach under her bed with the intention of drinking it after lights-out. Luckily, a fortuitous room search and debriefing exposed her plan. She was screened and admitted to the psychiatric unit of the local hospital early the next morning, before I even knew what had happened. She remained there for several weeks, and among other things was subjected to several incidents of sexual touching by a young man who had convinced the staff that he was too schizophrenic to follow rules of sexual conduct. When September called me in rageful tears, I directed her to file a complaint with the director of patient services, who was the designated patient advocate. She followed my suggestion. In fact, she filed 224 such complaints, exhausting the ward's supply of grievance forms. She actually had *stuffed* the complaint box with these forms, yet none of her complaints were addressed by the hospital staff. Instead, Hanna and the charge nurse conference called *me* the following day, livid that the girl was "acting out" in this manner. I asked if the director of patient services had discussed the sexual abuse with September.

"You don't understand!" the charge nurse said angrily. "He's just so psychotic. You can't expect anything from him!"

"The director?" I asked.

"No!" she snapped. "The boy . . . the patient."

"So apparently the only place a child can be legally sexually abused is while in custody of the state," I offered.

"That's not fair!" Hanna stammered.

"That's my point," I said.

The hospital saw things differently, of course. They transferred September a few weeks later to a psychiatric group home. Shortly thereafter, a much less emotional social worker from that facility called to make contact with me. In the interim I attempted to work with Hanna to find a foster placement for the girl, but she told me that no one would want September. It was clear that our professional relationship had become strained at best and equally obvious that Hanna simply didn't like September. Her reference would be needed for any foster home to take the girl, and I knew Hanna would do little to place her, even after the group home insisted September was ready for discharge.

In the meantime, September had much weightier matters to attend to—most notably the restoration of her family—which seemed to have been lost somewhere along the way. Late that summer she sent me a poem she had written during the week following her disclosure. She titled it "Life of Gold." Though rough, it evidenced the raw pain of a child nearly broken from the confusion between her love for and repulsion with her offender.

Once my life was the color gold
Now that color's begun to mold
There's a few spots of gray and a few spots of blue
Is it because of me, or because of you?

The color gets dimmer, it's almost black
Oh, how I need you dad, I need you back
Why won't you come and set me free?
The color's darker, don't you see?
My life of gold is just a dot.
Should I love you, or love you not?
My gold is gone, the black is coming,

I hear the angels above me humming.
Father, father, please come soon
I need you here before full moon.
How darker everything has become
I need more gold. Won't you give me some?

The day drags on, I feel so sad.
Dad you're making me so very mad.
I feel so small like I'm falling apart.
I don't believe that you have a heart

You said when I need you
You'd always be there
Right now I greatly need you
But you're nowhere near

As I read her commentary, I felt as I always do working with a child and family whose natural emergence has been interrupted by abuse, neglect, or sexual violation—quite small and inconsequential. Out of my own sheer helplessness in this case and hundreds like it, I came to see the need for a radical shift in my own thinking and approach. These young people were not simply abused by acts of sexual and physical assault. There was something more fundamental at play. Being deprived of physical, emotional, sexual, and spiritual needs violated her most basic human rights, creating a grave injustice in September's life. She could not simply go on, not unless and until those transgressions were set right. Moreover, the injustice in her family had now brought into play a much larger system, ostensibly designed to protect and defend her, that had not taken any better care of her than had her parents. And in this regard, her case was more the rule than the exception.

September and I did not know it yet, but in that first session we had each reached a turning point that would change our lives. For me, her case was about to become a critical step in the formation of this therapeutic approach. For her, our time together would begin the emergence of her identity from the darkest corners of family injustice.

NOTES

1. I use the term "child protective services" or "CPS" in this text as a generic term inclusive of social service agencies that remove children and place them in foster care. In many communities this is a specific designation for the department that investigates child abuse. However, to use the actual department names would decrease anonymity of both the workers and the families.
2. When I did read this exceptional book (Lowry, 1993), I found that September's account was not at all an accurate remembrance. In fact, the Giver places *into* the memory of his protégée all the painful (and joyful) memories of hundreds of generations. It was both poignant and diagnostic that September misremembered the story in this way.

CHAPTER 2

Justice Themes in Family Therapy

> **justice \Jus' tice\, n.** 1. Conformity to the principles of righteousness and rectitude in all things; strict performance of moral obligations; practical conformity to human or divine law; integrity in the dealings of men with each other; rectitude; equity; uprightness. 2. Conformity to truth and reality in expressing opinions and in conduct; fair representation of facts respecting merit or demerit; honesty; fidelity; impartiality. 3. The rendering to everyone his due or right; just treatment; requital of desert; merited reward or punishment; that which is due to one's conduct or motives. 4. Agreeableness to right; equity; justness; as, the justice of a claim.
>
> —*Random House Webster's Unabridged Dictionary* (1998)

EARLY THINKING IN FAMILY INJUSTICE

Ivan Boszormenyi-Nagy was one of the first theorists to introduce essential tenets of morality into coherent goals and techniques of family therapy. "According to Nagy, neither the pleasure-pain principle, nor transactional expediency is a sufficient guide to human behavior. Instead he believes that family members have to base their relationships on trust and loyalty, and that they must balance the ledger of entitlement and indebtedness" (Nichols & Schwartz, 1998, p. 52). Boszormenyi-Nagy suggests that healthy families practice the ethical treatment of all members, with mutual consideration and balancing of each member's welfare and interests, and he posits the emergence of symptoms as a response to the breakdown of caring and accountability in the family. It is at this very point that a problem of family injustice begins to crystallize. To avoid confusion with legal jargon, one might use terms other than "justice" and "injustice" to describe this dynamic. Boszormenyi-Nagy and Spark (1984) proposed "reciprocity imbalance" as one alternative.

However, they quickly dismissed it (as I have done), noting that "we purposely chose the word justice because we feel that it connotes human commitment and value in all their rich motivating power and meaning" (p. 55).

We gain much from this early work, particularly the authors' astute observations about the importance of the biological family even to the abused child and the need for intervention to restore justice to the child's life (Boszormenyi-Nagy & Spark, 1984, p. 275). However, the approach itself lacks the powerful techniques necessary to directly impact families in which severe injustice forms the core of family dysfunction well in excess of "reciprocity imbalance." Elegant phraseology such as "unresolved, negative loyalty attachments," "denied debt obligation," and "hopeless unavailability" seem quaint and inadequate in describing the acts of physical assault and sexual exploitation inherent in these cases. These injustices require not only a clear sense of right and wrong but techniques for restoring that sense to client families.

This point is underscored in Boszormenyi-Nagy's scholarly case study of physical abuse in a chapter replete with background data and interpretive statements about the family dynamics, but short on the technology of change. The authors describe the following high points over a year of office-based therapy with a battering mother and an additional year of telephone sessions.

- Therapy between the battering mother and her own mother, in which the former expressed feelings of loneliness as a child. This resulted in the grandmother's refusal to return to therapy even though the battered child was now placed with her.
- Couples therapy in which the mother and father were encouraged to be more open about their needs. Central to this was the husband's admission that he wanted no more children and resented the wife's current pregnancy. The pair agreed to a tubal ligation after she delivered their fifth child.
- A suggestion that the battering mother make more contact with her own mother and father—which she did, even though she continued to blame the grandmother (falsely, by report of the authors) for her children's misconduct.
- More sharing of feelings between the couple about their experiences of overburdening one another, resulting in the wife's reneging on the agreement to have her tubes tied.
- Sessions with the battered child that helped her share her feelings in appropriate ways (through expressive art) and redirection of the mother to allow her to do so.
- Anger and temperament management of an unknown style for the battering mother, which appears to have involved her assertive expression of feelings.
- A sixth pregnancy resulting in the father's subsequent abandonment of the family and therapy, despite the therapist's repeated requests that he continue.
- The mother's suicidal overture and emergency session with her parents. This included the disclosure (albeit late in the game) of the grandmother's tubal

ligation and substantial praise for her daughter's housekeeping. All agreed that the father's abandonment of the family "was not the end of the world."
- The mother going on public assistance and receiving items of daily necessity from her siblings and a subsequent reconciliation with same.
- Delivery of a sixth child, a tubal ligation, consideration of a divorce, followed by the father's brief foray into reconciliation, which apparently failed (Boszormenyi-Nagy & Sparks, 1984).

In short, though the authors' conceptualizations are presented in great depth, it is not clear exactly what sorts of face-to-face interventions were conducted with this family, nor even if the case was a success or a failure. To further confound matters, it appears that the child in question was never returned home though the other outplaced children, who were not abused, were reunified with their mother. In summarizing the case, the authors lament this ambiguity of outcome:

> It may appear as if at the conclusion of the treatment the family was worse off because the parents separated. However, one major improvement was that the children no longer were used as an arena to rebalance the parents' unfair exploitation.... The greatest change developed between Mrs. C and her family of origin. She changed from a critical, hurt, angry, distrusting individual into a much more active, reaching-out, loving person (p. 300).

Apparently she also stopped hitting the child—though this seems a bit of an afterthought.

A second shortcoming of the approach is Boszormenyi-Nagy's failure to propose intervention at the larger-system level, leaving us without a comprehensive or integrated treatment "package." The authors actually note this as one area of future attention, stating that the current child protective system (CPS) is "an important example of a major social activity in which reciprocity of fairness is inadequately considered" (p. 383).

Critique on these points in no way diminishes the importance of Boszormenyi-Nagy in the conceptualization of family injustice. However, the aforementioned schism between theory and practice has left it largely in the hands of scholars and away from practical use where it is needed most. The present text represents a pragmatic extension of this work from the trenches of family injustice.

SYSTEMS AND THE THERAPIST AS ADVOCATE

In their book *Working with Families of the Poor*, Minuchin, Colapinto, and Minuchin (1998) discuss therapy with disenfranchised families, including those caught up in CPS, emphasizing intervention both with the family and within the larger system to make it friendlier to them. They begin with a family systems perspective and expand it to the social service system, courts, and other agencies. They give considerable emphasis to what they term the *agency family,* defined as "those controlled by the courts, welfare system, and protective services," suggesting the system often focuses more on their most pathological characteristics and little on their strengths. Admitting that severe pathology is apparent in some families, the authors suggest that far too many are unfairly maligned. "One recurrent and disturbing fact about such families is that they do not write their own stories. Once they enter the institutional network and a case history is opened, society does the editing" (p. 23).

They also posit two levels of violence in such families: the obvious domestic kind that comes from within the family, and that which is externally imposed by larger-system interventions gone awry. This second type of violence comes from "intrusion, and from the absolute power of society in exerting control.... The rhetoric, and sometimes the reality, is that of protection for the weak, but the intrusion into the family is often disrespectful, damaging ties and dismembering established structures without recognizing that the procedures do violence to the family" (p. 24). The authors note that, when the system intervenes in a family, the system becomes the most powerful external influence in it, meaning that all interventions must be carefully devised to assist the family to help themselves.

In attempting to intervene in the interaction between family and larger system, Minuchin and colleagues have found many of the same obstacles that we have encountered in our work: the nature of the system itself, the training of the professionals, and the family-phobic (my term) attitude of society toward the populations being served. In response, Minuchin and colleagues focus most of their intervention on the "the details of interaction between professional workers and family members. That interaction is the bottom line of delivery, more fundamental in efforts to change the system than laws, social policies, or available money" (p. 30). Yet they find that even this micro, and ostensibly more manageable, level of intervention is fraught with obstacles, most notably the lack of experience and training on the part of professional staff in how to intervene from such a perspective. In response, they offer a primer on structural therapy conceptualization and intervention to include:

- Understanding families as being composed of individuals, patterns, rules, and boundaries.
- Recognizing the importance of transitions in family development and the way in which system intervention can actually serve to create positive or negative transitions, depending on the skill of the intervention.
- Developing a stance of optimism and hope, and an openness to the possibility of change in families (rather than a pessimistic and deterministic stance).

- Gathering information by listening, joining, and observing the family's interactions.
- Reframing family assumptions, challenging negatives, and exploring other perspectives.
- Examining alternative patterns of interaction and helping the clients to integrate them into their natural patterns.
- Helping clients to manage conflict between members in nonviolent or demeaning (we would say unjust) ways.
- Helping families at the juncture of the larger system to navigate its strange ways and interact with its more difficult factors. (pp. 33–63)

The authors close with a plea to work from the ground up to overcome a sense of "national impatience" with the poor and socially downcast and to "reverse the inertia and the punitive attitudes that maintain ineffective and destructive systems of intervention in the lives of poor families, and that complicate the already difficult task of professional workers who are trying to help" (p. 240).

I could not agree more. In fact, it was Salvador Minuchin who first got me interested in such cases, by practicing and writing about families who were, by the reckoning of other therapists and society at large, of little consequence. The impact of that work was for me what I hope this text will be for the reader—an inspiration for a change of heart and mind that encourages us to fight the good fight for these families and children in the therapy room, the courtroom, the living room, and anywhere else that we encounter family or social injustice. Yet despite the importance of this work, Wexler (1995) claims that the response among CPS and its subordinates has been discouraging. He writes, "when Salvador Minuchin, probably the nation's foremost expert on therapy with families, wrote to three hundred New York City agencies offering to train their staffs at no charge, he did not receive a single reply. He did a little better writing to foster-care agencies: Four out of thirty accepted his offer" (p. 260). Disappointing as this is, it is an all too familiar problem to those of us who have attempted similar, more limited interventions.

SOCIAL ACTION AND STRATEGIC HUMANISM

In 1993 a conference was held at the National Institutes of Mental Health (NIMH) on the integration of strategic and structural therapies, which was co-led by Jay Haley, Cloé Madanes,[1] and Salvador Minuchin. Before the 800 in attendance, Madanes set forth a list of ways in which the two approaches were kindred; in doing so, she asserted tenets of humanistic therapy, the applicability of which goes well beyond either theory. She argued that family therapists must take a just and active stand to:

- Advocate for children, families, and those living in poverty.
- End violence and abuse in families, institutions, and CPS.
- Oppose blaming and mistrust of families by therapists or CPS.
- Avoid therapist neutrality, advocating for what is right and opposing what is wrong.
- Accept responsibility for the process of directive therapy, and expect responsibility from our client families.
- Avoid, to the extent possible, the institutionalization of our clients.
- Deemphasize traditional diagnosis in favor of benevolent, change-oriented conceptualizations.
- Oppose constructivism in favor of the pursuit of an objective reality apart from perception.
- Guard against the misuse of circularity, recognizing that not every family member contributes equally to every problem.
- Advocate for a consistent quality of and access to treatment for all clients, regardless of economic status.
- Engender optimism and hopefulness in families and the larger system.
- Adhere tenaciously to a belief in the basic competence of people.
- Emphasize client-focused interventions with no generic technique generalizing to all clients and every situation.
- Advocate for a consistent quality of and access to treatment, regardless of socioeconomic status.

Later that same year, Price and Keim (1993) published a conceptualization of *strategic humanism* as "the practice of directive therapy within a certain framework of ethics, self discipline, and practice standards . . . which depicts the spirit as well as the technique of the model" (p. 1A), including such tenets as:

- A belief in the resilience of the human spirit and the ability of human beings to solve problems.
- The disrespectful nature of communication to clients that they are hopeless victims of fate, predetermination, or any other power, which takes away human intention and responsibility.
- An optimistic view of client abilities, knowledge, and competencies.
- A belief in the teaching power of experiences that take place outside of the therapist's office.
- Symptoms framed as attempts to solve problems in life rather than as "sickness" or "disease."
- The belief that the therapist should take an active role in motivating change. (pp. 1A–B)

Shortly thereafter, Madanes (Madanes, Keim, & Smelser, 1995) refined many of these concepts into what she termed "a therapy of social action," which became the standard to which I held myself in early work with cases of abuse and neglect. It also greatly influenced the approach outlined in this book, particularly in what we call the contrition process of apology, reparation, reconciliation, and forgiveness. This period of thinking is described quite powerfully by Madanes:

> Therapy has social consequences that go beyond the therapeutic relationship. If my therapy emphasizes the value of introspection, I am asserting the value of introspection for everyone. If my therapy emphasizes the value of negative feelings, I am encouraging everyone to express their negativity. If my therapy requires repentance and reparation, I am asserting the value of repentance and reparation for everyone. The responsibility of the therapist goes beyond the therapeutic relationship. If I believe in personal responsibility and I also believe that the only reality is in action—that not to act is to act—then I must recognize that in my therapy I need to protect human rights and prevent violence. To avoid action, to remain neutral, is to be on the side of violence and abuse. (Madanes, Keim, & Smelser, 1995, p. 9)

RESTORATIVE JUSTICE AND THE FAMILY THERAPIST

The court system typically focuses on crime and punishment as a fairly linear process, one following the other without an in-depth understanding of that process as it impacts the victim. Consistent with this tradition of *retributive justice* is the practice of separating from the rest of society, both physically and metaphorically, those identified as a risk to the common good. Thus, by its very design retributive justice focuses on the offender, leaving the victim as little more than a symbol for the risk or actual harm done to the greater society. From the perspective of retributive justice, the view of human nature is not kind. To be human is to be prone to harmful behaviors against others, unless powerful social forces coerce compliance with the rule of law through legal mandate, swift and careful judgment by persons unconnected to the direct consequences of the offense, and strict punishment. The victim rarely receives anything particularly helpful from the experience, except in some cases the satisfaction of retribution.

The value of retribution in the broader application of justice far exceeds the scope of this book, but its use in the CPS and family court system is the foundation of many systemic failures. More specifically, in this context retributive justice underlies the outplacement of the victim in cases of family injustice, criminal prosecution of the offender, and limitation or elimination of contact between child and family. This is, quite simply, not how justice works in the family. In cases of intrafamilial sexual or physical abuse or neglect, the wholesale isolation of offender and victim enforces physical and emotional cutoffs that typically continue only as long as the system is present before reverting to the preplacement stasis. Moreover, even as the expressed purpose of this isolation is to protect the victims from further abuse, it often places their greater emotional needs secondary to the punishment of the offender and family—especially when the offense is sexual—and puts them at greater long-term risk after the imposed isolation is withdrawn. Finally, total isolation[2] does nothing to lift the shame and guilt carried by victims, which exists regardless of and in many cases because of the punishment delivered to the offender.

In recent years, a movement within the American court system has endorsed an alternative known as *restorative justice* that dovetails nicely with our own therapeutic approach. Far from a radical or reactionary response to the stasis quo, this movement was taken up by the federal government in 1996, leading the National Institute of Justice, under sponsorship of the United States Department of Justice, to host a Web site on restorative justice (www.ojp.usdoj.gov/nij/rest-just/index.htm). It serves as one of best clearinghouses for information and resources on this topic. According to the institute, retributive justice leaves citizens disconnected from, victims dissatisfied with, court officers frustrated at, and policymakers disenchanted with the judicial system. In contrast, restorative justice involves these stakeholders and the greater community in an intervention that focuses first on the needs of the victim and second on those of society or the state.

Zehr and Mika (1997) outline the basic tenets of restorative justice with a clear recognition of what we would term the *interactional nature* of any harm done by one person to another, and their work parallels our own quite nicely. I have excerpted the most salient points in their paper:

- Crime is fundamentally a violation of people and interpersonal relationships for the offender, victim, and community, which must be addressed and restored.
- The primary victims are those most directly affected by the offense, but others, such as the family members of victims and offenders, the witnesses, and members of the affected community, are also victims. The state has a circumscribed role in this process (i.e., investigating, facilitating, ensuring safety), but the state is not a primary victim.
- Offenses create obligations and liabilities on the part of offenders to set things right, to which they should be held accountable using as much freewill and as little coercion as possible. The obligation is primarily to victims, not to the state, and victims should be invited to help define those obligations—which may be experienced as difficult, even painful, but are not intended as retributive or humiliating.
- Restorative justice provides a framework of recovery and healing in balance with victim protection, offering opportunities for remorse, forgiveness, and

reconciliation. Victim–offender encounters are used in some instances, whereas alternative forms of exchange are more appropriate in others. In determining the terms and method of exchanges, victims have the principal say and not the state or other external authority.

- Removal from the community and severe restriction of offenders is administered as much or as little as necessary to accomplish restorative goals and protect known or potential victims from further harm.

Often in cases of family injustice, the abstract threat of incarceration pales in comparison to the task of facing the victim(s) of one's acts and the family with the direct assignment to repair the damage one has created. The consequences are more real, clearer, and directly connected to the acts themselves. Thus, at its core restorative justice argues for ultimate accountability, not to an abstract system or a threat of punishment, but to the *actual impact and consequences* of one's actions. And like Madanes's (1990; Madanes, Keim, & Smelser, 1995) approach, restorative justice holds among its core tenets the value of apology, reparation, reconciliation, and forgiveness. To find these two remarkably different disciplines arriving at the same conclusions in near isolation from one another suggests quite powerfully the need for such work in both realms and cross-validates both efforts. Yet many family court and CPS systems have neither the training nor inclination to support these relatively new ideas. Even those who would otherwise support restorative justice in cases of theft or battery, shy away from its use in cases of family injustice where systemic, psychological, and emotional disturbance make it even more appropriate.

By far the greatest failure of the retributive stance in cases of family injustice is the way in which it reverses the contingencies necessary for positive outcomes by rewarding deception and punishing confession and disclosure. As we found in chapter 1, and will discuss repeatedly in later chapters, confession is a vital step in the contrition process for recovery of both the offender and victim. Yet the retributive model irrevocably discourages confession, particularly of sex abuse, by linking it to punishment and not treatment. Accordingly, abusive parents are advised by their own attorneys to have nothing to do with a therapy that demands honesty and candor. Given that it is the offender's word against the victim's in the vast majority of cases that lack forensic evidence, the unrepentant offender is not prosecuted and the victim is left in the position of questionable honesty, sometimes doubted even by her own family. Nothing is worse for a victim, or further from a just outcome, than an offender who avoids the consequences of his or her acts through denial. Many of our clients have said it is a fate worse than any form of exploitation they have experienced. Worse, if they are protective of their offenders, victims will tend to avoid disclosure as did September, choosing instead to suffer in silence with things "we'll *never* be able to deal with."

In such cases, justice is never the protégé of silence.

CONCLUSION: AN APPROACH IN CONTEXT

Strategic humanism and social action, in tandem with ideas from Minuchin, Boszormenyi-Nagy, and the parallel tradition of restorative justice, have formed the basis for integrating and organizing a working model to address the most severe injustices at the level of the family, the larger system, and the interaction between the two. In the current evolution of therapy, which sometimes resembles a frantic rush from one "big thing" to the next, most new approaches are really the culmination of many schools of thought or the refinement of one. Although this chapter has been far from exhaustive in this regard, it should serve as a reminder that very little of what we do in the art and science of therapy is new but instead has been repackaged, extended, updated, and differently applied. Thus, I would strongly encourage readers to resist the urge to chase this approach or any as the new end-all and be-all, but instead to study the history of these and other schools of thought on family injustice in forming their own implementations of the present model. I offer my own attempt in this direction as a synthesis and extension of this work, respectfully looking backward and hopefully moving forward.

NOTES

1. An overview of Madanes's offerings and a full bibliography of her work are available at www.cloemadanes.com.
2. Referring to elimination of contact of any kind, in any forum, including therapy.

CHAPTER 3

Curative Factors and Obstacles to Change

> It would be a serious contradiction of what we are if, aware of our unfinishedness, we were not disposed to participate in a constant movement of search, which in its very nature is an expression of hope. Hope is a natural, possible, and necessary impetus in the context of our unfinishedness. Hope is an indispensable seasoning in our human, historical experience. Without it, instead of history we would have pure determinism. History exists only where time is problematized and not simply a given. A future that is inexorable is a denial of history.
>
> —Paulo Freire, *Pedagogy of Freedom* (1998, p. 69)

An organized approach to therapy must at once explain the change process and the therapist's role in it, guiding us toward its curative factors and away from constructs and interventions that are, by that theory's reckoning and organization, antithetical to change. Drawn rationally from the strategic and structural perspectives and empirically from our practice, we have identified four factors that form the foundation of intervention in both the microcosm of the family and the macrocosm of child protective services (CPS). They are *personal influence, the belief in free will, utilization,* and *contextual change.*

As we have learned to enact each factor in cases of family injustice, we have also found a number of obstacles to successful conceptualization and intervention, some of which are actually popular aspects of the treatment and social service hegemony. Far from a dry academic issue, these are often the very concepts that directly contribute to case failure, increased injustice, and unnecessary time and effort being given to a specific case. By examining each curative factor and its antitheses, readers should be able to distinguish what sets this therapy apart from others and to make an informed decision as to whether they wish to work in this way.

PERSONAL INFLUENCE

We believe that a therapy of family injustice is by definition directive. Erickson, Haley, Madanes, and Minuchin were unparalleled in their development of the technology and techniques designed to elicit quick and substantial change. In that same vein we offer, as a necessary curative factor of this approach, the therapist's influence on the client. Given their use of specific directives (such as homework tasks, enactments, advice, assignments, rules, rituals, and ordeals), it is not surprising that the Haley/Madanes and Minuchin clinics and their followers were frequently referred the most difficult of cases. In fact, for many years Madanes's clinic in Rockville, Maryland, saw the bulk of the county's teen sex offenders and their victims for highly directive and successful therapy (Madanes, 1990).

It is now taken as inarguable that the relationship between the therapist and the client is central in any therapy. Anyone who suspects otherwise is both opposing a vast body of research and ignoring the daily experience of therapy. The error is to limit the definition of this relationship to conditions of empathy, genuineness, and unconditional positive regard, while ignoring the more salient issue of *personal influence.* Even in the early days of modern psychotherapy, Jerome Frank (1961) saw this in noting that all psychotherapies shared

> a particular type of relationship between the patient and a help-giver. . . . The essential ingredient of [which] is that the patient has confidence in the therapist's competence and in his desire to be of help. That is, the patient must feel that the therapist genuinely cares about his welfare. (p. 325)

Today's clients, especially those involved in issues of family injustice, come for many of the same reasons Frank noted more than 40 years ago—to vest in the therapist a sense of faith that he or she can suggest methods for solving problems that the client might not otherwise have considered or put into use.

Consistent with Frank, we consider personal influence a combination of two subfactors, expertise and benevolence. We do not apologize for taking the expert role: We accept that therapists have something valuable to offer clients beyond a kind presentation, empathic ear, and willingness to give them what they want. At the same time, expertise is not always found in strength. Sometimes the therapist yields to the expertise of a family member, particularly a respected elder, which is simply another form of personal influence. Indeed, being an expert can mean giving good advice and stating a clear understanding of a problem. It can also mean knowing when to keep one's advice to oneself and beg others for their perspective, direction, and participation.

Above all, professionals involved in cases of family injustice must be genuinely benevolent and good at showing it under the most extreme conditions, demonstrating a real understanding of and respect for the clients' position and circumstance, even while acting to help them change it. For example, when working with a powerful and rebellious teenager and his family, the therapist must be able to direct the family to lay down the law whether the teen likes it or not. If one has assessed the situation correctly (e.g., the child is not being secretly abused or subjected to some other injustice), the child will ultimately see the therapist pursuing his best interests, even as he rebels against that authority. In fact, it is benevolence that permits the therapist to join with the client and exert the necessary level of personal influence, even in very difficult cases such as domestic violence, child abuse, and sexual molestation.

The Dangerously Powerless Therapist

Those who consider themselves nondirective or postmodern often criticize the tack of personal influence as manipulative. Given their role in the lives of others, one would expect most therapists to accept the position of respected healer much as physicians and plumbers do. Puzzling therefore are therapists who assert that they are little more than catalysts in a naturally occurring process of change, or cocreators of a highly subjective reality. Although this is always an interesting philosophical debate, in cases of family injustice the denial of personal influence directly obscures the therapist's real juxtaposition to the client, the family, and the larger system. Under the supposition of powerlessness, the therapist with a doctorate or advanced master's degree, years of supervision and experience, and the ability to render life-altering diagnostic decisions is considered the equal of a poverty-stricken, poorly educated, socially oppressed family who has been court-ordered into therapy. Taking this position is condescending to the sensibilities of everyone involved and certainly out of sync with the rest of the system. One's power differential should not routinely be lorded over the client, but neither should it be ignored. Just as a skilled plumber has in his hands a family's hopes and dreams of water and waste disposal, so does the skilled therapist hold significant sway over the family's future of function, justice, and in many cases the simple act of living together.

Nevertheless, many therapists are often less comfortable with this power than are plumbers, or surgeons, or car mechanics. Perhaps this is not so surprising given that personal influence proposes that the therapist and not the client is responsible for setting the stage for change. Thus, with only a few periods of interruption, the historic trend in therapy has been to refuse the expert role. When calling the plumber, most of us would be distraught if asked what aspect of the pipe we wanted to address. Like the therapist, the plumber needs some important information to form a hypothesis (Where is the sink? What did you put down there?), but he would never expect the customer to be an equal in the pursuit of pipeline functioning. Consumer and plumber are not "cocreating" the plumbing situation. The plumbing is as it is, and the plumber is there to discover the problem and suggest action for change. Nevertheless, many therapists have begun taking a powerless approach under the rubric of collaborating with "the customer," and many are attempting to apply this tack to the work of family injustice.

In his study of power in therapy, Gregory Bateson was at once fascinated with and distrustful of issues related to power and influence, and he never overcame the contradiction between the desire to help clients and his stance of noninfluence, *nor was he interested in doing so.* His daughter Mary Catherine Bateson wrote,

> Gregory's distaste for politics came from a deep unwillingness to determine the lives of other beings or to let others try to do so; he would have made a terrible philosopher king, and he was an extraordinarily reluctant therapist. For us this created a dilemma, a double bind in fact. We knew that there were insights that needed to be passed on but were warned against doing so. Two decades later, I can see the fallacy in Gregory's argument: refusing to dominate, he extended his objections to the act of persuasion. (Bateson, 1991, p. 323)

True manipulation does not come from influence (known or unknown) but from *undue* influence, or domination, as Mary Bateson put it. *Random House Webster's Unabridged Dictionary* (1998) defines undue influence as "any improper or wrongful constraint, machination, or urgency of persuasion, by which one's will is overcome and he is induced to do or forbear an act which he would not do, or would do, if left to act freely." In other words, to be improper, therapists must force their will on clients in such a way as to negate the assertion of free will. This sort of manipulation is present in no theory with which I am familiar, but only in the character of certain practitioners. In other words, there are no manipulative theories, only manipulative therapists. Indeed, I have known therapists who were quite disingenuous and manipulative and who were thus not offering a *correct* implementation of directive therapy. I have also known "nondirective" therapists who were no less manipulative, but quite a bit less transparent.

As we shall discuss shortly, there is no doubt that the client's influence on therapy is and should be considerable. However, we can acknowledge this and still accept the imbalance of our role in that partnership. Further, our overriding goal in using influence must always be to return the client to a position of free will (e.g., sans probation, children in custody, or hospitalization), even when we may exert substantial personal influence on that journey. In fact, this is the ultimate paradox of any psychotherapy—its practitioners are the odd professionals who are fired by their best customers.

Our job is to take advantage of our influence, develop and implement strategies for change, take the heat when we fail, surrender credit to the natural social context and resources of the client when we succeed, and then pull back until we are needed again.

Value-Free Therapy

Another unhelpful way to be dangerously powerless is to claim and assert a belief in value-free therapy. Originally, it was believed that therapy's primary curative factor was the client's projection of thoughts, ideas, pathologies, and other issues onto the one-on-one relationship with the therapist. To allow for unmitigated projection, the therapist was encouraged to present herself as a tabula rasa, a blank slate. The actual client and his or her problem set were often relegated to a low priority. These projections were thought to emerge outside the impetus of therapy itself, to be reflective of intrapsychic rather than interpersonal happenings. The actual interaction of therapist and client was important only in that it was neutral and nonadditive, allowing for a more pure projection. Interestingly, the therapy community clung to this notion even after disciplines such as sociology, anthropology, experimental psychology, and even the "hard" sciences had come to accept objectivity in inquiry as little more than wishful thinking. This new view held that objectivity was illusory at best, and perhaps even represented an undesirable distancing of observer and subject that actually decreased the validity and reliability of the findings.

Therapist neutrality continued, however, and was greatly bolstered by the work of Carl Rogers. Rather than create a tabula rasa therapist, Rogers asserted a caring and concerned, but always nonjudgmental and accepting one. Though his actual neutrality was convincingly challenged by Truax (1966), the popularity of his value-free therapy fit well with the times, encouraging clients to feel okay in "doing their own thing" even when that went against the hegemony. In fact, it seemed just what was needed at the time to help clients and society overcome social repression in favor of new thinking, insight, and inquiry. However, the 1960s came and went, as did the 1970s and 1980s. The sense of openness and joyous abandon from social convention, begun in the era of protest and unrest, led to a realization that some rules of social conduct were still vital. The Kemp report identifying the "battered child syndrome" (Kemp et al., 1962) was published early in this era, and a burgeoning social welfare and child protective movement was begun to ameliorate what were believed to be the antecedents of child abuse—poverty, poor living conditions, and related social stressors. Well-intentioned psychologists and sociologists asserted the psychosocial underpinnings of abuse and family violence with a decidedly nonjudgmental flair. Though initially considered enlightened and hopeful, these perspectives eventually came to be seen as bleeding-heart excuses for all manner of antisocial behavior, and the pendulum began to swing in the opposite direction.

Even in the heyday of neutrality, there were persistent calls to reconsider the importance of values in the process of therapy. In summarizing his comparative analysis of the various schools of family therapy, Nichols (1984) lamented the absence of such discourse, noting "values are seldom discussed in the family therapy literature. The one exception is Boszormenyi-Nagy, but he considers the ethical dimension only in terms of the patient. There is too little consideration of the practicing therapist's ethical responsibilities, including the possibility of conflicting responsibilities to individuals, families, and the larger community" (p. 572). Some 14 years and 4 editions later, Nichols and Schwartz (1998, p. 499) made this same notation, suggesting little advancement in this critical area.

And then, all at once, things changed in the world of family injustice—and not necessarily for the better. The emergence of sexual abuse—or rather our growing awareness of it—added fuel to the public indignation over child maltreatment, and a backlash ensued (Gardner, 1991). This led value-free therapy to an all-time low in the late-1980s when the McMartin nursery school case illuminated the use of controversial and highly prejudicial techniques to elicit testimony from the alleged victims. McMartin marked the pinnacle of therapies of judgment wherein practitioners assumed the worst before interviewing their subjects and then worked diligently until the child's responses were consistent with the therapists' original hypothesis of sexual abuse. These zealous therapists also did a great deal to blur the line between evaluation and therapy. They were not simply value laden, they were wholly biased.

At its conclusion, this cart and horse reversal was so severe that the important juxtaposition of social justice and child protection was lost, and the integrity of sex abuse evaluation and treatment were damaged in courtrooms across the country. This combined with research on the suggestibility of young children has curtailed the investigation of sexual abuse, leaving very young children easier targets for offenders. Thus, by the early 1990s we were left with apologists on one side, psychological vigilantes on the other, and authors such as Wexler (1995) and Gardner (1991) critiquing the entire discourse. In the popular press, Christopher Darden (1996) exemplified the depth of this backlash against all psychological opinion in his treatise on the O.J. Simpson trial, writing, "I had never had much confidence in expert witnesses, especially shrinks. It seemed as if you could find a psychologist to say anything, and whatever your shrink said, their shrink would say just the opposite" (p. 185).

The strategic and structural family therapy models also evolved during the 1960s, 1970s, and early 1980s. Their amiable, utilization-based style was in sharp contrast to the discipline's early tendency to blame families for child pathology, which, as Haley noted (personal communication), was not particularly useful in getting families interested in change. Students were taught to be skilled diplomats, charming conversationalists, savvy mediators, articulate presenters, knowledgeable experts, and masters of subtle influence. This yielded family-friendly techniques specifically designed to increase the likelihood that clients would follow treatment directives, among them:

- Speaking the language of the client.
- Taking a deliberately one-down position in deference to a powerful family member.
- Finding common interest or experience with a powerful family member.
- Showing empathy for a family or any member of a family, examining their perspective as if it were one's own.
- Reframing a set of behaviors in a more positive light than the family might.
- Providing a humorous alternative to an inappropriately grave situation.
- Agreeing with the client until the client admits his real position in opposition to the agreement.
- Expressing helplessness if the family is unwilling to assist in helping the identified client.
- Apologizing for directives that have not been followed or expressing a willingness to resign the case if the client is not being helped.
- Normalizing frightening or upsetting situations as manageable problems faced by many people now and/or throughout history.

In the past 10 to 15 years the "postmodern" schools of thought have extended this position to suggest that the therapist should not only be amiable, but genuinely agreeable with the client's wishes and values. In fact, solution-focused therapists refer to the most motivated client as "the customer," and believe that the single most important factor in the early stage of therapy is to ascertain "what the client wants" and then to work diligently on that issue. There is good sense in this position. In cases of voluntary therapy with highly coherent problems and ambiguous issues of right and wrong, what the client wants should rarely contrast with the therapist's goals. Our only quibble might be in the extent to which this agreeable position can be considered nondirective. This is also a good way to *appear* successful, because the therapist takes what the client wants and then helps the client attain it, greatly reducing the likelihood of resistance.

In all, the directive nature of strategic therapy offers an excellent foundation for intervention. However, in confronting family injustice we have found its traditional diplomacy too subtle and too affable, and the solution-focused approach wholly unsuited and potentially iatrogenic. Though we have seen far less dramatic examples in common practice, this is powerfully illustrated by a case consultation I provided several years ago in a rural community. A husband and wife were referred for an intake by probation and parole. They were expecting their second child, and the court had ordered an intake and treatment process to determine whether the father should be permitted future contact with that child. The therapist took a social history on the case and learned that the man had killed his first child in a fit of rage a year prior. Although it did not appear that he intended to kill the child, his violent outburst and subsequent blow to the child's head had justified a plea bargain of manslaughter and a surprisingly short jail sentence. At the end of the intake, the therapist asked the couple what they wanted to get out of therapy. The man thought for a moment and then shared that they were fighting a great deal. When asked, he explained that he and his wife disagreed about how to divide the life insurance money from the dead toddler. He complained that his wife had selfishly chosen to retain the entire payment for herself. She felt she deserved it because she had not killed the child.

I consulted with a group of therapists trained in family therapy and Ericksonian methods. None seemed to know what to do with such a couple. A therapist trained in the solution-focused approach suggested that we attempt to bond with the couple around their grief over the child. I noted that they had shown no grief, and instead focused on financial squabbles. Another therapist, similarly trained, suggested that we tend to the couple's bickering and hope that it would lead to a more substantive issue, that of the couple's safety around their unborn child. I found this a very disingenuous approach, ignoring the elephant in the therapy room.

The most thoughtful response came from Mental Research Institute (MRI) family therapy historian Wendell Ray, referring to a case seen by Virginia Satir. According to Ray, Satir was referred a woman who had cast both her children into a furnace. The woman had remained mute since the incident, refusing to engage in any therapy process. Satir, known for her humanism and regard for personal dignity, opened her first session with the woman by looking her in the eye and saying "I want to begin by telling you that what you did is the most ghastly thing I've ever heard of." The stunned woman broke down, started talking, and therapy began. Ray finishes by noting how impressed he was by Satir's ability to distinguish between behavior and human worth (W. Ray, personal correspondence, 1998).

Attempts to "normalize" bad client behavior or consider it with a neutral eye can adversely impact cases of family injustice. Instead, when confronted with a sex offender, a violent teen, or a neglectful family, one must be prepared to assert the non-normalcy of the situation, sometimes quite vigorously. In such cases, the therapist must not normalize but *problematize* the behavior, thereby helping the client to perceive more fully its true nature, quality, and wrongfulness and then act to change it (Freire, 1970). For example, the therapist may point out that it is not normal to have sex with a child, to endlessly berate a child's mother just because she is your ex-wife, to allow 13-year-olds to have sex partners come for sleepovers, or to buy liquor for a minor so that he will "at least be drinking where we can keep track of him." In fact, the tacit acceptance of such conduct by a therapist suggests to the client that the behavior itself is acceptable. Subtler are cases where a family's high chaos, weak limits, and poor boundaries do not constitute abuse or neglect, but are irrefutably pathogenic. Yet the same tenet applies, even if more genial challenges are a better fit. Where there is injustice, there is a problem and most often a family that has chronically failed to recognize or act to correct it. If that problem is not noted and addressed, therapy cannot be considered a success, regardless of how satisfied the client feels.

Another example of the way in which value-free approaches miss the mark in cases of family injustice appeared at a consultation seminar with a noted postmodern therapist. A young clinical social worker presented the case of a teen boy who had, among other things, beaten up a teacher and later an old man in the park. The therapist admitted that the boy's reasons for this conduct were a bit of a mystery, but the therapist suspected the boy felt very angry. The boy had also disclosed to the therapist how oppressed he felt by forces at school and at home and how unfairly people were treating *him.*

Consistent with this consultant's popular approach, she asked what the therapist thought the boy had found helpful in their work together. The therapist said, "that I just listened to him. . . . And that I was nonjudgmental . . . about him beating up the old man." To this the theorist effused, "Oh! Wow. That is great. I really agree with you on that. If you had said anything about that he wouldn't have come back and you would have lost him. And besides he's 16 and he wouldn't have listened to you anyhow. It is great that you are able to be so nonjudgmental." This was quite astonishing for me, as it was for several participants who were sitting around me. Under the method discussed herein, I would have used the boy's own sense of injustice and pointed out how incongruent it was when considered alongside the unfair things he had done to others. I would have been clear in stating in a benevolent and noncondemning way the abusive nature of such conduct, and I would have promised to help him set about the task of making reparation as a matter of his own character development as a man. While I'm sure proponents of neutral approaches would disagree, it has been our experience that the youth most certainly would have listened, just as did Satir's client. In fact, an example is found in the second case study in chapter 5 and in September's case in chapter 11. I believe a correction of the injustices he had committed and an exploration of those injustices done to him would have been far more worthwhile than the warm, nonjudgmental acceptance of his conduct.

Aponte (1994) makes a similar case for values in therapy in *Bread and Spirit.* Taking direct aim at postmodern schools, he summarized the book, noting:

> If we split off "a separate world of language, divorced from any notion of relevant social and material realm" (Fish, 1993, p. 228), we destroy the basis for social and personal morality. There is no enduring basis in essential reality for justice or injustice, right or wrong. Since "both problem and cause are simply a set of constructions about reality" (De Shazer & Berg, 1988, p. 42), we have no moral basis for therapeutic goals outside of what therapist and client construct together in the moral and social vacuum of the office.
>
> Therapists communicate values in therapy, such as their views about justice in the abuse of power in personal relationships and the rightness or wrongness of yesterday or today's family structures. . . . Therapists can lend importance or insignificance to what gives meaning and purpose to client's lives. They can work with or around people's values . . . we are a part of that culture that reaches most deeply into people's lives, empowering or disempowering them and their values, morality and culture. This dilemma is in front of us as therapists all the time, whether we wish to acknowledge it or not. (p. 243)

Enacting Benevolent Power

In cases of family injustice, we have come to realize two things, well illustrated by the examples already mentioned:

- The customer is *not* always right.
- The therapist should learn how to tell the customers they are not right by problematizing the situation in a way that does not show contempt for the client or generate undue conflict or suffering yet still gets at the point.

Needless to say, this is easier said than done, and the reader should feel a bit perplexed at this point in considering how one can reconcile the amiable, diplomatic therapist with Satir's benevolent honesty. Having spent many an hour on such tasks, my colleagues and I have generated the following guidelines.

- It is vital to have an a priori discussion and consensus by therapist and client as to the goals of therapy. We do this in the form of an interview with clients before we agree to take their case. In this process, the therapist typically shares his or her values relevant to the case—that wife battering is wrong, allowing minors to drink alcohol in the home is poor parenting, blaming the system or anyone else does not exonerate poor conduct, and so on. If after some discussion the client and therapist cannot reach an accord, the therapist should not take the case. Of note, we have rarely lost a case this way, and more often than not such clients express their experience as one of refreshing clarity not found in the rest of their encounters with the system.

- The relationship is everything. In fact it is *more* important to relate well to those who have committed injustices than to any other client one might see. Further, as we will discuss later in this text, if one cares about victims one also must care about offenders—because quite commonly in cases of family injustice, so do the victims.
- As noted, power and benevolence must exist in careful balance and present themselves quite noticeably. Both offenders and victims respect interpersonal power. Some respect little else. Offenders rarely respect weakness, and victims never trust it.
- As Ray (personal correspondence, 1998) notes, it possible and necessary to condemn behavior while supporting the person. It is not easy, but it is a skill that must be mastered. He takes careful note of Satir's wording, "what you *did* is ghastly." In such cases, language is incredibly important in making distinct variables of behavior, character, and human worth. In reviewing the cases described herein, or examining our training tapes, attentive therapists will find a precision of language unique to this approach.
- Honesty is usually the best and most effective policy. Clients involved with the social or court service systems are often misled if not lied to directly. If they are told the truth, it is usually with a professional callousness borne of many years of redundancy in practice. Therapists who are unafraid to speak the truth to their clients, while maintaining the caring relationship, place them into a state of receptivity for change.
- A therapist should understand and use his or her own fallibility without becoming an apologist for the injustice of others. We shall discuss this thoroughly in the section on self-utilization.

Not infrequently, after a series of more modest techniques have failed, clients must be directly confronted with their own behavior. This is especially true of clients who are too volatile to participate in therapy or (in CPS cases) the reunification process, and of those who are sabotaging their children or themselves despite repeated punishments and dire consequences. Further, such confrontation is often necessary to bring offenders to the point of reparation.

In the most extreme of these cases, we have developed a "Hail Mary" strategy wherein the therapist becomes a desperate quarterback hurling a forward pass downfield hoping to hit any receiver in the end zone and win the game. In practice, this technique begins with the warning that the client will not like what is about to be said, and that he or she will probably fire the therapist or phone the supervisor, whose number is provided for that purpose. This is admittedly paradoxical, but it is also good risk management. The therapist then admits to having been much too diplomatic for the client's own good—that he can no longer be disingenuous simply to protect the feelings of a client he genuinely likes. In some cases, the therapist may even express fear of the client's rebuke, noting that this is why no one wants to tell her the truth, leaving her in perpetual ignorance about her situation. Of note, this is *rarely* an inaccurate observation, especially among CPS workers who do all they can to avoid such difficult people, even when they are the parents of children in custody. Needless to say, the client's state of attention is unparalleled at this point. The therapist then simply tells the client the truth—that the injustices in the case are the client's fault, that the client is responsible for fixing them, and that externalization of blame is futile in any efforts at reconciliation and reunification. And this is said in no uncertain terms. If the client chooses not to fire the therapist, he pledges to help her correct this terrible situation, but leaves responsibility for the initiative squarely in the lap of the client. A brief talk on the importance of free will is also useful at this point.

As we shall see later in September's case (chapter 11), we may be called upon to confront the ways in which victims often take over the job of self-destruction after their offenders have long left off. Needless to say, walks an especially fine line between the acceptance of personal responsibility and the distancing of the victim from the offense. It begins with the explanation that the victim is in no way to blame for what was done to her by others. Once this is clear, the therapist explains that others have historically treated the victim horribly, but that she is now free to make her own (age-appropriate) choices with the help and support of family, therapist, and community. When instead she has chosen to destroy herself through suicide attempts, running away, sexual misconduct, drug abuse, or a host of other maladies common in these cases, she is replicating the behavior of the offender. What the offender has begun, she now seems hell-bent on finishing. In extreme cases, where the relationship is strong, the therapist may indicate that he cannot tacitly support the victim's self-destruction and that he will refer her to a more restrictive environment if he cannot stem it. Of note, most ethical guidelines support this choice if the therapist feels that the level of treatment he is offering is inadequate or potentially iatrogenic. This point is explained carefully to the client along with the ethical requirement to make a referral.

These approaches may seem unusually brusque to readers, who have not encountered such desperate circumstances as these. It may help to consider this within the context of the aforementioned benevolence, or as Frank (1961) notes, "even stern and harsh therapists . . . succeed in conveying that they care" (p. 326). Of course these strategies are used much less frequently in our approach than more gentle means of confrontation. Yet, despite the name, even these Hail Mary approaches have rarely failed when used sensibly. And as we shall see later in the case of September, even when they initially seem to have failed they often show latent success. In one case, a mother called my supervisor and the agency director the next day to complain that I had been horrible to her and that she now hated me. A few days later, she suddenly reversed herself and called to express her appreciation for my honesty. "You know," she said sheepishly, "nobody's ever put it to me quite like that before." Her dangerous Munchausen syndrome by proxy also ended that week. In our last session many months later, I borrowed from Erickson and said in a closing moment, "My voice will go with you." The woman began to cry as did her husband. "Yes," she said, "and it will be right here in my heart." Her husband got up and hugged me.

The Paradox of Power in Larger System Interventions

The influence of the therapist is never more important than when cases of family injustice are inducted into the larger system. Paradoxically, however, therapists are both the most qualified and, in many jurisdictions, the least likely to have influence over the case. This results from a systemic arrangement in which those with the greatest power often have the least direct involvement with the family. For example, the judge may see a case for less than 30 minutes on a given docket day, yet all final decisions ultimately fall to her. The *guardian ad litem* and state's attorney may see the case for only 30 minutes plus an additional 10 to 30 minutes at some other point, giving them an hour of contact. Court hearings are usually scheduled for three- to six-month intervals. Thus, in the course of a foster-year, a judge may spend at most, 1 to 2 hours on a given case and the attorneys perhaps twice this. Court service workers may see the client as much as once a week in the office or as little as once every 6 months, depending on the level of supervision. The evaluator (if there is one) often sees the family between one and ten times. The CPS worker may come to the client's home, but even with high-need cases this will rarely exceed once per week. More typical is a once or twice monthly visit for an hour, a 3- to 6-month case planning meeting, and hallway contact during the wait-time before the court session. This point is not lost on foster children, as their most frequent complaint about their caseworkers is "They don't know me, and don't listen to me when I try to tell them anything."

Therapists typically have at least weekly contact with the family and sometimes several contacts a week or even daily in the most intensive cases. Further, the therapist typically has the greatest training and experience in child development, family psychology, and behavior change. Yet of all the professionals, the therapist has only as much power as the system will allow. Although some judges give extraordinary weight to the input of the therapist, others side with CPS when any dispute arises.

Conclusion: Benevolence and Expertise in Balance

In summarizing this section on personal influence, it is important to consider that balance is everything. Benevolence without expertise is impotent caring. Expertise without benevolence is heartless domination. As a harbinger of social convention, the authoritative, benevolent therapist can use personal influence and expertise to help a family learn or relearn a sense of normalcy that was not available in childhood or was interrupted by a traumatic incident. In doing so, he helps the family members correct their relationship with each other and with society, while resisting dominance by that society. In short, influence and values are to be embraced as guides in therapy, not feared as oppressors.

THE BELIEF IN FREE WILL

Having just detailed the importance of the therapist's influence over the client, it may seem paradoxical to now emphasize the therapist's belief in client free will. It is not. In fact, client free will exists in dialectical tension with the power of the therapist. Moreover, the therapist's use of influence to assert a belief in free will is itself curative. Throughout our philosophic and psychotherapeutic tradition, we have given a great deal of intellectual energy to understanding something as seemingly self-evident as our ability to take charge of our own lives. In one of the most famous and controversial treatises on the subject, Jean-Paul Sartre wrote:

> We were never more free than during the German occupation. We had lost all our rights, beginning with the right to talk. Everyday we were insulted to our faces and had to take it in silence. Under one pretext or another, as workers, Jews, or political prisoners, we were deported *en masse.* Everywhere, on billboards, in the newspapers, on the screen, we encountered the revolting and insipid pictures of ourselves that our suppressers wanted us to accept. And because of all this we were free. Because the Nazi venom had seeped into our thoughts, every accurate thought was a conquest. Because an all-powerful police tried to force us to hold our tongues, every word took on the value of a declaration of principles. Because we were hunted down, every one of our gestures had the weight of a solemn commitment. . . .
>
> And the choice that each of us made of his life was an authentic choice because it was made face to face with death, because it could always have been expressed in these terms: "Rather than death . . ." And here I am not speaking of the elite among us who were real Resistants [those who fought the Germans], but of all Frenchmen who, at every hour of the night and day throughout four years, answered "*no.*" (Cummings, 1966, p. 233)

This same radical belief in free will in the face of determinism must be held when confronting family injustice, for without it one becomes submerged in reality, bound to the whim of fate, and overwhelmed by external influence

(Freire, 1970). Far from an abstraction, we have actually used this passage and related language with clients in facing the oppression of family and systemic injustice, including September's case (chapter 11).

Unfortunately, this emphasis on free will is becoming less a part of modern therapy as other explanations for human thought and behavior ebb and flow. This poses a special problem for cases of family injustice in which humans deliberately and hurtfully impact one another, because it challenges the locus of responsibility that forms the core of our approach and questions our ability to change. There are many ways in which human behavior and responsibility can be externalized; I shall list the four forms of determinism that appear most often in our work.

Psychobiology

The growing emphasis on psychobiology as the core of human dysfunction emanates in large part from efforts by the pharmaceutical industry and the purveyors of "managed care" to market a hegemony of medication-based treatment. A short extrapolation from this premise is *psychobiological determinism* in which human behavior is separated from volition and assigned to bad chemicals.

It may come as a surprise to the reader who has been bombarded with expensive marketing, but this trend is not necessarily supported in objective research (Miller, Duncan, & Hubble 1997; Hubble, Duncan, & Miller, 1999). However, rather than debate the utility of medication per se, which already fills other volumes, it is more to the point of this book to understand that any intervention in a case of family injustice is a powerful one and those leading to further injustice are intolerable. Given the arguable claim that medication is a powerful cure for many or most psychological problems, this is especially true for its use in such cases. So numerous are the ways in which these clients can be disadvantaged by medication mismanagement that I can only cite a few examples, all of which actually crossed our doorstep.

- A woman in an abusive marriage became more depressed as her husband became more violent to her and her son. The woman began taking Prozac (fluoxetine) without result, and remained in the marriage. The psychiatrist responded by increasing the dosage to the maximum allowable. The woman finally experienced symptom relief but continued to stay in the marriage. Eventually, she came to therapy stating that she must go off Prozac noting, "Maybe I shouldn't feel so okay when my life is so terrible." The therapist agreed with her. She discontinued medication over a 4-week period, felt depressed again, and left her husband. A few months after attaining stability in her postdivorce life, her symptoms had remitted.

- Unbeknownst to anyone, a young teen was molested by her uncle. She struggled with nightmares and flashbacks but was not forthcoming about their content as she was afraid she would be in as much trouble as the uncle "for having sex before I'm old enough." She was placed on Zyprexa (olanzapine), which reduced her dreams and flashbacks, and given Zoloft (sertraline) for her depression. Thereafter she was better able to cope with her situation, which continued for several more months until she was hospitalized for a suicide attempt and finally disclosed the abuse.
- A known sex abuse victim was acting out severely and placed on lithium. At the same time, she experienced a therapeutic apology from her mother for not having protected her from her abuser. The prescribing psychiatrist was pleased that the medication had done its job and the bipolar symptoms were now gone. Several months later, the girl suggested that she should go off medication. The psychiatrist disagreed, stating that because of her illness she must stay on meds in perpetuity. The girl reminded the psychiatrist how well she was doing. He reminded her that the medication was working. The girl confessed that she had never taken the lithium after the first week and gave him the full bottles to prove it. The psychiatrist was upset with the girl and noted in the chart that she was noncompliant. The family had good insurance, and he suggested they put her in the hospital for a week to stabilize her meds. They declined.

This is not to say that medications are never useful. In fact, another way in which our approach differs from our therapeutic lineage is our belief that medication is not the problem, but rather medication's excessive or strategically incorrect application, often in isolation from the therapy process. When medication may reasonably help alleviate human suffering, therapists of all schools should support its responsible usage. However, when it is principally designed as a chemical form of social control, a "cheap alternative" to real problem resolution, or a method of avoiding a more just outcome, it is abhorrent. Especially in cases of family injustice, pharmacologic therapy should never function like psychological pain pills, masking symptoms that the client, family, or society do not care to deal with directly.

Strategic use of medication can actually bring about more just outcomes than might otherwise have been possible, especially when prescribed in-house as an adjunct to therapy and in careful consultation with therapists. In our practice, we can now carefully assess each client on medication and closely monitor his or her behavior over time to report back in "real time" to our board certified advanced registered nurse practitioner (ARNP). Of particular importance, our ARNP is also a therapist trained in this model and thus quite responsive to our feedback, and our client families are frequent and direct observers of the case. Following are a few examples of how we have used medication to increase justice and avoid psychobiological determinism.

- A father was very neglectful of his wife and family despite several interventions designed to improve the situation. The use of Effexor (venlafaxine) decreased his depression and improved his energy level, and he became "just like a new dad" by report of his family.
- A teen was outplaced to foster care because she had attacked her stepmother with a knife. In custody, she was so out of control that she could not be seen in the office because she would verbally abuse the other clients. Small children were afraid of her. She engaged in incredibly dangerous sexual conduct and drug abuse. When she arrived on our doorstep she was on a cocktail of medication designed to tranquilize her into submission, a strategy that was clearly not working. We modified her regimen and commenced a meaningful therapy; however, before either approach could impact the girl, she disrupted her placement and was hospitalized for her unremitting anger and manic behavior. We got her released a few weeks later after our revised medication scheme had had a chance to work, and eventually she even returned to the same foster home a very changed girl. Had we not been able to closely control her medication, we would never have gotten her through the initial stages of therapy and she would have undoubtedly been hospitalized repeatedly or perhaps not released at all.
- In a complex case, a 14-year-old was failing every class in school. She was losing interest in social activities and looked very depressed and tearful. She then quit eating and was referred by her doctor for anorexia. Our careful evaluation determined that her depression appeared reactive to her deteriorating life, as her failure in school was costing her friends, activity time, and her parents' patience. She came from an intact family with above-average parenting skills. There was no history of abuse, neglect, or failed attachment. Extensive intervention helped a great deal with the depression and eating problem but not the school failure. The girl was assessed for attention-deficit disorder (ADD) and found to be positive across several settings. These were substantiated through classroom observation, the Continuous Performance Test, and the Conner's instruments. She was given a trial dose of Adderall (amphetamine and dextroamphetamine), which caused her to focus bit more and eat a great deal less[1] and it was quickly discontinued. Continuing to struggle in school, the girl and family worked closely with the therapist but could not overcome her school failure. She did overcome her anorexia however, and on doing so began a trial of Concerta[2] along with a careful regimen of calorie intake to keep her weight up. After a few days, she was like "a whole different student." Her grades improved slowly at first, and by the end of the year she was getting As and Bs in most of her classes. She finished 9th grade on the honor roll for the first time since 5th grade. More important by her reckoning, she won a position on a very competitive high school pom-pom squad because she could now follow and learn the steps more easily. She is continuing with As and Bs in high school.

The primary difference in the first and second set of cases included: (1) thorough evaluation of the client's psychosocial, family, and phenomenal reality as well as the theorized psychiatric condition; (2) careful, long-term follow-up to determine efficacy, and (3) close integration of medication and treatment. Additionally, we are always explicit that medication is a tool, not a cure-all, and certainly no substitute for the rectification of family or social injustice. Because of the frequent overuse of medication and misdiagnoses, we have even developed a placebo trial system for any child or adult with an ambiguous diagnosis of attention deficit disorder, which has greatly improved the accuracy of our diagnosis and intervention.

Integrated wisely into a larger program of care, medications can assist in bringing about just outcomes. Isolated from that process, especially in cases of family injustice, they can victimize those already afflicted and exonerate those who afflict them. Taken as a replacement for volition, psychobiology easily encroaches on the primacy of free will by allowing clients to rely on their chemical makeup as an explanation for all manner of mismanagement and misconduct.

Diagnosis

The reification of the American Psychiatric Association's *Diagnostic and Statistical Manual of Mental Disorders* (*DSM*) codes took a great leap forward in the 1994 4th edition, which includes a significant research basis; thus, deserved or not, it has taken on the mantle of science. The 2000 *DSM-IV-TR* (text revision) represents the next stage in this process. However, at its core, the *DSM* remains more a political and economic document than a clinical one, determining which mental health diagnoses will be paid for by insurance companies, just as the current procedural terminology (CPT) coding system determines what treatments will be covered.

Kurt Vonnegut said the moral of his story *Mother Night* (1966) was "We are what we pretend to be, so we must be very careful about what we pretend to be." A slight paraphrase relevant to diagnosis is, "We are what we are pretended to be, so our therapists must be very careful about what they pretend us to be." At its core, diagnosis must always be remembered as nothing more than the pretending of a person licensed to do so. Unfortunately, because of the way in which diagnosis is used—to generate third-party payment—this pretending becomes "the truth" rather than one interesting way to view a client. There are even those who cling to the notion that a future DSM will generate prescriptive treatment, despite research that argues against such a position (Miller, Duncan, & Hubble, 1997).

As with psychobiology, we have encountered many misuses of diagnosis, the most prominent of which fall in the Axis II category. While in the hospital, September was not only diagnosed as bipolar and medicated with lithium, she was also given the Axis II diagnosis of borderline personality disorder. Were this not so common it would be considered absurd, posing numerous nosological errors including the fact that a child of 15 has not crystallized a personality, let alone a disorder thereof. *DSM-IV* (and Theodore Millon, expert on Axis II diagnosis) actually caution against this use of diagnosis, noting that Axis II disorders may begin in adolescence, but they should not be routinely assigned due to the instability of identity and personality formation during the teen years (Millon, 1999). Yet in practice we have frequently seen teen girls who were diagnosed with personality disorders while in custody but recovered with good therapy by young adulthood. Because Axis II disorders are defined as unremitting, these youths must not have been diagnosed correctly to begin with. Radical proponents of formal nosology will forgive such errors, noting that it is unfair to use 20/20 hindsight to criticize the original diagnosticians. We strongly disagree. In research, hindsight is known as post hoc analysis and forms the cornerstone of experimental design. If you assume, as we do, that every intervention is an experiment, then each of these treaters should have become aware of their errors and correct their procedures in future client contact, a rare occurrence indeed. There is, however, no excuse for the next example, which goes well beyond error.

A defense attorney requested my review of a psychologist's report concluding that a 14-year-old boy had an antisocial personality disorder. She did not say he might someday have this disorder, she said that *he had it now*. Moreover, the psychologist did not bother to offer evidence for this supposition, nor did she seem aware that *DSM-IV* expressly *prohibits* use of this diagnosis for children. Worse, she determined without any stated criteria that the boy was a sexual predator and should be committed to a lock-down facility indefinitely. Though the trial judge accepted the recommendations of the psychologist, the appellate judge threw out the conviction on reading my rebuttal questioning the quality of the diagnostics in the evaluation.

Diagnosis *may* be a necessary conduit to communicate with others; however, like medication, the very act of generating a diagnosis is an intervention that can itself create injustice just as it did in the cases discussed here. It must be remembered that unjust environments and human transactions shape behavior. Diagnosis does not.

Environment

Family therapy of any sort takes a decidedly contextual approach to understanding human behavior. In fact, environmental influence is one of the oldest explanations (or excuses) for symptomology, dating back to the belief in evil spirits as pathogenic. Freud emphasized childhood environment as central to the formation of the adult psyche, and many therapies still focus extensively on this process. Others, especially behaviorism, have deemphasized the impact of childhood, positing instead ongoing social learning as the principal influence in personality development. However, taken to its logical extreme, the radical belief in any environmental theory becomes deterministic when it ignores the imperative to exert free will within that social context.

Though they may use a different language, clients are quite fond of environmental determinism and the freedom it offers for excusing the injustices they have committed against others. Many offenders explain early in treatment that they cannot be expected to change or improve because they are products of a flawed upbringing. For offenders, the more negative their own behavior toward others, the more likely they are to attribute blame in this way. Likewise, victims may take the stance that their social context has irreversibly damaged them, as a way of self-handicapping and avoiding Sartre's "condemnation" to be free.

An example is found in Justin (chapter 5), a 15-year-old who claimed, in a belligerently philosophical tone, that he was a victim of circumstances, not responsible for his actions and incapable of meeting any expectations. He *had* lived an unjust life in which his addicted mother left him in the care of his grandmother for years at a time. However, Justin was on the verge of moving from victim to offender, and thus the issue of free will was paramount. While preparing him for an apology session with Justin's mother, his therapist, Greg Tangari, took charge of Justin's excuse making using a method we have replicated many times hence. He asked Justin if he was not in fact a puppet. The oppositional youth launched into a heated argument about free will in which he stated emphatically that he was no one's puppet! Greg reiterated all the evidence of determinism Justin had presented, concluding again that Justin was nothing but a puppet, a little fellow who looked like a real man but was really just a toy on the end of somebody else's string. This paradoxical intervention provided hours of thoughtful and intense discourse. Moreover, it made it easy for the boy to exercise a healthy attributional style by *externalizing* the origin for his problems onto his offender ("the puppetmaster") while *internalizing* the locus of control for overcoming them. Whether working with a victim or an offender, this is the core intervention for reducing a client's projection of volition onto bad environments.

Perhaps the most valuable single phrase I ever learned from studying with Cloé Madanes came when we consulted on cases in which young men and women were recapitulating the very same problems their mothers had faced—poor parenting, underemployment, bad marriages, violence. "Here is what you need to tell her," Madanes said in response to the desperate plight of a pregnant teen. "It's hard for a young woman to let herself have a better life than her mother." How elegantly she summed up the position that, regardless of the powerful context of our family of origin, we are free to struggle to *let ourselves* have a better life than they lived or gave us. In this phrase, which I have used successfully hundreds of times since, the client is both validated for her experience of determinism and challenged to transcend it.

The System

The involvement of any powerful external system creates the potential for a unique form of determinism. In this text, the organism of interest is the child protective system, which even persons of extraordinary intellect and education have trouble tracking and understanding. One can only imagine the struggle faced by the poor and undereducated, creating a fertile ground for families to surrender to the will and authority of a larger entity. As we shall discuss later, some level of surrender is crucial if families are to have their outplaced children returned. But often families surrender not only their dysfunction and conflict, but also the better aspects of their free will, and many systems are specifically designed to encourage such deference and dependency, which may remain long after its brief utility has faded.

Unfortunately for therapists, CPS exerts this same level of influence on them, particularly if they advocate for just outcomes and due process between the system and the family. As noted, a therapy for family injustice is also a therapy of personal responsibility in which a therapist may remind a client of the ghastliness of her behavior or state that wife beating is simply wrong. This same direct and reasonable critique inevitably targets any system that denies its own responsibility or attempts to shift blame for errors or inconsistencies onto the family. On the whole, CPS prefers instead to use the therapist as a tool of family reunification or termination and does not much appreciate any objection to its own conduct, even when it applies directly to the mental health and well-being of the child. When things get particularly contentious, all factions of CPS tend to denigrate the therapist, at times sabotaging and redirecting therapy or even discharging the therapist to return the system to stasis.

Beyond simply running interference for the family's due process in the system, the therapist is usually the only person willing and able to educate the family about that same system and to coach them through it. As I shall do for the reader in a later chapter, the therapist must explain the players and their roles, discuss whom to trust and not trust, analyze the flow of information, explain how the family should present itself to others, and interpret the strange psychosociolegal language that is ever present. At every moment the potential for systemic determinism keeps the therapist walking a very thin line between helping the client meet reasonable social expectations and norms, and becoming controlled by arbitrary authority that threatens free will. And all this must be negotiated and under way before, during, and after any reunification plan.

Conclusion: The Power to Choose, No Matter What

The issue of free will is always important in therapy and never more so than in cases of family injustice. Madanes (1993a) provides a nice summary to conclude this topic: "Without ever denying the importance of the family, and of chemistry, and of social context, we believe in the power to choose no matter what the circumstances" (p. 70). And with that we turn to the next curative factor, utilization, which modulates and interprets the will of the client and the influence of the therapist.

UTILIZATION

I was once attending sessions with Jay Haley, behind the one-way mirror at the Family Therapy Institute of Washington, DC. A family did not arrive for their session, so Haley showed a tape of a man and wife being seen by a former minister a few years before.[3] The couple was well balanced in their arguments, each acting in a pattern to counter the other. Haley saw nothing happening in the therapy except tit-for-tat bickering, so he asked the therapist to come behind the mirror. He noted that the couple would go on in the same conflict indefinitely if something was not done, so he asked the therapist to go back to the session and blame the husband for all the marital problems and to demand that he court the wife more frequently and effectively. For a fair man, the minister did an amazing job of being unfair. The husband was outraged and, of course, the wife came to his rescue, allowing him to prove by the next session that he was a good husband in many and various ways.

In discussing the tape, a young psychologist in our group noted, "I have a friend who tried that intervention on a couple and they never came back." "Well," Haley said not missing a beat, "you wouldn't use it on someone it wouldn't work on."

As the core of strategic therapy, Haley taught his students to become experts at learning what works and how to help the client execute it. Obviously, the trick is figuring this out with as few trials and errors as possible. In later writing, Haley (1996) noted that he knew that the therapist had a good enough relationship with the couple that they would accept this intervention and not flee. But how did Haley know this? How did he find and use just what would work with this couple? Can this sort of clinical intuition be taught or was Haley simply good at what he did? The answer is *utilization.*

Drawn from Erickson's work in the late 1950s and heavily emphasized by Jeffery Zeig (1992), the concept of utilization originated in hypnotic phenomenon. Zeig notes that Erickson (1980) considered utilization to involve the use of "the subject's own pattern of response and capacities, rather than an attempt to force upon the subject by suggestion the hypnotist's limited understanding of how and what the subject should do" (Erickson, p. 22). Like the hypnotist, the therapist works to involve the client's environment, experience, patterns of response, and even resistance to treatment rather than make the client fit the therapist's conceptualization. Failure often derives from treatment of the client as less than unique, and the expectation that the client will respond to the therapist's limited understanding of what the client should do.[4]

Utilization is to any Ericksonian therapy as analysis is to dynamic approaches, as conditioning is to behavior therapy (Zeig, 1992). In our approach utilization is nothing less than a catalyst that allows personal influence to work in dialectical tension with free will in the service of change. Given our focus on family injustice, it is vital to note that utilization *does not* require positive regard for or acceptance of the client's worldview as has been advanced in the postmodern interpretation. It does mean being ever responsive to that worldview. As Frank (1961) notes, "Caring . . . does not necessarily imply approval, but rather a determination to persist in trying to help no matter how desperate the patient's condition or how outrageous his behavior. . . . If not for what he is, then for what he can become" (p. 325). Even when the family's conduct is reprehensible, utilization allows the therapist to use their experience, behavior, and perception not just as grist for a therapeutic mill but, as Zeig (1992) puts it, as fuel to "propel the client forward into new space" (p. 261). With this all too brief introduction, we shall now review aspects of utilization that especially impact and inform cases of family injustice.

Utilization of the Past

The incorporation of the past is another point of divergence between our model and traditional "here and now" approaches of family therapy. In working cases of family injustice, one cannot set aside the past because that is always where injustice began. Often the offense is no longer occurring and may have occurred briefly or only once. Thus, without an assessment of these issues over time the therapist may make the fatal error of offering an intervention that does not fit because the problem is not apparent in the here and now. This is most tragic when a child presents with oppositional behavior and the therapist attempts to resolve the problem before recognizing that the child has been victimized and is in part rebelling against that. Asking a child to obey and respect a parent who has committed an offense and not shown contrition is a form of emotional abuse in and of itself. To respect a parent, the child must first see the ledger as balanced, that the injustice has been corrected. An especially salient example is found in Justin's case in chapter 5.

An astute historian, Harry Truman nevertheless struggled to compile his own memoirs for publication. He wrote, "the past has always interested me for use *in the present* and I am bored to death with what I did and didn't do some nine years ago." So it is for the therapist treating cases of family injustice, who rehashes history only when past injustices account for the current maintenance of a given problem. If one applies the theory properly, those occasions become more obvious and recognizable and the proper approach to them more apparent.

Self-Utilization

We have learned through experience that proper utilization requires the therapist to be aware of his or her own self as a part of each session and case conceptualization, and to put personal qualities to productive use. The value of self-utilization is apparent in any therapy case, especially in those described herein, and may include race, background, gender, ethnicity, sexual orientation, life experience, or professional credentials. It should also include the therapist's knowledge of his or her own responses to a given client or client-type and the way in which those responses might be used deliberately in the service of change—or inadvertently against it. Throughout the work of Erickson we also find self-utilization in the form of self-disclosure as a central mechanism of joining with and influencing and guiding the client.

Illustrative of this point is an actual case I later used as an essay question to screen interns.

> A 23-year-old single mother of three comes to your mental health clinic at the direction of a social worker. She has a history of committing minor child abuse (i.e., she uses excessive physical discipline given the age of her children). She wants to learn better ways to parent her children as well as receive personal counseling to resolve family of origin issues. In her initial interview she shows mild paranoid symptoms, including a concern that cameras are watching her both in your office and when she is in other public places. She has no other symptoms of thought disorder, but she remains somewhat suspicious for the first few sessions. Nevertheless, you are able to skillfully build rapport with the woman and influence her parenting skills, emotion, and cognition. Through this process you realize that she is becoming very attached to you, though she is never inappropriate or excessively dependent. At the next session, the woman brings a list of issues she wants to discuss in therapy. The list also includes a number of personal questions she wants to ask you. She timidly asks such questions as "Why did you go into psychology?", "What was it like growing up in your family?", "What do you look for in people you like . . . your friends?", and "How did you meet your spouse [partner, paramour, etc.]?"

> Briefly explain how you would conceptualize this client and her psychotherapy. How would you respond to her questions and what outcome would you expect from your responses? You must defend your strategy with a solid rationale.

The most common answer to this question was the obvious one, as taught in most training programs. Though it was phrased many different ways, it summed to "maintaining boundaries" with the client by "refusing to answer and telling her that therapy is about you not me." However, the interns we accepted answered the question differently and from an intuitive understanding of utilization. The best answer in this vein was from then-graduate fellowship student David Barnum (coauthor of two chapters in this book): "It would be disrespectful not to answer her questions. I would tell her an appropriate story about my life in response to each question that answered the questions she hadn't asked." Barnum hit the nail on the head. In each of the questions, the client mother was not trying to pry into my personal life, but rather was asking me for advice on how to live hers. She had bestowed on me referent power—the influence of one whom you wish to emulate. By utilizing myself and my own experience in responding to her questions, I was able to offer important psychological concepts in a personal and approachable language, maximizing my influence over her. I might also add that she listened to and incorporated these concepts into her life.

Self-utilization is not limited to the therapist's best attributes. The benevolent, authoritative therapist is willing to bring his own imperfections into the session to join with and influence the client. Typical of this is a male therapist sharing with a battering husband his own successful struggle to contain his temper in a difficult situation. In working with teenage girls and young women, one of my greatest strengths is the ability to share both the best and worst aspects of my youth as a true "insider" on the issue of how young men think and behave. In working with parents, a great asset is my less-than-perfect adventures as a father. Of course, therapists should never pretend to be "just like" their clients, but instead should use disclosure as evidence of empathy with their struggle even if that struggle is disagreeable. Proper self-utilization precludes the use of disclosure as a way to help the therapist; we all grow and change from our contact with clients, but the hierarchy must be clear and favoring the client, and any personal disclosure should come in the form of an Ericksonian story and not intimate sharing. Aponte (1994) describes the profundity of this exchange quite aptly:

> Today people like my mother—of Latino, African American, Native American, and white European origin, all poor and in some pain about their lives—look for some answers from professional counselors. . . . Our

> therapy can seem presumptuous before the depth of personal struggles these families bring and the social conditions that so test their powers. These are people working for their bread to survive and looking for the nourishing strength of love for their souls from their families, their communities, and their God. This more-or-less commonality with us, their therapists, gives us a ticket of entrance into their lives. If we can risk some memories, emotions, and mutuality, we can join them in the human experience. Then we can use our professional learning and skills because we have also used ourselves. (p. 241)

On this eloquent note of support for self-utilization, we now turn to its most substantial threat—countertransference, one of the few tenets of Freudian psychoanalysis that is applicable to cases of family injustice. In fact, it is central to nearly ever aspect of these cases from the level of the CPS caseworker to the voting public, and thus we shall give it the attention it deserves and rarely receives.

Countertransference

The *American Heritage Dictionary* (2000) defines *countertransference* as the surfacing of "the psychotherapist's own repressed feelings in reaction to the emotions, experiences, or problems of a person undergoing treatment." In emotionally evocative cases of family injustice, we find that much of what goes on throughout the system relates less to the facts of the case and more to the reactions of the therapist and involved professionals. Using a more Ericksonian language, we can think of countertransference as self-utilization gone wrong. In responding to it, the therapist is not telling an illustrative story or finding an echo of the client in himself, he is foisting upon her his own internal agenda. This results in interventions and opinions that are unsound because they result not from an empirical act of therapy, evaluation, or social service but from raw emotional reactivity and false intuition.

Countertransference can emerge in any number of emotional expressions, such as anger, guilt, resentment, pity, or love. However, the most prevalent and controversial is the professional's inappropriate utilization of his own unjust history in conceptualizing a child's experience of his or her family. In one case, a young individually oriented play therapist repeatedly asked her 8-year-old abuse victim if she would be "okay with seeing her dad in therapy" with another therapist assigned to do these sessions. After several iterations of trying to reassure the therapist, the child finally said, "*I'll* be okay with it . . . will *you*?" The therapist said she would be fine, though she knew she would not. The session went well, but a week later the individual therapist contacted CPS to file a child abuse report against the family therapist conducting the conjoint sessions, even though the therapy had been court-ordered. She also told the family that she had "stayed up all night crying" because the girl would be "forced to see her father in therapy." CPS discontinued the therapist on the case, recognizing the potential threat she posed to child and family progress. Unfortunately, most cases of countertransference are not so obvious and are less likely to be addressed so decisively.

Apart from its other benefits, proper implementation of self-utilization can mitigate the effects of countertransference by allowing the therapist to make clear to himself, the family, and the system exactly who he is and where he stands on issues of importance. Consultation and supervision is another important hedge against countertransference. Interestingly, with the notable exception of the Bowenian model, family therapists have not traditionally looked deeply into the psyche of their supervisees, favoring instead an emphasis on development of the therapist's capacity for understanding and intervening with clients. However, to the extent that the therapist's self may impact his or her effectiveness in such cases, one must examine how it is best utilized.

Also critical is adoption of a stance of empiricism and rationality in conceptualization and intervention rather than emotionality. This requires the therapist to consider each case a mini-research project wherein data are gathered, hypotheses tested, interventions implemented, more data collected, interpretation made, and interventions modified. This goes on until the project is successful in finding the correct hypothesis and testing its susceptability to change. Even so, the therapist cannot consider or present herself as objective and wholly free of external bias. She is a product of all that she has experienced since birth, and the best she can do is to be clear to herself and everyone around her where her predispositions lie, especially on the most fundamental bias in any case of family injustice—her perspective on the very nature of families in the system.

Friend or Phobe?: Critical Optimism and Family Nature

No aspect of self-utilization is more central to just outcomes or prone to the effects of countertransference than one's core view of the *nature of families* in the system. At the risk of being reductive and turning a continuous variable into a dichotomous one, most players in the system, from the judge to the foster parent and most certainly the therapist, can be viewed as either family-friends or family-phobes. If one wishes to extrapolate, we can even apply this to the legislature, executive division, and voting public of a given jurisdiction because they ultimately set the agenda for the state CPS.

The extreme family-phobe is a sociological functionalist. He assumes that families in the system have arrived there because they mistreat their children as a matter of character and personality. As such they are unlikely ever to treat them properly, and if they do it will come only under the greatest scrutiny and control. When he encounters a benign family in the system, the family-phobe explains it as an exception to the rule but does not modify his core assumptions. This leaves him submerged in pessimism, which in turn seeps into every other assumption he makes in his practice of law, social work, or therapy. Family-phobes tend to be fatalistic and deterministic, seeing most problems as ego-syntonic, expecting very little of the families they serve. They often dismiss apparent change as "a show" put on by the family to escape the confines of the system, ignoring the fact that most behavior change in any client is a show of psychological compensation and not the result of deep personality reconstruction.

Some family-phobes entered this work grinding the axe of their own dysfunctional childhoods, a clear expression of countertransference. Others grew up loving and caring for children, seeing a move into this field as a mission of salvation for abused and neglect kids. They are referred to in other critical texts as "child savers"—and not with a positive connotation (Wexler, 1995). Still others began with a naïve sense of hope and optimism about families that was not very realistic to begin with. At some point they are invariably "burned" by a family, creating countertransference anger and retribution. Once may be all they need to become family-phobic, or it may take several such cases before they adopt a "never-again" attitude toward families in general. I myself have sent children home and lived to regret it—though thankfully not a fraction of those I have successfully kept at home or brought to reunification—so I know how easy it is to become discouraged and angry out of a countertransference sense of betrayal. One must not ignore or flee from such feelings, but work through them openly to avoid overgeneralization. It is also helpful to remember that therapy as an empirical act offers learning from both success and failure.

The family-friend does not acknowledge a qualitative family or human nature, but sees in each person the potentiality for a humanizing good or dehumanizing evil (Freire, 1970) in dialectical tension. She approaches cases from a position of *critical optimism* (Freire, 1974), which "requires a strong sense of social responsibility and of engagement in the task of transforming society[5]; it cannot mean simply letting things run on" (p. 13). Critical optimism allows the therapist to perceive reality for what it is without becoming submerged in it or determined by it, and to lead the clients toward that same stance. Unlike some approaches discussed later in this chapter, this sort of optimism does not view family injustice through rose-colored glasses, but engages in the reflection and social "response-ability" necessary to transform it. It also balances a radical belief in free will with an informed appraisal of the reasonable limits of change in any given situation.

The critically optimistic therapist begins with the assumption that families in the system are benign by character, but influenced by certain social, family, and personal variables, which lead them to malign *behavior*. If these variables are changed the therapist hypothesizes that the family will function adequately without external influence. The therapist then works carefully to see if this assumption is accurate through dialog, reflection, and action in the family. In this way, therapy becomes an empirical act, which proves or refutes the assumption of benevolence, pointing the way for further intervention; therapy is not guesswork on the part of the therapist based more on his own perceptions than the data at hand.

If they are not critically optimistic, family-friends are every bit as prone to countertransference as family-phobes. They must manage pity for the family and anger at the system by following the guidelines and priorities outlined in chapter 8. Failure to do so generates equal bias in the opposite direction, making them no friend at all to the child, the family, or society. Family-friends have the same concern for children as the "child savers," but put their energy toward just and safe outcomes for *the child in the context of the family*, strengthening damaged homes, wherein they believe children will grow up best.

The Problem of Constructivism

The postmodern therapy movement predicates a great deal of its approach to utilization on constructivism, a concise definition of which is inherently reductive. Behaviorists view knowledge as a passive, largely automatic response to external factors in the environment. Cognitivists view it as an abstract symbolic representation in the perception of individuals. Constructivistics consider knowledge a constructed entity created by each and every person through each person's unique process of learning. Therefore, knowledge cannot be transmitted from one person to the other as it is—it must be constructed, transmitted to, and reconstructed by each person. It is not as absolute but relativistic, varying according to time and space and yielding a "truth" that can never be taken for granted. Most notable for our purposes are the social constructivists who stress collaborative effort as the source of all knowledge, an essential characteristic of a constructivist therapy process.

As a nearly pure approach to utilization, constructivism has utility in a great many cases. There are times when we are free as therapists to explore a client's problem from many angles and realities. There can be fluidity in our thinking as we take the parent's perception and then the child's, walking a mile in each person's shoes and then deciding how to proceed. We can bask in the positive reframe of a client problem, challenging it with a hopeful perspective. Yet as useful as constructivism may be for common family therapy and evaluation, it is so easily misapplied to cases of family injustice that it is best dispensed with at the onset.

Rather than seeing things as a constructed reality, in these cases the therapist must first see things as they really are or come as close as humanly attainable. This involves what might best be termed praxis (Freire, 1970), as the therapist undertakes a dialectic of critical reflection on and action toward an understanding of reality through dialog with the client. In this model, praxis is the only source of all true knowledge and creation. Through this critical reflection on reality, the therapist comes to understand family injustice as a process of who did what to whom and how much each person suffered for it, as well as who was in a position to prevent it. This requires a posture in therapeutic praxis that the truth is best said and lies are to be avoided at almost any cost. It also requires the therapist to be as certain as possible that he is right before intervening because his influence can create greater injustice through ill-informed or errant action. And because we all make mistakes, he must always be ready to state when he was wrong and make rational changes in his approach.

In short, a great part of the utilization process in such cases is the investigation of reality, not reality's construction. We will later put this concept into practice as we discuss the evaluation of families in CPS over three levels of scrutiny.

Conclusion: Making Therapy Relevant

In one language or another, utilization is at the core of any modern therapeutic intervention. It is literally the way in which the act of therapy becomes relevant to the client, thereby improving generalizability of generic techniques to the real world of the client and enhancing the chances of success. As with any important construct, utilization can be and often is taken too far, creating a sort of therapeutic relativism that is unhelpful, especially in cases of family injustice. However, properly applied utilization of the client's past and present reality and the therapist's self while avoiding constructivism is a potent and necessary curative factor.

CONTEXTUAL CHANGE

As family therapists we share a historic belief that meaningful and lasting change in an individual typically requires a change in that person's larger life context. This necessitates an interactional perspective, seeking first to understand how people involve themselves with one another and the world around them, making the construct especially suited to cases of family injustice. From this perspective, client behavior is seen as an encoded message to the natural environment, requiring a determined effort on the part of the therapist to decode it and utilize it to render change. Although this may seem unwieldy, the focus on context actually makes therapy briefer and more enduring than individual approaches, which seek to change the client's feelings, thoughts, or behaviors outside their natural context and without its input. Moreover, as Madanes (2000) notes, if a therapist believes that a person has a problem because of his social context, she must also believe that she might conceivably have the same problem were she in similar circumstances. This yields a very special kind of empathy in which the therapist finds "an echo in yourself for each person in the room. You must realize that the person could be you." Needless to say, this in turn sets a foundation for mitigating countertransference and maximizing self-utilization while leading the therapist to focus not on the intrapsychic world of the client, but his context as the focus of change.

The factor of free will requires attention to personal responsibility, but contextualizing therapy extends this responsibility to the social world. As Madanes (1993a) notes, "When we say that the individual is responsible for himself, we not only mean that each is responsible for his or her own individuality, but that he or she is responsible for all human beings. . . . When we choose for ourselves we choose for all human beings. Every single one of our acts creates an image of the human being as we think she or he ought to be" (p. 71). Thus, we become both products of and contributors to a vast web of human interplay from which we cannot extract ourselves by an egocentric and false individualism. For even as we are each free to choose, so are we obligated to choose for our social context. We are not individuals, but part of a human network, each aspect of which influences the others. Our therapy must reflect and act on that reality.

In stark contrast to this contextual approach, traditional models of intervention are commonly imposed via separate individual or group modalities for victims and offenders. This seems a very odd response to victimization, which is by definition an interactional process that does not exist outside of human interplay; it is hard to imagine how isolating people from one another can ever resolve it. Yet predicated on this specific view of family violence and an understandable desire to protect victims from further physical or emotional insult, it has been common to treat family violence as if it were an intrapsychic phenomenon. Following a contextual approach, there may be good reasons to have separate sessions at times for all family members, but it is rarely sensible to conduct the entirety of therapy this way, especially if the therapists are not all on the same clinical team.

Circularity in the Misunderstanding of Family Context

An enduring cybernetic construct of family therapy, circularity holds that everyone in a system contributes something to the greater sum of its functioning. This idea may be helpful in understanding family context in common therapies, but circularity has no place in cases of family injustice. Yet because she is looking so hard for strengths and avenues of intervention, the family-friend may be the most vulnerable of any professional to its allure, leading her to intervene at the wrong point in the family system, potentially creating more injustice than she has resolved.

For example, a husband and wife are having marital difficulties. Their son sides with the mother and the daughter with her father. The daughter pierces her tongue to the horror of the mother, a PTA president for 3 years. The father thinks "it's cute" that his little girl is becoming her own person and admits he signed for the piercing. They argue intensely about the girl while the boy steals money from the father's wallet. The father grounds the boy, the mother lifts the grounding and increases the boy's allowance, saying that the father is too stingy with money. The father stays away one night. The girl blames the mother and announces she is now gay. The boy hits the girl. And so on.

Using a circular model, the therapist can approach this family from any of several perspectives. The therapist could get the father to spend more time with the mother (an approach we would favor). Or she could get the mother to spend more time working with the daughter, and the father more time working with the son. She could get the two children into the superordinate goal of helping the parents' marriage, or use a behavioral plan to draw the parents together to work with their children. In short, one might enter the sequence at any point, as everyone has a reasonable level of contribution to the problem.

Cases of family injustice have almost nothing to do with this example.

As Madanes (1993a) notes, "Many family therapists adhered to their concept [of circularity] trying to escape from ideas of bad parents or bad chemistry, only to find themselves mired in the concept that no one has responsibility. The abusive father is the same as the abused child in that both are part of a system that functions as best it can . . . and this is the best of all possible worlds" (p. 70). So let us modify the above case to say that the marital problems and father/daughter alliance lead to failing boundaries and sexual abuse by the father. By altering this one very serious variable, we have rendered moot the idea of everyone contributing equally to the problem. We cannot suggest to the daughter that she quit having sex with her father—that would be a horrific example of blaming the victim. We must first focus on the offender and offense. Yet errant conceptualization of such cases from a circular perspective can metaphorically do just that, misconstruing the comparative responsibility of victim and offender.

September was the subject of two such misattributions, one by the veteran CPS worker involved in the case and one by a psychiatrist who saw her during one of her hospital stays. In the first example, September's father spoke to his daughter's caseworker about his guilt and shame over his sex offense, wondering aloud if he was responsible for all the problems the girl was having. Amazingly, Hanna Winthrow consoled him, noting that she had known the girl since she was 6 years old and that she probably would have turned out this way anyhow. The father was so dumbfound by Hanna's response that he called to ask me the same question. I responded that the caseworker was wrong—he was 100% responsible for what he had done to her and that, even if she had problems before, which was arguable, his treatment of her had made them infinitely worse. "That's what I thought," he said. "But Hanna thought September was just, well . . . screwed up somehow before all this even happened."

The caseworker's response might be one of ignorance, as she was not trained in the mental health professions. However, there was no excuse for the staff psychiatrist at the hospital who informed me of a most remarkable development in September's case.

"You know that September wanted to have sex with her father," she commented, almost as an afterthought.

"What?" I said with obvious shock. "I'm the one who took the disclosure. At no time has she ever said anything like that to me. What did she say that leads you to think this?"

The psychiatrist became uncomfortable. "Well I'm just telling you this because it's something that you need to be aware of in working with her."

I could feel the presence of arbitrary conjecture hidden behind the hubris of psychiatric opinion. "Dr. Smith," I said. "Could you please provide me with the data upon which you base that supposition?"

"She consented to it," Smith said.

"How did you learn this?" I reiterated.

"Well," Smith said, now completely flustered. "She didn't tell him 'no.' "

I attempted to retain my composure, without hiding my dismay. "Dr. Smith, I am an expert in the treatment of sexual abuse and thoroughly familiar with the research on this topic, and I have never heard anyone assert that a 14-year-old girl being molested by her father was 'consenting' because she didn't say 'no.' "

Fortunately, the girl was discharged and never saw this doctor again, nor was she privy to this detail of the case until adulthood. But it was buried somewhere in her record, where I am sure it was read and pondered by others in the system, who then joined Dr. Smith as careless advocates of a circular conceptualization of family dynamics. In viewing September as partially responsible for her abuse, they were revictimizing her and actually distancing her father from responsibility for his offense.

The Outplacement of Children

The most radical form of isolation, the outplacement of children to foster care, inextricably changes every aspect of the child's natural context and will thus receive attention throughout the remainder of this text. We will begin with a critical examination of the concept and the practice of outplacement contrasted with a therapy of contextual change in which the family is changed and strengthened to retain or reintegrate the child. On one far end of this debate is CPS, which in its most family-phobic form tends to see itself as a bastion of safety and goodwill for children cursed by violent and neglectful parents. This represents an enactment of the fundamental attributional bias—that good and successful things come from me and that bad things are the fault of others. One of many clinical examples was found in the comment by a CPS director that what was really needed was a therapy that would "disconnect these kids from their biological families." When queried further, one of the caseworkers agreed, noting that it had taken "5 years for one of my kids to finally give up on her family and by then she was well into her teens." At best, such opinions have no empirical or rational support, ignoring the vital importance of a child's family, regardless of her placement status. At worst, they are the root of family-phobia in the social service and mental health systems and the basis for many errant decisions on reunification versus long-term foster care.

Dave Pelzer, perhaps the best-known former-foster child in current popular culture, actually takes this same position on behalf of CPS in his follow-up to *A Child Called "It"* (1995). In *The Lost Boy*, Pelzer (1997) details his trek through at least five placements from removal to young adulthood, including numerous examples of carelessness and callousness in the system from a child's point of view. Yet adult Pelzer concludes that CPS and the foster care system are unfairly maligned, referring to social workers as burned-out "angels—whose sole goal is the saving of children" (p. 308). This reflects in part from his belief that his abusive mother would have ultimately killed him, a tenable assertion based on his earlier work. However, with the hundreds of cases we have seen over the last 10 years, only a tiny number of offenders are as severe or disturbed as Pelzer's mother. The author makes this point himself, claiming that his case was then "identified as one of the most severe cases of child abuse in the state of California" (Pelzer, 1999, p. 288), which means that it cannot be generalized in any way to the remaining majority. Still, Pelzer (1997) is unrelenting in his praise, claiming without any evidence beyond his own experience that "while the system is not perfect, it does in fact work" (p. 313). In fact, I have rarely if ever seen a foster child as grateful to be a graduate of "the system" as is Pelzer, and more often children are ill served by and resentful of their experience in custody. And lest the reader diminish the greater importance of this very personal and wholly nonacademic perspective, it should be remembered that Pelzer's books have sold far more copies than any of the more contrary accounts of foster care we shall now discuss.

At the most opposite extreme is Scott (1994), who portrays the entire child protective movement as a liberal governmental conspiracy to extricate children from loving parents. The author actually describes the book as a series of "horror stories" about the system and offers strategies for the "best defense" of innocent families from the "foster care nightmare." These views are particularly common among neo-conservative and fundamentalist groups who distrust governmental intervention at any level. More mainstream, academic and well researched but no less critical, is the work of Wexler (1995), which has become somewhat the bible for foster care reform. In its second printing, the text emerged in the early 1990s right after the McMartin hearings and during a growing backlash against what Gardner (1991) termed "sex abuse hysteria." Taking a rather bitter stance on the "child saving" and family-phobic mentality of the system, the author offers an extensive critique not only of outplacement and foster care but also of mandatory abuse reporting and investigation. Not simply a gadfly, Wexler compiles no less than 35 highly specific recommendations for the improvement of the system, many of which have come into practice in a number of jurisdictions since the book's first publication. Space allows only a brief excerpt of those most relevant to this text, but the majority are tenable and well reasoned, and the book is an important read on the topic. Wexler suggests:

- Reversing financial contingencies to encourage permanency and reunification.
- Eliminating educational neglect from CPS jurisdiction.
- Narrowing the grounds for intrusive intervention to include only situations of child endangerment and imminent risk.
- Basing all findings and decisions in a CPS case on the idea of the least detrimental alternative, taking into account the iatrogenic effects of foster care as a part of that formulation.
- Raising the burden of proof on the state to clear and convincing evidence.
- Maintenance of regular visitation between parents and children unless it can be proven to the court that such visits would be seriously harmful.
- Six-month reviews of the child's case by the court at the clear and convincing standard of evidence for retention of outplacement.
- Assistance to the family for at least 6 months after reunification.
- Termination of rights when exhaustive efforts have failed.
- Court processes to review termination cases and to offer legal redress for families who have been harmed by the system.
- Minimum requirements (a bachelor's degree) for the practice of social work and better pay, better conditions, and improved training for workers.
- Aggressive advocacy of family preservation as both a concept and a program of intervention.

Many of Wexler's assertions are reflected in later chapters of this book, and a number of others are consistent with our own work and experience. Moreover, a healthy distrust of foster care is supported in the scientific literature (Anonymous, Connors, Fribourg, Gries, & Gonzales, 1998; Barth & Blackwell, 1998; Benedict, Zuravin, Brandt, & Abbey, 1994; Blome, 1997;

Cook-Fong, 2000; Gillespie, Byrne, & Workman, 1995; Herman, Susser, & Struening, 1994; Lewis, Walton, & Fraser, 1995; Mangine, Royse, Wiehe, & Nietzel, 1990; McDonald, Allen, Westerfelt, & Piliavin, 1996; Pilowsky, 1995; Smucker, Kauffman, & Ball, 1996; Spencer & Knudsen, 1992; Susser, Lin, Conover & Struening, 1991).

Yet even as I applaud critique of the system and support its reform, a more pragmatic and clinically informed perspective challenges both ends of the wide spectrum of opinion on outplacement and isolation of children from their families. Any political treatise (Scott, 1994) that holds families collectively innocent and vilifies the system is indulging in a fantasy of intrigue, conspiracy, and purposive corruption well beyond the evidence. Even the better-reasoned and documented work of Wexler (1995) comes not from daily clinical contact and training but from his experience as an investigative journalist writing in an exposé format. Decrying child saving by offering hundreds of disturbing stories of systemic abuse, he extrapolates directly and by implication that (1) systemic abuse of families is the norm; (2) the family as a concept is so maligned by the system that many innocent parents are the subject of excess child abuse reporting and systemic intrusion, a practice so pervasive that each of us should beware; and (3) family preservation, specifically of the homebuilders model (Kinney, Haapala, & Booth, 1991), is the primary clinical solution to the problem of outplacement.

Wexler is on the right track. Consistent with the tenet of contextual change, a great many difficult families are manageable sans outplacement and few if any CPS systems are without flaw, some with flaws as profound as any seen in the families they serve. Yet his suppositions often appear more like those of the idealistic young therapist who has learned to be naïvely optimistic, snatching CPS's self-defined halo and dropping it squarely onto client families who become little more than bystanders or victims and not participants in the experience of injustice. As noted, Scott takes this same view to an almost ludicrous degree. First of all, despite some of the stories I will share later, systemic abuse of innocent families is not the norm, and when it does occur it must be addressed without minimizing the scope of the problem of family injustice. Of course, the system does not work and outplacement has been greatly overused to the detriment of children and families. Yet most of the system-bound families we have encountered over the years *have* committed injustices against their children that require significant intervention to resolve.

At the crux of his position in this regard, Wexler returns to the origins of value-free intervention by focusing on poverty as the explanation for abuse and neglect, downplaying personal responsibility. He notes, "Fundamentally, the programs that are needed to reduce child abuse are programs that are needed to ameliorate the worst effects of poverty . . . with an emphasis on 'hard' services and meeting needs identified by the clients themselves" (p. 251). This is both unproven and an extension of circular reasoning to the larger society. Poverty may well lead to improper placement by CPS, and the poor are increasingly underserved in our nation, but economic stratification is not a de facto precursor to child abuse and focus on this issue detracts from the offense. We must remember that the vast majority of poverty stricken families *do not* sexually or physically abuse their children, and a fair minority of middle-class and upper-class families do. Family injustice is simply not the stepchild of poverty, which brings us to my final critique of Wexler's position.

The homebuilder's model is a fine program for a certain client population, mostly families who need to learn skills and find resources to maintain safe and attentive homes and who need what Wexler calls "hard services" typically defined by the families themselves from the realm of social service offerings both public and private. However, despite its success at keeping children out of custody, its case management style and surface-level interventions are not designed to deal with the complex interplay of physical and sexual abuse, which are by far more common in our experience than families who simply lack access to services. The model would have been ideal for Bobbi and Zach (chapter 10), but its strategic misapplication in other cases can expose children to greater risk, as it did for Leia in chapter 5, thus increasing family injustice.

This is more than an academic argument. Extreme admiration of outplacement renders status quo, because the system is portrayed as working as well as can be expected when it certainly is not. Extreme critique renders chaos, as reactionary forces advocate disposal of baby and bath water, or in more moderate works curtail the legitimate functions of child protection in favor of preservation models or reversed contingencies that are perhaps valuable but far from panaceas. Neither position does anything to render justice, because neither critically reflects on the real successes and failures of the system. Whether examining the unjust family or the failure of the system to render just outcomes, it is important to maintain critical reflection and optimism in an effort to fully perceive reality and act on it. This balanced perspective is consistent with Minuchin and colleagues (1998) and Madanes (1990; Madanes, Keim, & Smelser, 1995), and fits Toth's (1997) extensive and critical case study of 5 children in foster care:

> [The case studies in this book] point directly to where the system is going wrong. The children in substitute childcare today have all suffered trauma. They are all at greater risk than the general child population. Yet they are given less care, when they need more care. Many thousands of children are lost and millions of dollars are wasted each year because no one . . . takes full responsibility for them. (p. 24)

As the most intrusive intervention available in the treatment of family injustice, outplacement should demonstrate efficacy in improving outcomes for children, but it has not. In fact, foster children are at a significant disadvantage when compared with the general population, regardless of the reason for placement. Whether this is a product of placement itself or reflective of the circumstances that led to it might only be determined in larger, controlled studies, which cannot ethically balance experimental research and child protection. In absence of data to the contrary, foster care is best considered a necessary evil in the overall process of child protection. As such, therapists must learn to work with it and within it, while striving to find alternatives before placement, and toward reunification after placement has occurred.

Conclusion: Family as Friend

The tenet of contextual versus individual change is so important that it underlies the entire remainder of this book. While we cannot always engage the family, in the vast majority of cases we have found the greatest obstacle to be the failure of the therapist to ask or the unwillingness of the system to allow it. A close second is the therapist's failure to ask properly, in a way that increases the likelihood of engagement. In other words, if properly invited, most families will come and try to win back their children from the unnatural context of outplacement. Some of these will fail to rectify their injustices even with the best of efforts, and these are the saddest cases of all, for we as a system fail with them. But failure should never lead us toward family phobia. As critically optimistic family friends, we must always look for ways to succeed, to make things better not worse, and to strengthen and advocate for every family who can reasonably make it. We are never more powerful in the life of a child than when we are the allies of that child's family. We are never weaker than when we become its foe.

NOTES

1. This is a known side-effect of all stimulant medications, not just this product.
2. A time-released form of Ritalin (methylphenidate).
3. This case is fully discussed in Jay Haley (1996) *Learning and Teaching Therapy* and on the video tape *Unbalancing a Couple* (1998). Both are available from www.jay-haley-on-therapy.com.
4. This forms a core conceptual error for most CPS agencies. They are not schooled in utilization and thus tend to do exactly this in the majority of cases.
5. Freire is speaking here of social injustice, but the point is equally true in the microcosm of the family.

CHAPTER 4

Contrition, Forgiveness, and the Restoration of Justice

WES CRENSHAW AND DAVID BARNUM

> Who had mama been, what had she wanted to be or do before I was born? Once I was born her hopes had turned and I climbed up her life like a flower reaching for the sun. . . . Her life had folded into mine. What would I be like when I was fifteen, twenty, thirty? Would I be as strong as she had been, as hungry for love, as desperate, determined, and ashamed. . . ? I would be thirteen in a few weeks. I was already who I would be . . . someone like her, like Mama, a Boatwright woman.
>
> —Dorothy Allison, *Bastard Out of Carolina* (2000)

As Madanes (1990)[1] notes, family injustice invokes the basic human need to repent and forgive. Regardless of the nature of the injustice, only the most sociopathic offenders are beyond repentance, and even some of them may be reattached to it for brief periods in treatment. Likewise, if they have not been redirected by powerful others, most victims yearn to forgive. The need for repentance in the restoration of family justice led Madanes to develop her renowned apology process, first for use with adolescent and adult sex offenders and later with a wide range of family injustices. Not surprisingly, given the intrapsychic treatment slant of the times, these strategies were met with controversy. The idea of a victim, especially one who had been sexually abused, *forgiving* her offender seemed at best outside the realm of therapy. At worst it was seen as wrong-headed and traumatizing, as well as a de facto softening of the hard line against offenders. But none of this was what Madanes had proposed or implemented, and those who practiced the approach were genuinely surprised by this criticism. In fact, the emphasis on forgiveness was actually superimposed by the model's opponents on a technique that focused squarely on offender responsibility and against pressuring the victim to do anything, least of all forgive the offense. In response, proponents found themselves defensively distanced even from the idea of forgiveness. While necessary at the time, this tactical position prevented full exploration of the way in which an *invitation* to forgiveness does not exonerate the offender, but releases the victim from a life of perpetual connection to the offense. By the mid-1990s the idea of apology was becoming more widely accepted and integrated into other approaches at the same time the legal community began experimenting with restorative justice models. In this new light, we felt ourselves released to explore the possibility of forgiveness and to modify our thinking and practice within the context of treating family injustice.

Any approach to therapy with a victim of injustice must seek to reapportion the shame of the offense, contextualize and distance her[2] from the experience, release her from culpability, and protect her from further abuse. Any therapy with an offender seeks to prevent reoffense and move him from denial and blame toward responsibility, compassion, empathy, and self-control (Madanes, 1990).

Where we differ from other models is in our belief that without a transformation of *the relationship* between the victim and offender, these outcomes are difficult to achieve and shorter lived. Moreover, we believe a conjoint transformative experience synergistically produces these outcomes more efficiently and with greater durability than any other method. Beyond this we propose a superordinate goal in the treatment of all victims, which we refer to as *putting the offense in context.* We define this as the victim's perceptual transformation away from seeing the offense as central to her life, and toward viewing it in a greater life context—no more or less important than other significant life events. It bears noting that the superordinate goal for offenders is also to recontextualize the offense—seeing it as existing within a context of free will so that whatever his violent, sexual, or neglectful impulses, he is solely culpable for his actions and associating an appropriate sense of shame with them.

Using the language of our Ericksonian tradition, we consider the victim's relationship with the offender to represent a sort of "trance state" foisted upon her at the point of offense. As underscored in the opening passage by Dorothy Allison, this fascination is borne of the need to understand the complex answer to the two questions asked by nearly every victim regarding her offense: "Why did this happen to me?" and "Who will I become because of it?" These questions lead abused children and adults to spend inordinate amounts of time considering what they have done to deserve this fate. Responding directly to this predicament, a core intervention in the restoration of family justice is a ritual of repentance on the part of offenders toward their victims (Madanes, 1990; Madanes, Keim, & Smelser, 1995) at which time the invitation of forgiveness is extended to the victim via the offender's apology.

When it is even considered, forgiveness is often seen as a sort of duty to either oneself or the community, especially when taken within a religious framework. We do not see this as particularly healthy or therapeutic, and in fact attempt to mitigate this sense of obligation in therapy. Instead, when repentance is offered, we believe forgiveness will naturally emerge from the victim's yearning to become free of the offense, move away from pathology and toward health. The emergence of forgiveness in this manner results from a *contrition process*, which can be described through six levels of completeness. The more complete the process of contrition experienced by the victim, the greater her experience of true healing and rectification of the injustice. Each level of completeness can be identified by the juxtaposition of the offender and victim in how contrition was offered and received, and observed in the extent to which several dimensions common to the experience of victims are addressed. The more direct the apology, the more complete the process, and the more healthy the victim will be across several dimensions:

- The fascination of the victim with the original and subsequent offenders.
- The degree to which the relationship between offender and victim is transformed from pathological to healthy.
- The expectancies and attributions of the victim about the offender, which often extend to her greater world context.
- The role the victim takes in relating to others (e.g., passive, caretaker, etc.).
- The extent to which the victim remains stuck in a "victim" or "survivor" mentality.

These levels of contrition are not stages in the sense that people must move through them in sequence, but discrete circumstances, at least one of which will appear in any given case at any given time. The illustrations are provided as a visual organizer for the six levels of contrition, which will then be discussed in greater detail. Each includes a victim (V) and an offender (O). Some levels also include an interceding therapist (Tx), and one includes a substitute (S) for the offender.

LEVEL 1: ISOLATED

As noted in chapter 3, the isolated level of contrition (Fig. 4.1) is fairly common in cases involving CPS, often forming the core unit of intervention, especially when the injustice is one of sexual abuse. At this level the victim voluntarily or involuntarily experiences what Bowen (1978) termed an "emotional cut-off" from the offender, often an important person in the child's life. The victim is afforded no opportunity to transform the relationship away from trauma, adopting instead a hateful stance toward the offender with no means by which to express the resulting anger. The victim might initiate isolation of her own volition, but it is more commonly encouraged or imposed by external forces. These may include estranged parents, CPS,

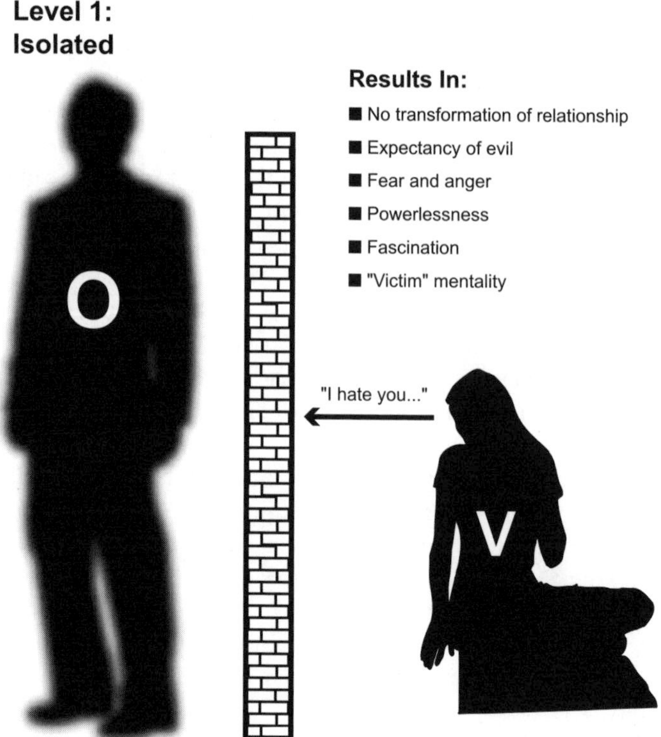

FIGURE 4.1

therapists, or well-meaning family members who advise the victim to "move on" and distance herself from the offender. In therapy and in many social service interventions, such communication implicitly or even explicitly suggests to the victim that she must maintain a certain level of hate to prevent further victimization and to set "good boundaries."

With no opportunity for transformation, the victim remains stuck with the offense as perhaps the most critical event in her life. Not infrequently, she spends many years and considerable energy focused on and recapitulating her own abuse in an attempt to understand and master it. But like Sisyphus, her plight is unending as she rolls the rock of her shame up a hill of false responsibility, only to have it fall back down upon her each time. In the process she develops an expectancy of evil and approaches the world with a combination of fear and anger, overgeneralizing this event to other aspects of her life. As inferred from the figure, the victim's experience of the offender becomes "fuzzy" and confused. This is because the trance state is never stronger than in a level 1 case, as the victim remains fascinated by the offender, who in isolation becomes larger than life, requiring tremendous emotional energy to put in check. In a worst-case scenario, this fuzzy memory and perceived imbalance of power can yield a victim-turned-offender, as she overidentifies with the offender and his hold over her and recapitulates it with others. More commonly, the victim simply remains passive and deferent to those in her life who then reoffend her in one way or another.

As discussed in chapter 3, family-phobic therapists and social service systems support family dismantling and isolation as a matter of theory and practice. An example was found in Debbie, a gentle, attractive, and intelligent young woman of 26 (see Leia's case, chapter 5). Toward the end of the first session, Crenshaw asked her a common intake question in our approach, "What's the worst thing I haven't asked you?" Debbie immediately broke down crying and disclosed that her father and mother had sexually abused her quite severely from age 8 to 14. It was now clear why she had remained in an abusive and unproductive relationship with her current husband, a man who was responsible for the loss of her 5 children, one of whom he had sexually abused.

Debbie had sought treatment for depression in a psychiatric hospital a year before her intake at our institute. At that time she disclosed her sex abuse history, and that therapist had hypothesized a connection between this and her depression. When asked what had been done to help her with this problem, Debbie said she had been instructed to write a letter to her mother telling her that she never wanted to see her again. Crenshaw expressed curiosity as to how this directive had gone, and Debbie admitted that it did not sit right with her. However, she knew that therapists were educated professional people, so she complied. In fact, for the next year her mother had come at least once a week to the discount store where Debbie worked and stood about 20 yards away from her, never approaching and never being asked to approach. The two remained in suspended animation for 30 minutes and then separated again until the following week. It was a strange ritual that metaphorically reminded Debbie that she was both connected to and disconnected from her mother. When asked how well this arrangement had worked in dealing with her problems, she thought for a moment and then, with a tinge of embarrassment, admitted that she was now more depressed than ever. Debbie even wondered whether she had not been ignoring her mother enough.

A classic example of poor utilization, this intervention built upon Debbie's lifelong feelings of isolation and made them worse. She was not allowed to experience the apology and repentance of her mother, leaving her to deal with the ordeal of her abuse virtually alone, which in turn led her farther into an unproductive and dependent relationship with a husband who also turned out to be a sex offender. In reality she felt like she had damned and then abandoned her mother—a woman who was also a victim of abuse and of her own limited intellect.[3]

Crenshaw took a very different tack. He asked Debbie if her previous therapist had attempted to bring her mother into session. When Debbie indicated she had not, he asked her to schedule a conjoint session as soon as she felt she was ready. She did so the next day. In fact, Debbie later commented in the preparatory session before the apology that she was rather surprised that this idea had not come up before. Clients intuitively understand the importance of such interventions. Only therapists must learn the hard way.

Perhaps the greatest irony in support for victim/offender isolation versus contextual change is the frequency with which it fails after the system withdraws. Often when external forces are removed, victims return of their own volition to the scene of family injustice, usually without benefit of the therapy or other intercession, and face the entire ordeal alone. As we shall discuss shortly, this unmitigated and impromptu reconciliation is rarely in the best interests of the victim, and often leads to further injustices outside of the purview of the system; and the result is well short of a complete contrition process. It does, however, set the stage for the next level of contrition, which is just slightly more complete than total isolation.

LEVEL 2: ARTIFICIAL

The artificial level of contrition (Fig. 4.2) occurs when a victim has without due reflection made the unilateral decision to "just forgive" an offender without any act of contrition on his part, at times while still in total isolation from him. This is often influenced by a very unsophisticated version of the aforementioned sociocultural emphasis on forgiveness rather than placing it in a larger process of contrition. As such, it leads to what we term a "reverse transformation," where the victim goes directly from being mistreated by the offender to being gracious and accommodating in offering unrequited forgiveness. This may seem magnanimous at first blush, but it ultimately leads the victim toward resentment and hostility across many domains of her life. Because they have accepted the burden of unilaterally correcting their relationship to their offender, these victims tend to invite reversed hierarchies, especially in poorly bounded and codependent intimate relationships. In this they go "over the line" to forgive and reforgive people who have not earned it, often becoming involved in a cycle of violence. This tends to veil the fascination of the victim with the offender (e.g., forgive and forget), creating a state of denial and repression, because acknowledging the offense and surrounding issues would force the fragile artificial forgiveness to crumble. This takes considerable focus and energy, at times even requiring an unhealthy dissociative state around the offense to compensate.

Some victims will state from the onset that they have "just forgiven" the offender as a part of coping with the offense, but most level 2 clients do not even mention forgiveness unless the therapist raises the issue. Instead, they may speak of having "gone on with my life," or of "trying not to think

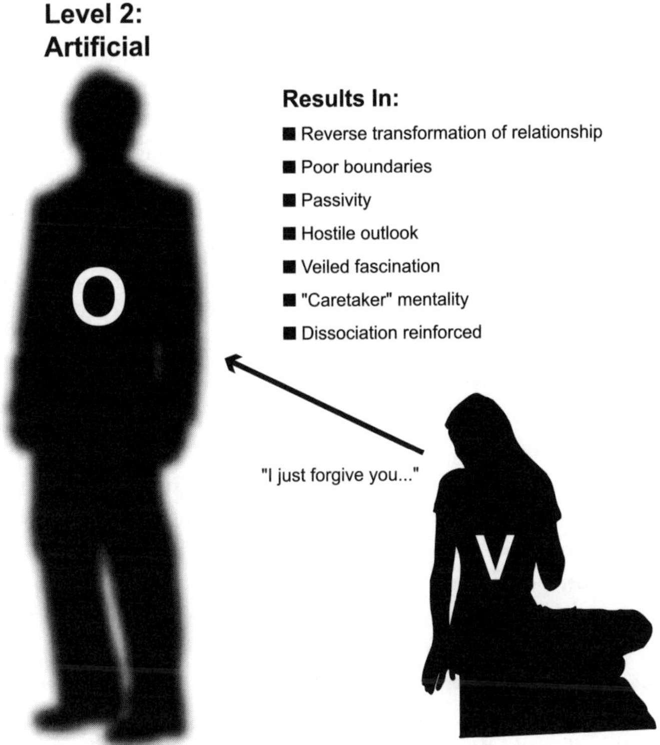

Level 2:
Artificial
Results In:
Reverse transformation of relationship
Poor boundaries
Passivity
Hostile outlook
Veiled fascination
"Caretaker" mentality
Dissociation reinforced
O
"I just forgive you..."
V

FIGURE 4.2

about it." As we shall see later in the case example, they may also make a series of positive statements about the offender within the same conversation in which they reveal details of the offense, even coming to the defense of the offender when he is criticized. It is especially disturbing to hear a victim first describe horrible sexual abuse, then comment that the offender was a "great dad to me except for molesting me," then comment on how she used to imagine killing him until she forgave him. She will often recycle this same commentary in therapy and in life because, as noted above, she is doing all the work and the offender is doing nothing.

At times victims at this level of contrition even create an artificial apology memory for themselves. The client may say that she knows that the offender feels sorry for what he did because "he couldn't look me in the eye" or offered some imagined reparation like buying her a car or giving her college money. Particularly common and odd are the cases where the victim has experienced a deathbed apology, which often seems to have nothing to do with the offense. In more than one case a victim has stated that her offender had, in his final incoherent moments of life, uttered, "I'm so sorry. I'm sorry," which she is sure pertains to the offense. In one case the victim said, "Just before he died he looked at me in this really funny way and I could tell that he was sorry for what he'd done to me."

Examples of artificial forgiveness are replete in cases of family injustice. However, they are less common among children and families in the system, because the offense is still a core part of real life thus not as easily prone to the necessary distancing. When it does appear, it usually does so in the context of a victim desperately trying to portray herself as unharmed by the abuse so that she can be returned home. Otherwise, when they involve CPS at all, most level 2 cases appear among graduates of the system who go home after release.

Though it does not involve CPS, an excellent example of artificial forgiveness is found in the case of Sarah and Ron, published in Crenshaw and Cain (1998), excerpted herein. Sarah presented as quite verbally abusive to Ron, accusing him of infidelity without reason and using sexual relations as a tool of manipulation. Worse, she had begun to stay out until 2 A.M., shooting pool alone at seedy bars in clothing she readily admitted to be sexually provocative. Ron begged her to come to therapy and finally threatened to divorce her if she did not. Kim Cain had been seeing the case for several weeks and sought live supervision because she could not get the couple to stop shouting expletives long enough to conduct any form of meaningful therapy. But when placed in front of the mirror the couple was surprisingly cooperative, and we took the opportunity to finally learn something about them other than their full repertoire of curse words. Suspecting a history of abuse at play, we explored Sarah's previous relationships to see if they played into her anger and hostility with Ron. It did not take long for this lead to payoff.

"Sarah, tell me in about two sentences how you feel men have treated you," Kim began.

"Like shit! How about two words? Like shit."

"Ron, when you hear your wife say that, how do you feel?" Kim asked, beginning a process of empathy generation.

"I feel like I'm takin' the rap for those sons of bitches."

"But how do you feel?" Kim reiterated. "I understand that's kind of frustrating for you. How does it make you feel to know that your wife has been hurt the way she has by other men?"

"It makes me feel sad for her. It makes me want to help her get over . . . her demons so she can live a happier life, you know . . . and not have to worry about that kind of stuff all the time. Let it go or whatever she needs to do to be a happier person."

"I have to have a good example first," Sarah said in an odd tone of both sarcasm and hope. "You're that man. I chose you. I put stock in you."

"And you still have some stock in Ron, huh?" Kim said.

"Yeah, but I got slapped upside the head with it too. . . . I just thought you'd be that one."

"Well, dear, I'm not the *perfect* one," Ron said, adding to the edgy tone of the session.

"God, there's not a perfect person in the world," Sarah said.

"She's not really asking for that," Kim intervened before the couple could escalate. "Actually, you're a pretty good guy."

"Yeah, I'm not gonna fight that, believe me," Sarah said, to everyone's surprise. She had never praised him before. "I just felt like you'd be the person to understand me and try to meet me half way. . . . You know, I wasn't born hating men. I was born innocent just like everybody else. The things that you go through teach you that."

"Ron, what do you know about the extent to which other men have hurt Sarah?" Kim asked.

"I don't know . . . her dad leavin' her when she was 6 months old . . . and then her mom married a drunk that molested her. . . ."

"For all the right reasons!" Sarah shot back. It was a remarkable response. This was the first time since Kim had started the case that Sarah had spoken directly of the offense. And now that she did, she moved quickly to exonerate her mother, who was still married to the offender. Befuddled at her own words, Sarah stumbled on trying to clarify herself, only to underscore her confusion. "She didn't marry him knowing that was going to happen! You know, I can't differentiate between that either, because I protect my mother in many ways and to a certain point my stepdad. I won't let Ron hate my stepdad 'cause he didn't do nothin' to Ron." She turned abruptly to Ron. "So I can't deal with you and your feelings toward him or the decisions my mom made, 'cause I'll stand behind them."

In one desperate statement and without any visible impetus, Sarah had now extended her artificial forgiveness from her mother to the man who molested her. With a few more queries we learned that in fact she had an ongoing relationship with her stepfather and her mother. Although everyone knew about the abuse, no one had done anything about it; in fact, Sarah refused even to discuss it further. She had forgiven all involved and now wanted to move on. What she was ignoring in this decision were the dire consequences to her marriage and herself.

Kim honored her refusal to discuss the matter, focusing instead on the pain it had caused. "What Ron needs to understand is the *extent* to which it hurt you. Can you tell him about the extent? We're not talking about the situation or the people, but what the pain was like. What did losing your dad and being molested do to your heart?"

"It broke it," she said solemnly before returning to the defense of her forgiveness. "But I need to solve that on my own—Ron doesn't need to know about it. I mean he wants to go with me. I can't deal with that on top of things I need to get off my chest."

"You know, Ron," Kim said, "This whole situation kind of gets hard and confusing because Sarah has, in a way, been set up by other men. She has been hurt, and you know that holds you somewhat responsible to help your wife get over some of the pain that she feels. Would you be willing to help her do that . . . to do whatever it takes? It's not going to be easy."

"Help her get over the pain? Yes, I want to do that. I mean that's my goal." He seemed surprised that Kim might actually give him that chance.

We had suspected Ron's rescuing mentality as a central theme in his approach to Sarah since they first met, and we were prepared to put it to the best therapeutic use we could find by moving to a level 5 substitute apology. We shall return to Ron and Sarah's case in that section of the text and discuss how we were able to render for her a more complete experience of contrition, opening the door for Sarah to get these painful and self-destructive feelings off her chest once and for all.

Desperate to forgive, victims at level 2 extrapolate anything offered by their offenders (or sometimes nothing at all) into unilaterally perceived acts of contrition, which they rarely are. This becomes the basis for artificial forgiveness, which often seems more healing for the victim than it actually is over time and distance. With therapy, however, it can at least set the client on a journey toward a higher level of completeness, as we shall see in the next section.

LEVEL 3: ILLUSORY

The illusory level of contrition (Fig. 4.3) is similar to level 2 in that it does not involve any real act of apology on the part of the offender. However, rather than "just forgiving" the offender arbitrarily and without reflection, the victim undertakes a rigorous process of developing her own private path to forgiveness. Not infrequently this emerges from therapy, religion, or a highly disciplined self-help process. Therapists working in traditional forgiveness models typically see this as the highest attainable level because they simply don't believe in apology. They see forgiveness as so essential to health and well-being that it should be a focus of the client's treatment and lifestyle.

Often bolstered by a decidedly Christian perspective, such therapists and clients come to see repentance and forgiveness as distinct and separate entities rather than connected and sequential.[4] It is critical to note that a process of reflection and personal growth toward forgiveness typically yields a more healthy and functional client than at lower levels, because these victims are not simply going on as if things were now set right. They are instead actively trying to set them right on their own. And thus the illusory level may be the best

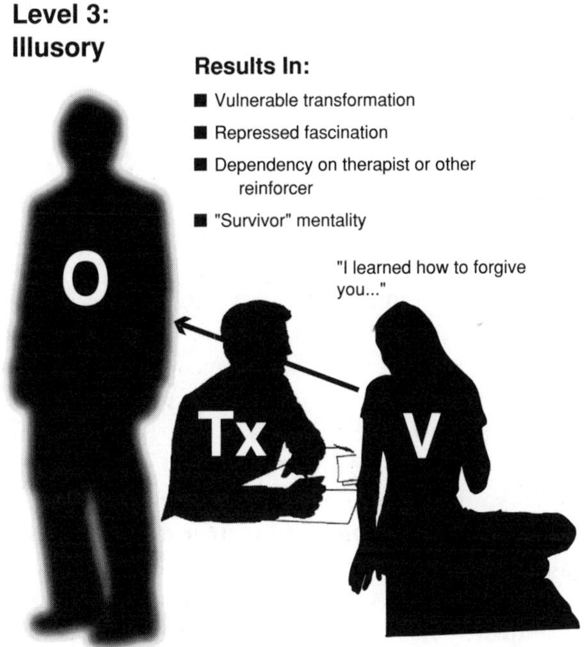

Level 3:
Illusory
Results In:
Vulnerable transformation
Repressed fascination
Dependency on therapist or other reinforcer
"Survivor" mentality
"I learned how to forgive you..."
O
Tx
V

FIGURE 4.3

some clients can hope for, particularly when the offender is dead or irrevocably isolated. But rarely is it enough for a complete transformation of the relationship, because the only thing that has changed is the way in which the client views the offender and attributes the offense. Moreover, maintenance of the illusion involves the victim shifting her attention from the offender and offense onto the act of forgiveness itself and her own personal or moral strength in offering it unconditionally. The fascination with the offense is thus systematically repressed by the illusion, which in turn consumes a great deal of the victim's emotional energy and makes it subject to threat from external forces, especially family members who remain in denial. This in turn keeps the victim in therapy, church, or self-help to reinforce her disconnection from the offense; in fact, such victims are often very loyal to their therapists and may remain in regular contact with them for years on end. When the illusion begins to fail, they are as vulnerable to fuzzy, larger-than-life memories of the offender and offense as any other victim who has not been offered the justice of contrition. As such, illusory forgiveness is a part of a valid "survivor" mentality, but never the equal of a complete contrition process.

We have seen this condition many times in our practice, but never as dramatically as in the inspiring work of Terry Anderson, the news reporter held in Beirut for several years by members of Hezbollah. At the National

Conference on Forgiveness where we first presented this model (Crenshaw & Barnum, 1996), Anderson provided an eloquent and moving keynote on how he came to forgive his captors. During the question and answer period, he was asked what role he thought sorrow and repentance played in the process of forgiveness. Anderson responded out of character, actually scoffing at the question and stating with a tinge of anger, "These people aren't going to apologize for what they did to me."

Surprised at his take on this issue, we reviewed his work in its entirety and realized Anderson was maintaining a level 3 illusion by the very act of speaking publicly on the subject of forgiveness. By becoming one of the nations' foremost experts on this topic, Anderson had created and sustained a powerful and very healing sense of forgiveness. It did not change our model, but it did require us to acknowledge the value of illusion for victims who, for one reason or another, cannot experience sorrow and repentance from their transgressors. At the same time, the yearning for apology does not ebb simply because a person has made the active and reflective decision to forgive, so the therapist should not assume that the illusion is sufficient if a chance for greater resolution can be found. In fact, a year after meeting Anderson we saw him on a CNN special entitled "Return to the Lion's Den" that documented his return to Beirut. Partway through the 2-hour program, Anderson was filmed in a meeting with Sayyid Hassan Nasrullah, Secretary-General of Hezbollah, the Lebanese party responsible for his internment.

Filmed en route, Anderson opens the segment asking himself, in an aside for the camera, "Why would I want to come back here and talk to these people?" In a manner hauntingly reminiscent of victims of family injustice, he answers, "Islamic fundamentalism is a question that is going to face us for a long time. We need to understand them. We need to talk to them and to listen to them . . . the fact that this is personal, in a way very personal, is there and it's a bit disturbing. I'm not entirely comfortable right now." Like many victims approaching the point of reconciliation, Anderson was drawn to the moment, yet afraid.

Shortly into the interview, Anderson asks the question we had been watching for: "Can you say, Sayyid, flatly, that this was wrong or a mistake?"

Nasrullah responds, "I can't make such an absolute judgment."

Perhaps this conclusion to his long-anticipated encounter only confirmed Anderson's claim that Hezbollah would never apologize, even as it illustrated his desire for their repentance. Yet we suspect that even the lack of contrition on Nasrullah's part served the therapeutic function of distancing him from the offense, placing the Secretary-General on a moral level beneath his former victim, thus restoring a sense of justice to the offense. We have seen the same thing happen on occasion during less-than-adequate family apologies.

In a strikingly similar account, abuse victim David Pelzer recalls his own attempt at reconciliation with his violent, alcoholic mother. In *A Man Called Dave* (Pelzer, 1999), he recounts traveling to see her as an adult because "I had so many questions, and now I felt I was ready. . . . I could not imagine how a person, let alone a mother, could concoct ways to dehumanize and torture their own child. As much as I craved closure to my past for myself, now as a father I felt I owed it to [my son]. . . . Of all my tests, perhaps seeing Mother was the ultimate one for me" (pp. 174–175). With little conversation between them, his offender senses what he seeks and remarks, "I want you to know it [attempting to kill him] was an accident." Doing his own therapy at great psychological risk to himself,[5] Pelzer confronts her alone and unshielded and, of course, she is intractable. He notes, "For years I had believed if I ever confronted Mother as an adult, she would finally have to grasp the magnitude of the problem . . . but now Mother was carefully rationalizing her actions, guarding every word, making her treatment of 'It' seem like nothing more than a parent disciplining a disobedient child" (p. 179). But, like Anderson, even this untoward encounter appears to have created a similar outcome of release for Pelzer, as he notes, "Although I harbored no hate or ill feelings against Mother, breathing in the fumes from her lair, while surrounded by objects from our mutual past, made me feel nothing but pity for the person who was once my mommy" (p. 187). Yet his contrition process was far from complete; it continued on to an inevitable deathbed scene, in which Mother performed a classic non-apology by telling him, "I, uh, I'm proud of you. You turned out fine. I'm proud of you David Pelzer" (p. 212). At the graveside service, Pelzer recounts praying for her soul to achieve eternal peace: "And as I finished, I could feel a gigantic weight lift from my soul" (p. 213).

We would have wished for child-Pelzer a far more effective child protective system, which would have brought to bear upon his mother the power of the state in support of the interventions we discuss herein. Even if this had been in the context of a parental termination session, with professional intercession we believe his long and tortured contrition process might have come sooner and with greater completeness than the one he describes.

LEVEL 4: SYMBOLIC

The symbolic level of contrition (Fig. 4.4) shares with the first three the absence of an offender to offer direct apology, but includes a symbol of his repentance carried via the therapist or occasionally another family member. Usually these symbols are or are accompanied by written documents and prove especially valuable when the offender is not available to the victim, but is or was contrite in the presence of another party. Level 4 is thus more complete than the lower levels of contrition because there exists tangible evidence that the offender is actually sorry for what he did.

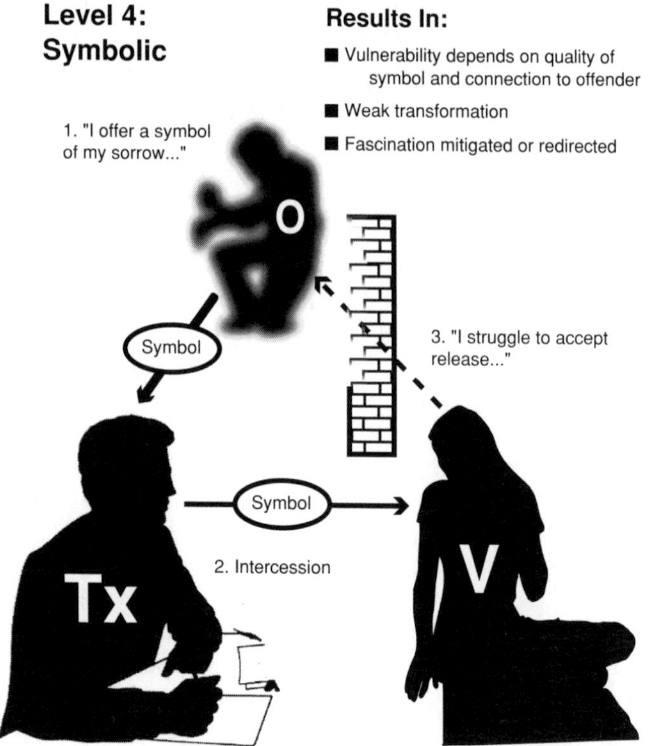

FIGURE 4.4

However, the extent of healing is highly dependent on the quality of the symbol and its metaphorical representation of the offender's sorrow. The less meaningful and direct the symbol, the more the victim must struggle to accept release from her fascination with the offender and transformation of their relationship.

This approach has been both used and misused by therapists in directing offenders (often sex offenders) to write letters of apology to their victims. If these letters are solely executed to provide symbols of sorrow and repentance and are overseen by a therapist who understands and works with victims, they can be extremely effective. They can even set the stage for a more complete apology in the future using the level 6 apology process. However, if these letters include specific descriptions of the molestation or abuse as required by some programs, they simply increase the trance state and retraumatize the victim at a distance. Such letters should always be reviewed and edited by the victim's therapist as well as received in his company. We believe that precious few young people need a clarification of the abuse as much as they need an apology; a clarification letter (or session) can actually be damaging without one, as the victim may come to believe that the offender has finally learned just how terrible his behavior was and is still not sorry for it.

An example of a very successful symbolic apology is found in the case of a teen girl presenting numerous problems with the law. She would frequently sneak out at night and go to a nearby convenience store to engage in petty theft within easy range of the security camera. At the suggestion of the juvenile justice system, the father brought her to see Barnum for this and other persistent misbehavior. At intake the father reported that the girl's mother was in the last stages of terminal cancer and was living in the home with the family in preparation for her impending death. The father complained that his daughter would not listen to him even though she had usually obeyed him before the wife's illness.

While the girl's behavior was now more understandable, further investigation suggested an even more serious issue in the mother–daughter relationship. The father reported that his wife when healthy had frequently taken the daughter to bars while she drank with her girlfriends from work and met other men the father assumed to be extramarital affairs. She would also hit and yell at the girl when she was angry, especially when intoxicated. In fact, the father had been secretly preparing for a divorce and custody dispute when the mother fell ill, but on learning of her condition had terminated the filing to care for her and support the girl through the death. With this information we suspected that the girl was involved in more than a simple grief process and was desperately in need of an apology before her mother died. Given that she was bedridden, we arranged for Barnum to meet with the clients in the home. Our initial approach was to attempt a therapeutic apology session. The mother was very willing to engage in this process, but the daughter absolutely refused to meet with her conjointly. Understanding that we had a very short time in which to work and attempting to be respectful to the victim, we devised a symbolic method of apology that would be durable beyond the death of the mother and would depend in no way on the victim's cooperation.

Twice Barnum went to the family's home and conducted individual sessions with the mother. He asked her a variety of questions consistent with the essential aspects of the therapeutic apology (level 6) along with a gathering of the hopes and dreams the mother had for her daughter. He transcribed and edited the tapes into a written document that he printed and arranged to have the mother sign. But on the morning of their final appointment the father called to say that if Barnum planned to do anything with the mother, he needed to do it quickly. He arrived at 4:00 P.M. The mother had died at 3:30.

After the funeral, the father took the daughter and her younger brother away for a 2-week vacation while other family members cleaned and prepared the home for their return. Barnum decided to keep the mother's empty signature line to symbolize the important but unfinished nature of the document. At the next scheduled session the girl arrived in her usual surly and incommunicative style. Barnum handed her the unsealed envelope while explaining the origin of its contents, uncertain whether she would tear it up, stare blankly, or take in what she could of the experience before becoming overwhelmed. Instead, she quietly took the letter from the envelope and spent the next 20 minutes in rapt attention to it. She appeared to read it more than once.

Upon finishing, she looked up. "I already knew all this," she said without emotion, as she folded the letter neatly, put it back in the envelope, and placed it carefully in her purse. Barnum agreed that she must have known those things, and that it was certainly good to know that her mother had known them too. He asked if there was anything else she needed to talk about regarding the letter. The girl said "no," and they ended the session.

A week later, the father called to cancel the girl's appointment, stating that her behavior was now normal. She was obeying his rules and requests with no acting out. In fact, he was as pleased as he was puzzled. He had expected the worst and the daughter was not delivering. Barnum suggested it might be best not to point this out, but offered further help whenever the girl or anyone in the family wished to come in. The father said that this was good because the girl had liked Barnum (which was news to him). However, we heard from the family only once when the father unexpectedly came by the office to ask if he could have the tapes of the conversations with his wife. Barnum explained that the tapes belonged to the daughter. The father clarified that he absolutely intended to give them to her. "I just think she may need to hear them sometime in the future," he said.

Barnum gave him the tapes in a sealed manila envelope on which he wrote the girl's name. "I'll be sure she gets these when she needs them," the father said.

When interventions truly fit the individual and the problem, the family often works to keep the benefit going into the future. This is the core idea behind the symobolic level of contrition—that even if the transgressor cannot provide the ideal show of repentance, he can offer a symbol that will be available to the victim in the future. As illustrated, this intervention also works when the victim is actively choosing to have no contact with the offender, putting herself into a de facto level 1 state. Sometimes this symbol actually takes on a human form; when it does, it moves to the next level of contrition.

LEVEL 5: SUBSTITUTE

At the substitute level of contrition (Fig. 4.5) we again have an offender absent, unable, or unwilling to apologize. However, someone who metaphorically represents the offender in the mind of the victim offers an apology on

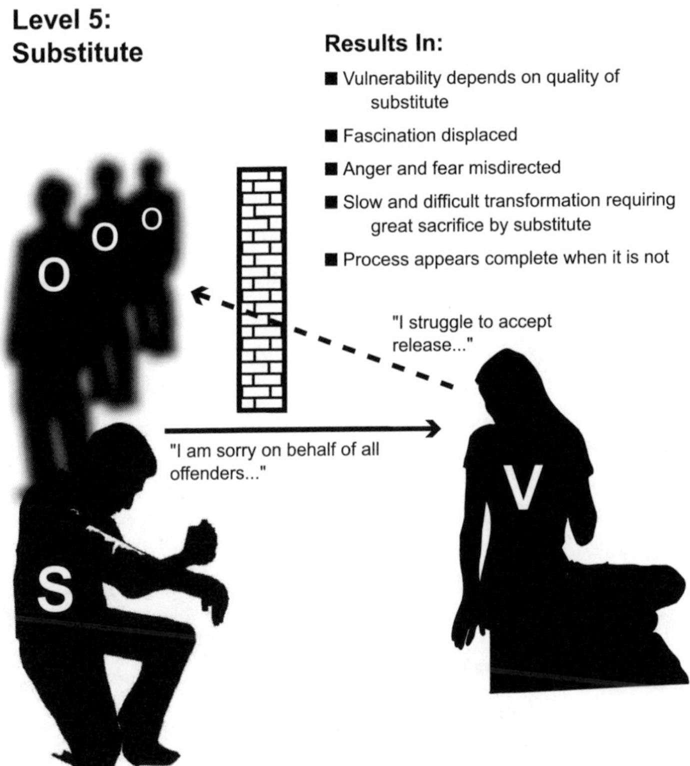

Level 5:
Substitute
Results In:
■ Vulnerability depends on quality of substitute
■ Fascination displaced
■ Anger and fear misdirected
■ Slow and difficult transformation requiring great sacrifice by substitute
■ Process appears complete when it is not
O
O
O
"I struggle to accept release..."
"I am sorry on behalf of all offenders..."
V
S

Figure 4.5

his behalf. When the victim is a child, a family member of the offender might offer the apology. When a member of the clergy perpetrates abuse—a particularly sad and ironic situation that has become all too common of late—the repentant party can and should be a bishop or even the congregation or subset thereof. Most often these cases begin at a lower level of completeness and quite outside of the therapy process, as the victim displaces her fascination with the offender onto an unwitting substitute, often an intimate partner. This results in the same anger and fear that was previously focused on the offender being misdirected at the substitute, and resultant therapy must address the ensuing conflict. This sets a foundation for resolution that might not otherwise be present, but it can be quite taxing to the relationship and not infrequently destroys it, consuming a great deal of emotional energy from the substitute without fully transforming the real victim/offender relationship. Not surprisingly, many of the presenting victims have been afforded only a level 1 process of contrition, and thus remain in perpetual fascination with and hatred of their offenders. In other cases, they reach level 2, having unilaterally and artificially "forgiven" their offenders but turning their anger against their partners.

Because most substitute apologies occur among adult victims and their intimate partners, there are few examples involving children in or out of CPS custody. For a practical illustration of how we work in the more common cases described above, we return to Ron and Sarah as Kim Cain attempts to evoke a substitute apology from a beleaguered Ron.

"Sarah, would you be willing to tell Ron one thing per day about what other men have done to hurt you?" Kim asked.

"I do, don't I?" Sarah said, with a nervous laugh. "When he tells me I hate men, I tell him why." She caught herself. "Now, wait. Are we going to get to the sexual abuse thing, 'cause I'm not getting into that? He can't go there."

"No, I'm not asking about that." Kim again respected Sarah's boundaries on this issue. "I'm going to have you do something, Sarah, and in doing it I want you to focus on *other men,* because it's easy for you to revert to Ron and say '*you* do that and *you* do this'—in this exercise, it's your job to say what *other* men did to you. It can be any other man in your life. Once a day I want you to tell him something, from now until the next time you guys come back. And at that time, Ron, I want you to apologize for what they've done to hurt your wife. I want you to apologize for what *other men* have done. I want you to apologize on behalf of all those men—and I want it to be sincere."

"Can you give me an example?" Ron asked.

At this point, a remarkable thing happened. Going against convention and Crenshaw's supervision behind the mirror, Kim decided to roleplay the apology with Sarah. To the team's astonishment, this portrayal was so effective that Sarah actually became emotional—almost imagining Kim to be a valid substitute for the real perpetrator.

"Woah," Sarah said, putting her hand between her face and Kim's in a gentle "back-off" gesture. "That's getting a little bit too close there."

Kim continued, "Maybe it's a good thing to do this whenever you feel comfortable . . . or maybe you'd want to set a time in the morning and you'll spend 20 minutes talking about the one thing that other men have done to hurt you."

Sarah smiled and looked at her husband as Kim took Crenshaw's phone call into the room. "You got into an awful lot when you married me didn't you? You poor thing."

"I don't think that." It was exactly the right thing for Ron to say.

"Ron, you're bearing a symbol," Kim continued as she hung up the phone. "You are a man in all of this. You are bearing the responsibility for other men and the pain that they have caused, and you are doing it in a way this time that you can help Sarah get over it. You are apologizing for what they've done to hurt her. I know you hurt inside because of the way that they've treated her, and you have an opportunity to talk about that now and apologize for them. I want you to try once before we leave so it's not confusing. I want you to practice looking at your wife and making an apology for what other men have done. It's kind of hard, but I know you can do it. I have a lot of faith in you or I wouldn't make you go through this . . . 'cause it's serious. Take her hand and tell her."

Ron took Sarah's hand. A few moments passed as he gathered his thoughts. "Sarah . . . I apologize for the way men have been to you and the wrong things they've done. I don't want to be in that group . . . I want to be there for you. I don't want you to ever be hurt like that again by any man—including me."

"I don't want to be hurt either," Sarah said quietly, thoroughly entranced. " 'Cause it sucks." A few moments passed and then she turned to Kim with an entirely new expression—one of joy. "Oh! You know what! I forgot to tell you. I went to go to work this morning and he'd used sidewalk chalk to put this big old heart on the driveway and it said, 'Be my Valentine!' "

It was the first time in five sessions that Kim had seen Sarah express anything but contempt for Ron. The case had been raised to a higher level. Moreover, she now became free to talk with Kim privately about the previously forbidden topic of sexual abuse, which she began to do in the coming weeks. Ron reported later that this technique was "the only thing we've ever done that worked," and he lamented Sarah's predictable request to discontinue the apologies shortly thereafter. Kim attempted to organize a level 6 apology between Sarah and her stepfather, but was unable to obtain Sarah's buy-in. Nevertheless, she continued to improve, and on this topic the case remained successful.

Just as the symbolic apology succeeds only with a meaningful symbol, the quality of the transformation at level 5 depends on the quality of the substitute and his meaning to the victim. Because it too is dependent on a type of illusion, level 5 contrition is vulnerable to challenge, and the process can appear complete when it is not. Often, the substitute apology must be repeated over time, a tall order when the substitute may feel terribly aggrieved by the original offender and unappreciated for his sacrifice by the victim. Of course, these are precisely the sorts of issues that will be addressed as therapy unfolds after the substitute apology session, and in every case where it is possible, the ultimate solution is to move to the final level of completeness.

LEVEL 6: THE COMPLETE CONTRITION PROCESS

The most complete level of contrition (Fig. 4.6) is the one that comes closest to the source of the victim's pain by taking her through a process of apology and repentance as described by Madanes (1990) and Madanes, Keim, & Smelser (1995) and extended and refined in our own work. At this level, the client is released from the relationship with the offender *by the offender*. The trance is broken, and the offense is placed in a broader life context. The transformation is complete, and a new relationship is formed, even as this may

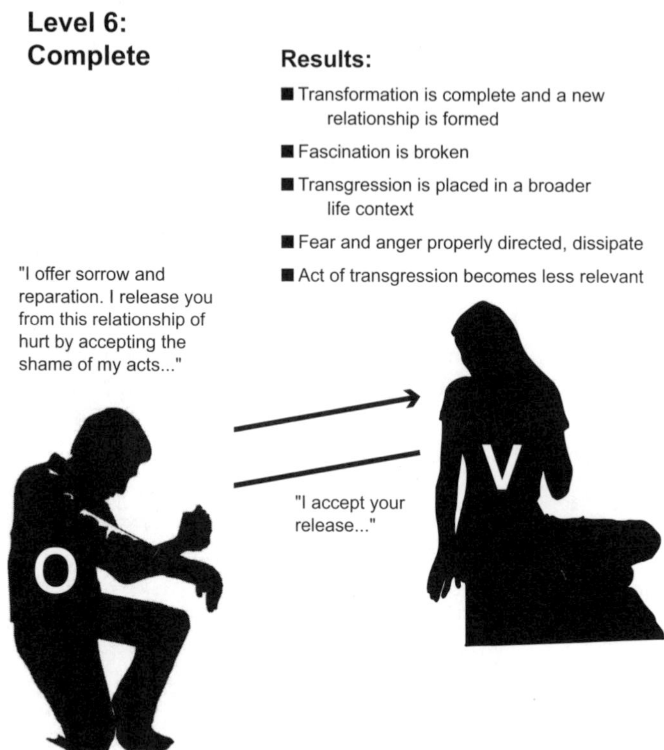

Level 6:
Complete
Results:
Transformation is complete and a new relationship is formed
Fascination is broken
Transgression is placed in a broader life context
Fear and anger properly directed, dissipate
Act of transgression becomes less relevant
"I offer sorrow and reparation. I release you from this relationship of hurt by accepting the shame of my acts..."
"I accept your release..."
O
V

FIGURE 4.6

mean no interaction at all. With the fascination broken, fear and anger—previously the bonding ingredients of that relationship—dissipate, and the victim is free to choose for the first time how she will respond to and relate to the offense.

Madanes originally conceptualized the apology process as a series of steps occurring in sequence over the course of family therapy. With 10 years' experience as a guide, we have made several amendments to this approach, reflecting implementation in a broader range of settings (see chapter 12). For one, we have moved from "steps" to "themes" in conceptualizing the contrition process. The idea of steps implies a very linear process that occurs in a discrete time period, which is rarely how things play out in the rancor of CPS and court-ordered treatment. Additionally, we have found the idea of themes to translate more easily to multiple modalities of treatment (group, individual, couples, family, etc.), allowing these critical concepts to move from a single therapy process to program-wide protocols that will repeat themselves in each therapeutic contact with a high degree of consistency. We shall now examine each theme as it impacts a typical case of family injustice.

Estimating "Readiness" and Treatment Length

We are often asked how one knows when an offender—particularly a sexual or physical abuser—is ready to undertake apology and reparation with the victim and family as well as when the victim is ready to receive the apology. These questions are necessarily linked to the issue of treatment length and intensity, particularly in an era of managed care, reduced budgets for social services, and a trend toward briefer models. In short, if one is going to apply this or any model in a managed care environment, one must plan the timing carefully, always balancing safety and brevity. Yet traditional therapies, especially those involving sex offenders, have greatly emphasized the importance of long-term, high frequency sessions without any real empirical support for that position. Some programs have required offenders to purchase two or three sessions of therapy per week for a minimum 2-year period before allowing *any* contact with their victims, even in therapy. As this is required of all offenders, it must be assumed to be arbitrary. In contrast, we believe readiness for any stage of therapy should take exactly as long as necessary to maximize the likelihood the child will be safe from emotional, physical, or sexual insult. In general, we find this varies more often than not from case to case, though we expect to see families for 1 to 2 years, with as much of that time as possible coming *after* apology, reintegration, and (if appropriate) reunification has occurred. Even then we do not typically terminate these cases. For those so interested, the cost-savings in this model are realized at the level of *intensity* over time, not in the premature truncation of services. This is because we may begin seeing clients one to four times a week, but never end this way. Instead, we decrease the frequency of contact as the client's circumstances improve, again tailoring our interventions to meet the myriad situations we face in cases of family injustice.

Regardless of any time frame externally imposed, we always begin with an assessment of readiness both of the victim and offender and continue this theme through the entire therapy process. We have learned that it is important to bring about the apology as soon as is safely possible. When the process is delayed for more than 3 to 6 months after treatment begins, the offense begins to crystallize among all members of the family, the emotion is greatly reduced, and the apology experience will not be as meaningful. Worst are cases of sex offenders who have been in treatment for years before an apology session. Regardless of their intended sincerity, they have learned an entire language of sex offending that pervades their apology, and they often deliver it without much feeling. In chapter 12, Bruce Laflen discusses this problem and how his sex offender treatment program made it a point to conduct apologies within the first 3 to 6 months of treatment—"the sooner the better," as he notes. As with brevity, swiftness should never overcome good sense. However, it is important to understand that children experience time differently than we do, and what seems like a "couple of years" to an adult is an eternity for a child.

To those unfamiliar with this model, it may be surprising that the assessment of readiness for apology is rarely difficult. For the offender, these are the necessary conditions:

- Admission of abuse generally consistent with that disclosed by the victim(s). If there is doubt, a successful polygraph should be completed or, if necessary, a 6- to 8-week period in a therapy designed to confront denial. This is where restorative justice courts make their greatest contribution by reinforcing treatment and punishing duplicity.
- Expressed awareness of the nature, quality, and wrongfulness of the offense, even if the offender is lacking insight as to its etiology.
- Willingness and ability to express sincere repentance *on his knees* as judged by the therapist, victim, family, and community.
- Openness to acts of reparation.

On satisfying these requirements, the offender can be expected to offer a sincere apology and participate from that point forward in the contrition process. Even when there is some discrepancy in the reported level or frequency of abuse between victim and offender, one can proceed if the offender is willing to accept as the working truth whatever the victim has disclosed or will disclose in session. Simply put, the pristine and rarely attainable conditions of readiness mandated by other protocols are not necessary for this model to work for the victim. In fact, we have seen many offenders who did not seem ready going into an apology session, who were more than ready coming out. More important, their victims emerged quite transformed.

As for the victim readiness, we are absolutely deferent to her wishes and protective of her status in the process. We have never pressured a victim toward an apology, though we sometimes suggest a symbolic apology as an interim measure. We once waited 2 years for a teen to become willing to receive an apology from her stepfather. In retrospect, she was exactly correct in her timing, as the offender turned out to be more than a bit difficult to treat during that time span. On the other hand, we have had very few victims who stated any reluctance. In one case a youth of 16 showed up at our clinic for exactly that purpose; she'd had no idea of our interest in this area, and it was by sheer luck that she came to a group specializing in apology.

Generally, the greatest barrier to readiness is neither victim nor offender, nor even the time frame of the family. As we will find in chapter 11, CPS or retributive court interventions more often impose delays and obstructions out of countertransference or arbitrary policy that does not reflect the needs of victims, families, or offenders.

Didactic on Forgiveness

We have become especially sensitive to subtle issues of power and influence in our work, finding that a victim who has been asked to receive an apology and then been told she need not forgive (Madanes, 1990) may find herself in a cultural double bind. As a society we tend to see "unforgiving" people as lacking in character themselves. Instead, we teach the victim and family that forgiveness can never be requested or expected because it is an experience not an act and certainly not a moral or cultural obligation. As such, it will come or not, now or later; the victim must be quite free to let this process unfold. In fact, one indicator that the family, victim, and offender are ready for apology is their acceptance of this condition. When opposed by the Christian tradition of universal grace, we invite pastors to come to therapy to explain from a theological perspective why atonement is important for earthly sin. Because of all this, we do not routinely experience spontaneous expressions of forgiveness during the apology ritual, even as we nearly always see the facet of forgiveness that we call "release" in the process.

Openness and Honesty: Evaluation and Practice

In normal families, secrets can be an appropriate delineation between individuals and generations, respecting the privacy inherent to a normal hierarchy. In families where members harm one another, secrets are a principal mechanism by which mistreatment is maintained, so secret keeping must be systematically disallowed for all family members (Madanes, 1990). At the onset of treatment, the therapist must bring forth and discuss all that is known about the offense in as much detail as necessary to clarify the situation. It is often quite difficult for the offender to speak of his offense, especially in front of his family, but he must be able to do so in clear but general terms before the other themes can be enacted.

Over time, we have learned several things about this theme of honesty.

- As previously noted, retributive justice does little to encourage this theme and at times makes it impossible to achieve, because offenders will be advised against honest participation if their attorneys believe it puts them at greater risk of consequence. As noted in chapter 12, there is no substitute for court support of this model.
- In any conjoint session the victim is not required to speak, but is allowed to do so if she wishes. Sometimes she takes a very active role in the process, which becomes quite empowering for her. In other cases, she does not. We have found no way to know a priori what will happen.
- Madanes's original approach conducted this step solely in conjoint sessions, but we have found many modern methods of assessment that increase the

truthfulness of offenders and make courts more open to these interventions. We favor a comprehensive evaluation, including the use of a clinical polygraph when there is any inconsistency in stories. Because this is critical in the movement toward normalizing relationships in the abusive family and because offenders are not known for their honesty prior to treatment, these methods should be used before conjoint therapy. This again reduces the reliance on the victim's statements and increases the responsibility of the offender for the contrition process.

- In multi-therapist situations, the therapist conducting conjoint sessions should always be the victim's therapist, or very well connected to her through previous contact. The nuances of conjoint abuse treatment are such that one must be able to read a client very well, to recognize signs of distress, and to know how much she can take. We have never had a victim retraumatized in a conjoint session, and we believe this is owed to our use of the victim's therapist as director of the process.
- Diverging from earlier thought, we do not find it important to provide explicit detail during these sessions, particularly when the abuse is sexual and it would offend the victim or younger children. For example, it is more important for the offender to say that he "touched her privates with my thing" than to say "I simulated intercourse with her by rubbing my penis against her vagina." What is important is that all known incidents be brought to light so secrets are not kept. This is not to shame the offender but to bring his behavior to light where it can be addressed and prevented in the future.
- We always have the offender thank the victim for her disclosure by explaining that without her courage he would not have been able to get the help he needed to stop his damaging behavior.

Defining the Offense as a Spiritual Pain and Injustice

We find great meaning in Madanes's (1990) emphasis on the spiritual pain of abuse and injustice in the family. Second only to the apology itself, this is the most important of all the themes to reiterate throughout therapy. In an early conjoint session, each member of the family is asked, in age-appropriate language, why the offense was wrong. Depending on the circumstances, most answers are acknowledged and open expression is encouraged. The process begins with the offender and works away from the abuse (e.g., nonoffending parent, siblings, grandparents). It is important to take as much time as is necessary but remain mindful of the various attention spans of the children involved in the process. After others have spoken, the victim is casually asked if she has anything to add. It is actually less common for the victim to remain silent at this point, but she is always supported if she does.

The therapist then adds that the offense was wrong for another reason—because it hurt the heart of the victim. In cases of sexual abuse, we spend considerable time talking about the spiritual pain felt by the victim, explaining how sexuality and spirituality are closely linked in people. We may put less emphasis on this issue in less severe transgressions, but we always set the frame for the problem as a pain in the heart that makes it difficult for the client to carry on normally. We also discuss the idea of the offense as a special form of injustice to emphasize the right and wrong of the situation.

Once these ideas are firmly planted, the therapist asks the family "who bears the shame" for the given offense. Almost always the family assigns blame to the offender; if it does not, the therapist has not adequately completed previous themes. At the same time it is important to be sure that the clients understand the phrase itself, as it can be honestly misunderstood as an invitation to acknowledge the unjust shame felt by the victim, resulting in the answer "she bears the shame" at a very inappropriate moment.

Addressing Experiences of Injustice among Other Family Members

In the original model, Madanes found it common in the apology session for the offender or other members of the family to share their own abuse histories, sometimes for the first time. However, in practice we have found it more typical and quite a bit more helpful for this important information to come to light in advance of the apology session, preferably during a comprehensive evaluation. This is because failure to address the unjust treatment of the offender or other family members before the apology session makes it more difficult for them to offer appropriate apology to victims. In many cases, the value of family members going through their own apology process before apologizing to the victim cannot be overestimated; to do otherwise can prove a serious error. However, if new disclosures unexpectedly emerge in the apology session itself, it is wise to stay with the specific offense at hand and return to this issue at a future session.

Defining the Offender as Experiencing a Spiritual Pain

While carefully avoiding constructivism and circularity, it is important to provide a better framework for the offense than evil and malevolence. We follow Madanes (1990) in suggesting that the offender be viewed as tormented and spiritually wounded. In practice, the therapist notes that the offender must have experienced great spiritual pain to do something so terrible to the victim. Far from exonerating the offender, who is still held accountable for his behavior under the tenet of free will, this frame helps the victim reach a level of peace when facing the persistent "why" and "who" questions. Seeing the offender as carrying a pain in the heart effectively answers each question by giving the victim a sense of distance from the offense in both her attributional style and her own ego development. This is especially important in cases where a child is physically or sexually abused by a biological parent. As we shall see in Justin's case in chapter 5, great dissonance is generated in children between their natural love and loyalty for their parent and the view of that same parent as evil or perverse. Moreover, it is quite disturbing when the essence of one's self is inextricably tied to a person one considers evil. Framing the parent as spiritually wounded also mitigates the confusion and fear children experience when confronted with the pervasive idea that a "bad parent" cannot produce a "good kid." It is also helpful for the offender, who comes to associate the transgression with terrible things rather than pleasure or expediency. Finally, and perhaps as important, any offender who is perceived as spiritually flawed is also seen as weak, which in turn suggests a radical decrease in anxiety on the part of the victim, who perceives the offender for the first time as less powerful than she.

Spiritual Pain and Injustice toward the Family

We typically ask the offender's family to attend sessions to help him face his own shame under witness of the family and to apologize for the spiritual pain he has caused them. Consistent with our focus on free will, this theme is predicated on the assumption that violence is not an impulse or an isolated action, but a social intervention that impinges on everyone's life. When extended family members are not available, we access the social network of the offender, including friends, spouses, Alcoholics Anonymous sponsors, or respected elders. In the case of clergy, we would consider the way in which the offense has caused pain for the church and its members and direct an apology to the congregation.

The Ritual of Apology and Repentance

Given the serious nature of most family injustices, we almost always follow Madanes's approach of asking the offender to apologize on his knees for the offense. However, after considerable experience we have modified our approach to be one of an invitation rather than a directive, which generates a much more natural experience for the family. In this, the therapist typically states, "In our society, when people want to make a very sincere or serious apology they take a certain position to show that they really are sorry." He then pauses. After a few moments, we find that someone will comment, "You mean like kneeling?" Thereafter, most offenders typically drop to their knees without further suggestion. This may seem astonishing to those who have not experienced such sessions, but we have far more examples of this than any alternative outcome, particularly among adult offenders. Teenagers are a bit more difficult and may require more pressure *by the family* for them to follow through on the kneeling apology.

The benefit of a kneeling apology is nothing short of crucial for myriad reasons, so we shall briefly review only the most important. First, kneeling places the offender in the position of humbleness and respect relative to the victim and family—literally on a physical level below them. Second, it increases the drama and seriousness of the session. Time and again, offenders who showed no emotion in numerous sessions of group or individual therapy have broken down to their emotional core in apology sessions. Even in the most severe cases, burly men, oppositional teens, and intractable mothers have all wept uncontrollably when previously assessed to be without feeling for their offense or empathy for the victims. Finally, by making the experience humbling[6] we are able to transfer the shame from victim to offender, often with dramatic and immediate results.

As appropriate, we also ask the nonoffending adults to kneel and apologize for not protecting victims from the abuse. In this we are not asking anyone but the offender to *take responsibility for the abuse*, only for not having created and maintained a supportive and protective environment for the victim. In some cases it is also appropriate to ask siblings of the victim to apologize, but only those who were old enough and had some reason to have known about the abuse, and who were themselves not victimized. For example, we would not have a child of 7 apologize for her 16-year-old brother's molestation of a 9-year-old sister. She is too low in the family hierarchy to have been responsible for anything. We would permit the child to spontaneously apologize and thank her for her contribution, but would then direct the offender and family to explain that it was never her responsibility to protect the sister.

Reparation as the Enactment of Apology

Some have considered reparation an afterthought to an apology process. Others, particularly those who favor a more forgiveness-based model, see it as unnecessary or even unhelpful. Consistent with Madanes (1990), we have come to view it as being nearly as important as the apology itself. First, active reparation is a constant reminder of the offender's obligation to set things right. Over the long haul, this helps supplant the emotional memory of abuse with one of restored justice. On a more practical level, an offender's willingness to follow through on reparation is one predictor of his true repentance and thus the extent to which he should be reintegrated into the lives of the family and victim. For offenders in active treatment, reparation helps them to remember the offense and to avoid reoffending by giving a constant reminder of the offender's status while impelling him to maintain change. Finally, and far from incidentally, reparation is useful because it is simply the right thing to do.

In the initial stages of reparation, the victim and family are asked to think of proper reparation to help repair the damage done to the child. The therapist is clear to point out that nothing can truly make up for child abuse, but a show of good faith on the part of the offender is crucial. We encourage families to be future-oriented in deciding on reparation, because abuse tends to rob children of normal development and jeopardize their future education, sexual relationships, family life, and careers. Often, the family will direct the offender to set aside a savings account in the name of the child that will be used for a college fund, downpayment on a car or house, or some other item that will enhance the child's future. If money is used, the amount must reach the point of sacrifice for the offender but not exceed his means. Although it is ideal to therapy that the offender do this of his own volition, we are aware that the best laid plans and intentions sometimes go by the wayside. Thus, an article of restitution agreed on in therapy is best included in any diversion, probation, or reintegration plan to ensure its execution. This is another area where restorative justice courts can greatly support treatment. However, as noted by Bruce Laflen in chapter 12, the metaphor of a business transaction or exchange must *never* enter the process. In fact, Laflen notes that money is by no means the only form of reparation available, and sometimes it is the least preferable. The nature of reparation is as varied as the cases we see, and the exact nature of any given process depends entirely on *utilization* of the client and family's reality. Creativity within the parameters of safety and reason is the best tool for developing a reparative experience for victim and offender.

Consequences and the Safety Plan

In our revision, discussion of consequences begins well before the apology session, and usually during conversations with the offender and other adult members of the family. After a successful apology, the family meets to discuss specific consequences if another offense occurs. To the extent possible, these consequences should emanate from the family, but the basic theme will be expulsion from the life of the family through outplacement, divorce, or other banishment (Madanes, 1990). Sessions with the offender should include clear communication that a reoffense will result in a report to police, and the court system is nonamenable to this type of treatment. Of course, one must always assess the level of threat to the child and respond without over or under-reacting in the setting of consequences. For example, in Leia's case (chapter 5) the family failed their safety plan after Laird struck one of the children, they were removed from the home instead of the more obvious response of removing Laird from the home, a clear example of overresponding.

As a part of the safety plan, it is important to find a reliable protector for the victim—someone she feels comfortable with and can go to if offensive patterns begin to reemerge. It is typical to engage the nonoffending family members in this process to maintain a proper hierarchical arrangement and to act as an informal type of reparation to the child. Though we have found exceptions, we generally follow Madanes's suggestion to avoid putting the nonoffending parent in this role because they have not usually been reliable before. The protector may be an extended family member (grandmothers are particularly good) or a trusted teacher, minister, "auntie," or neighbor. In adult cases (e.g., domestic violence), a brother or uncle is useful. One can even set up a committee of protectors, allowing for more response options for the child. We once brought 13 people into therapy to protect a boy from his violent father who was demanding visitation be restarted after a custody dispute. The family members (some of them from the father's side) signed an agreement to bear witness to the abuse in court if the father should press the issue without first seeking therapy. The father backed off.

The protector, child, family, offender, and therapist work together to brainstorm warning signs that might suggest the need for the protector's involvement. This has the added advantage of forcing the offender to hand over his metaphorical "owner's manual" so that all can understand his unique red flags and be ready to intervene. According to Bruce Laflen (chapter 12), this specifically involves the offender clarifying to the victim that he is not to be trusted in certain situations.

Recontextualizing the Offense

As noted, the ultimate goal of therapy is helping the victim place the abuse within a greater life context. This theme of recontextualizing the offense may be expressed in any and all modalities of treatment, including individual therapy. As we shall see in Leia's case (chapter 5), this is always easier and more successful after an apology, but it is important from the moment of disclosure until the client has been experientially released from the offense. We have found a number of subthemes particularly helpful for the victim at this point, all of which we work to integrate into the consciousness of the family. Some are drawn from Madanes and others from our own experience. All require reiteration, restatement, and recapitulation over the course of therapy, especially if the victim is a child attaining new developmental milestones. However, they are otherwise altered only by translation into age-appropriate language. These subthemes are as follows:

- *Special sensitivity.* When bad things happen to people they develop a special type of compassion that raises them to a higher level of being, and they can empathize more deeply with the pain of others. It is vital in this subtheme to discuss healthy, well-bounded ways to enact such sensitivity and to redirect tendencies toward codependency and caretaking (Madanes, 1990).
- *Existentialism.* Nietzsche wrote, "What does not destroy me, makes me stronger." This concept is invaluable in helping victims overcome their sense

of brokenness, leading to a deeper awareness of their own resources for future challenges. It is also a remarkable reframing device, empowering the victim by the very act that had disempowered her. If one avoids overemphasis on the utility of being abused (which, of course, has no utility) this is a powerful strategy.

- *Self and systemic protection.* With the secret out in the open, the victim can now be better protected, enhancing her sense of safety. She should be praised for her disclosure. It is important not to say, "And now you are big enough to fight back," as this implies that a portion of the abuse is still the fault or responsibility of the victim. In more than one case, it has also yielded angry, offender-like behavior in the victim who "fights back" indiscriminately at anyone who crosses her. We say that the victim and her family have learned a great deal about terrible things in this ordeal, and from this point forward everyone will work together to protect her.
- *Abuse is not your defining moment.* Consistent with Madanes (1990), while acknowledging the abuse as traumatic and unjust, we point out that it is also a very small part of all one's life experience, past and present. One way to invoke this is to focus on the positive things in the victim's life that occurred during the same time period as the abuse (e.g., school, friends, activities). Another involves helping the victim to find beauty and meaning in her current life, including perhaps her art, photography, or poetry. Yet another is helping the child and family do guided imagery of the future in which they will experience many wonderful and new things, as described in Leia's case in chapter 5. The therapist must not minimize the depth of what happened, but instead suggest a greater context along with limitations on the long-term negative consequences of the offense. Eventually we may even suggest that the experience will be mostly forgotten at some point, though it will always be available when the victim needs it.
- *The impossible question.* The therapist directs the victim away from obsessing on the question of *why* the abuse happened. Though it is usually less critical after the apology, this is a natural area of concern and must be addressed. However, too much focus on the motivations of the offender will fascinate and torment the victim. Invariably, a "mythology" will emerge to explain the inexplicable, so the therapist should work with the child and family to exert some influence over its content and direction. In truth, no one, including the offender, actually knows the true answer to "why," so the mythology should offer a reasonable conceptualization consistent with the idea of torment, which avoids the concept of evil and helps break the trance state. Of course that myth will be reviewed and refined as the child grows and develops, as do all mythologies. In personal correspondence, Madanes suggested that Arendt's (1976) thoughts on the banality of evil are a useful conceptualization for coming to accept that acts of violence and abuse are simply insipid and inexplicable.

Restoring the Offender

The therapist who also sees the offender must help him find a new metaphor for his life and conduct in the context of the family. This is a slow process undertaken under the rubric of apology and reparation. It often begins by addressing his own history of abuse to help the offender associate violence and abuse with horrible, negative things and associate love and compassion with kindly deeds. When the offender dwells on his own suffering as a child, we show appropriate empathy and even agree quite honestly that his life has been even a bit more horrible than he thought it was. This ratifies his legitimate negative feelings toward his own abuser before a simple point is posed to him: "With all these terrible things that have been done to you, you must feel even worse that you've done them to someone else . . . someone you love." Reiterated at every discussion, the more the offender resists being like his own perpetrator, the more he is forced toward empathy for his victim and away from excuse making. In this, we are attempting to make sex abuse ego-dystonic, outside the offender's image of who they are. This might include challenging statements, such as "You know, it just doesn't seem like you're that kind of a person. I just don't think it's who you are . . . a man who by his nature abuses children." This phrase defines the problem as solvable and not ego-syntonic.[7] We then work on relapse prevention with the use of various strategies, including bringing in the offender's extended family members to support him and assist with maintaining scrutiny of his behavior.

I recently saw an adolescent sex offender case fail miserably because the therapists had not restored the offender in the eyes of the family. After nearly 4 years of having committed no act of abuse or even coming close, and in a home where all children were sensitized to their own protection, the parents remained such rigid enforcers of the safety plan that at age 16 the boy emotionally imploded and forced a disruption simply to "get out of that home where I couldn't even move without somebody watching me." I suspect he was right, and in my postmortem of the case I suggested that the boy's conduct had required the development of greater trust and encouragement. There is no excuse for carelessness in this regard, but reintegration, if it is a reasonable case plan goal, ultimately involves acceptance of the offender back into the fold, with eyes open but arms out.

CONCLUSION: CONTRITION IN CONTEXT

Among the numerous misunderstandings of Madanes's apology process has been an assumption that it was designed as the end-all and be-all intervention in a family therapy of injustice, which it is not. This view came from both intrigued proponents, who thought it could offer a quick cure in the service of managed care, and opponents who saw it as a cheap and overdramatic parlor trick lacking the depth of their own endless and complex interventions. To either faction we can say with considerable experience that *it is neither panacea nor melodrama.* It is what it is professed to be—a remarkably powerful tool on the road to a much larger process of contrition, which is itself a part of a larger intervention in the restoration of family justice. For those who have not experienced it first hand, it is a bit difficult to capture in such technical analysis. In an attempt to go beyond the didactics of the model, we will next examine two cases in which the contrition process was completed through sessions of apology and reparation. We will then return to September's case to examine how an impromptu phone apology from her father had a lightning-strike impact at her moment of greatest desperation.

In all three cases, we have the gift of transcripts provided by remarkably articulate young people, who do much to explicate the victim's experience of the process. Although they are no substitute for the real experience, each case offers a dramatic example of the successful interventions that have become ubiquitous in our experience over 10 years in using this approach.

NOTES

1. This chapter is intended to be a companion to Madanes' earlier work. It is recommended that the reader study both Madanes (1990) and Madanes, Keim, & Smelser (1995) to fully appreciate the original model of apology.
2. In the interest of clarity, most generic victims in this chapter will be female and offenders male. We recognize that these are arbitrary assignments, though they do favor the statistics on many victims and offenders. The reader will note the case studies of apology in the chapter include offenders and victims of both sexes.
3. Unlike her daughter, Debbie's mother had an IQ just above mental retardation. She was easily controlled by her abusive husband and was used to satisfy his improper and destructive sexual needs.
4. This is not meant to be critical of Christian beliefs, but only to acknowledge that many victims attempt to use such theology to forgive others in a Christ-like manner, which fits well into this illusion. The extent to which it is successful or healthy is another matter. Offenders have also been known to refuse apology by citing universal grace through Christ, denying their victims here on earth proper atonement for those sins.
5. We never recommend an encounter like this to any victim outside of a carefully orchestrated therapy process. The probability of success is minimal, and the potential cost enormous. Yet if the therapist does not offer to assist, these are the sorts of scenes the client may fashion for himself, desperate to maintain or perhaps move beyond the illusion.
6. We categorically disagree that it is *humiliating,* as some critics have suggested, and no repentant offender has ever stated it to be so.
7. Needless to say, we do not use this technique with persons identified as pedophiles. In fact, pedophilia is properly diagnosed as ego-syntonic, and part of its treatment involves the offender accepting that condition.

CHAPTER 5

The Power of Apology

> Oh yes, the past *can* hurt. But the way I see it you can either run from it or learn from it . . . so what are you going to do?
>
> —Rafiki, *The Lion King* (Disney, 1993)

The first case study in this chapter describes the apology session of Laird Larson, who physically abused his biological sons and sexually abused his stepdaughter, Leia. It is a good illustration of the intervention's utility in cases of sexual abuse and especially its use with very young children. We also found both child protective services (CPS) and the court system unusually willing to allow therapy to take precedence over other factors in the case. As we shall see in chapter 6, this priority is not always so apparent. The second case involves a neglectful alcoholic mother and her son, Justin, who presented a number of conduct disturbances. It is very different from Leia's case because the boy is a teenager and well on his way to delinquency. As such he would more typically be the target of power-based interventions emphasizing his role in offending against his grandmother and society at large. However, as with so many of his peers, Justin is a victim in the garb of an offender, lashing out at the injustices done him by his mother whom he outwardly despises and inwardly cherishes.

LEIA AND THE TERRIBLE CHILDHOOD EXPERIENCE

The Larson family included 2 parents and 5 children, all under the age of 8. Debbie's 8-year-old daughter, Leia, was born when Debbie was barely 18 and shortly before she met Laird. Leia's father had abandoned mother and child before her birth, so the girl had always considered Laird her father. Debbie and Laird had borne 4 children, Eric (age 7), Joey (age 6), Tara (age 5), and little

Julia (age 2). The family came to our institute as a discharge referral from a program based on the homebuilders model (Kinney, Haapala, & Booth, 1991) of intense home-based intervention and case management over 6 weeks. Within days the family collapsed on our doorstep, as the sudden reduction of services left them without the level of support to which they had adapted. After 6 weeks of abstaining from violence, largely because of the scrutiny of the home-based therapist, Laird had hit Joey again and was reported to CPS. The blow was comparatively minor and left no physical injury, but Laird had verbally and physically mistreated the children before and the family had been through the CPS mill several times. With this history clearly in mind, CPS not only banished him from the home but also took all 5 children away from Debbie and distributed them in 3 different foster homes around the state.

Ask *Him*

Though the girls were kept together and placed with exceptional foster parents, they were now living some 80 miles from their mother and a very new therapy process. Moreover, because she lived well below the poverty line and had no reliable transportation or telephone, Debbie had no way of visiting the girls, making visitation and a meaningful reunification therapy rather difficult. Having made a commitment to the family and given few other options by a CPS system that was quite put-out with the family, I decided to travel twice a month to do home-based therapy with the children. Recognizing this extra effort, the foster parents offered transportation to our office once a month for therapy and visitation, which I was able to stretch to 3 hours on each trip.

When I met with her for the first time, I asked Leia what she would like to work on during our time together. Her sign-in response was unforgettable. "Well, you know," said the precocious 8-year-old, "I've had a terrible childhood experience."

"Really?" I said both stunned and amused at her verbal prowess. "Tell me about it."

"I've just grown up much too fast. You know, my dad has a terrible temper and he doesn't take very good care of the kids. I had to do most of it!"

"That's pretty difficult for a young lady, huh?"

"Young lady!" She laughed. "I'm just a little kid!"

"An excellent point," I smiled, pleased that she would correct me. "How'd you feel about that, having to take care of the kids and all?"

"Terrible! I mean I'm really mad at him for what he did."

"What *did* he do?" I asked, genuinely wanting to get her story. "I mean why are you so angry at him?" It seemed an obvious question, well known to all. But Leia took it much more deeply. Rather than listing all the things on Laird's known list of misbehaviors, she made a very cryptic response.

"I don't remember," she said.

This caught my attention. For this intelligent, talkative girl to suddenly forget why she was angry with her stepfather was out of character, to say the least.

"Did he ever mistreat you?" I asked.

"Hm," she said thoughtfully, but without anxiety. "I don't know."

"Well, what I mean is, did he ever hurt you or. . . ?"

"*I know what you meant,*" she said sternly.

"Well," I said, "I mean, it seems like that'd be hard to forget."

Leia changed the subject.

Whatever it might be, I attempted in our next session to help Leia put her "terrible childhood experience" into context by imaging the possibility of a better future. As we sat on the porch swing in front of her foster home, I had her imagine a tear-off calendar moving forward in time as I described all the wonderful things that would happen to her as she grew up.[1] I portrayed her completing elementary school, going to junior high, attending dances and sports events, graduating, dating, shopping with her mother, playing with friends, and a host of other wonderful experiences. Leia giggled as she visualized these things, and I was confident in my intervention. At the end, I asked her to imagine living in the future and having two boxes just the right size to hold all the important things that had happened in her life—one to hold all the bad things that had ever happened to her and the other for all the wonderful things.

"Now," I finished, "how big do you suppose the box would be with all those good things in it?"

Her eyes closed and she measured the air as wide as her arms could reach, and equally high.

"And," I said, "how big will the box be with all the bad things in it?"

Leia's eyes came open and she looked at me oddly. "Why, it would be humungous." She stretched her arms to show a box far too big to measure. "It would be . . . like as big as this house."

We talked a bit more about how, little by little, the bad-things box would get smaller and the good-things box would get bigger, but she was noncommittal. For now, my view of the future as a good place to live was far too radical a leap.

Suspecting that Leia still had more secrets to tell, I returned to the issue of her anger at her stepfather.

"I sure wonder why you're so mad at your dad," I offered.

"I just am." This sudden shift in conversation seemed to make perfect sense to her.

"I'd think he'd have done something to get you so mad," I offered.

Leia did not respond and I knew I needed to ask a very difficult question.

"Has your dad ever touched you, Leia? Has he ever touched your privates in a way that you didn't like or you didn't think he should have?"

"I don't know," she said, once again feigning an ignorance that was absent in any other aspect of our discussions.

"Do you understand what I mean?"

"Yes," she replied firmly.

We had established a good rapport, and she had shown no discomfort with the question itself. But, once again, she changed the subject, and it remained changed for the rest of my visit. However, as she walked me to the car, Leia spontaneously and very deliberately added, "Make sure and tell my dad that I'm mad at him. You can ask *him* why."

Leia's "supervision" informed my work with Laird in the coming week and every week thereafter as I continually asked him why he thought his daughter was so angry with him. And each week he came up with another nervous explanation, which I then refuted. Finally, after the third week, he called me on the phone.

"I should have told you this in person . . . but I just couldn't." His slow voice was filled with shame.

"You can tell me now," I offered. "Have you thought of why Leia is so mad at you?"

"Yes," he said, pausing for a long deep breath. "Its hard to talk about . . . but . . . well, I touched Leia . . . when she was 5 I touched her, her privates."

"You touched her sexually?" I asked.

"Yes," he said hesitantly. He went on to debrief the experience further, explaining that he had touched Leia sexually on at least two occasions and perhaps more often, and had directed Leia also to touch his penis.

I met with CPS the next day and several times thereafter to report and staff the case and determine the best course of action. After a reasonable debate, CPS agreed to lift the no-contact order to allow a conjoint apology session among Debbie, Laird, and their children at whatever point I found him ready. This did not automatically extend to visitations, which we all agreed would occur after a successful apology and be supervised in perpetuity. The request for the apology session was granted largely because Laird had been so forthcoming, thus preventing Leia from having to disclose the abuse herself. What was far more surprising was that CPS and the district attorney found Laird amenable to treatment and decided not to prosecute the case for reasons I have never been able to ascertain, particularly given his confession. The system simply turned Laird and the family over to me with the understanding that Laird would not have unsupervised contact with any children and would remain in treatment until he was finished. In response they would not file charges, creating a sort of de facto diversion agreement. Following each of the themes discussed in chapter 4, I worked intensively with Laird in the coming weeks to build his philosophy of contrition.

I also saw Leia regularly. When I told her that her father had admitted what he had done to her, she was pleased but noncommittal. We did not discuss the matter further, however, as she continued to keep the boundary, but both of us knew that we were on the same sheet of music. She said that she was more than ready to meet with him, particularly after I briefly explained the agenda of apology for the session. When Laird was ready to apologize, we set a date.

I Give to You from My Spirit

I began the conjoint session by thanking the children for their help in exposing Laird's misdeeds.[2] I then asked Laird if he thought it was a good thing that the kids told what happened, so that he could get help.

"Yeah," he said starkly.

"He told me before that he thought it was a good thing," I said to the kids.

This seemed to serve as an invitation to Leia as she proudly and spontaneously shared how she had disclosed the abuse to her teacher. "He needs to learn how to control his temper and not hit kids," she concluded thoughtfully. "He needs to not be . . . "

"To not be getting so angry?" I prompted, as she struggled for words.

Leia nodded. "Yeah . . . he gets too upset."

"Laird, do think you should thank Leia for what she did?" I asked.

Laird swallowed hard and reached his arm out to the girl. "Yeah," he said, "you did the right thing, honey. I know I scared you and telling was the right thing to do." It was just the right thing to say, and Leia responded by giving him a hug and sitting on his knee. I allowed her to remain in this position for only a moment, sensitive to both her need for Laird's touch and the inappropriateness of this posture for a sex offender. Despite the still-secret sexual abuse and all of Laird's well-known physical and verbal abuse, Leia still loved her father very much. To believe otherwise would have led one down the same errant path as her mother's previous therapist, who had recommended Debbie simply fire her mother.

"Kids," I said, moving toward disclosure, "you need to come over here, because there is something else big that we need to talk about. We need to talk about something else that happened, because another thing that is not going to happen in this family any more is for anyone to have any secrets about things. 'Cause when you have secrets in a family, then things happen that shouldn't happen."

I paused, waiting for the children to gather around their father and me.

"Your dad told me that about 3 years ago, when Leia was about 5, that your dad . . . " I paused. "Actually, Laird I'll just let you tell it. Let's listen close to your dad. He has something important to tell you about."

In the place of disclosure and, however, Laird began a nearly infinite pause and seemed to be gathering his courage, which did not appear quickly.

"It's a hard thing to talk about," I said. "It's a very hard thing."

The pause continued so long that I began to wonder if he would proceed or fall into an impotent stupor at the very moment his daughter most needed him. As if to underscore the importance of this moment, Leia began to weep gently. And with her, Laird began to cry. The pause continued until it had become quite oppressive, when Leia suddenly reached over and took her father's hand.

In another situation this might have been lovely—the innocent child comforting an adult with a simple gesture of love. But here and now it was only poignant. The little girl's act of kindness symbolized the reversed hierarchy of a family in which the children took charge and the adults remained pathetically insubstantial. At the same time, it spoke of the attachment this girl felt for a father who had earned only her pity.

Stumped for a long moment, I regrouped to acknowledge the girl without reinforcing the hierarchy failure. "Laird," I said, "I think you need to be giving Leia the kind of support she is giving to you . . . even if this is difficult for you." I waited only a few more moments and then began feeding the opening words to Laird. "When you were 5, I . . ."

"Come over here, Joey," Laird said slowly, reaching for the boy who had wandered away, impatient with his father's struggle.

I ushered Joey back into the huddle. "Your dad wants to make sure you hear this. He wants to make sure you know about this so that it will never happen again."

"When Leia was a little kid," Laird said haltingly. "I, uh . . . I touched her in a way that an adult isn't supposed to touch a little one. I shouldn't have done that. Do you understand?"

Certain that they did not, I asked, "Do you understand how he touched her? He touched her privates."

The children nodded, as if they had some inkling of what this might mean.

"Eric, do you know why it's wrong for somebody to touch someone's privates like your dad touched Leia?"

"'Cause it's bad," he said, a good answer for a 7-year-old.

"It is," I said. "It is a bad thing. Joey do you know why it's wrong?"

"'Cause it could give you something bad," he offered.

Leia and Eric giggled.

"It could . . . it could give you something bad," I said in a supportive tone. I thought this a rather intelligent response. I then asked Tara why she thought it was wrong, but at 4 years old this was a bit beyond her grasp. We simply agreed that it was wrong.

But even before I could get to her in the circle, Leia interjected her own response. "He could get sent to prison for it," she said with great conviction. I could not tell at the moment if she was more concerned for his fate than her own, or if she was reminding him of the seriousness of his offense. Perhaps, as is often the case, it represented a mixture of both. In any case it was clear that Leia understood clearly the nature, quality, and wrongfulness of Laird's actions.

"Yeah, Leia, that's right isn't it," I said, ratifying her perception. "Why else do you think it's wrong?"

The girl remained silent. Even when coaxed she would not acknowledge the way in which Laird had afflicted her, only the way in which it could affect him. It is at these moments that the strength of the apology session truly shows through in offering words of the heart—words few can find for themselves, but each knows to be true in this time and place.

"You know another reason that it's wrong what your dad did to Leia? Because when a big person touches a little one . . . touches her privates . . . it hurts her heart. It hurts her inside . . . her spirit. Leia's got a spirit. You ever hear about that?"

The kids nodded vaguely as I struggled for the proper language to speak to their young minds. Reflexively, Leia's tears returned and increased as the words made sense to her at a level she could only experience.

"Leia's spirit is a special place in her heart where she loves people," I continued. "And when your dad touched her, that hurt her heart."

"Do you understand what he means about her spirit?" Laird suddenly added. As a man of American Indian heritage, this language had caught his attention.

The younger children nodded, entranced by the moment. I caught a glance of Leia and realized that it had all become too powerful for her. Feeling precisely what was being said, her weeping had became sobs and she went to the arms of her foster mother for comfort. She needed this break, and I did not redirect her. Without prompting and after only a few moments of hugging, the little girl turned herself around on the foster mother's lap so she could continue to follow the proceedings.

"Laird, how has it felt for you to know that you hurt your stepdaughter's spirit?" I asked. " 'Cause you knew that you did that didn't you?"

"Uh huh. Really bad. . . ." he said. There was far more emotion in his voice than his simple words could convey.

"And who bears all the shame for what happened?" I asked.

"I do."

"Does Leia bear any shame?"

"No . . . none." His voice was grave as he turned to directly face her for the first time. "You didn't do anything wrong," he said.

"Does Joey bear any shame for what you did to him?" I asked, driving home this important point as I spoke about each child.

"No," Laird said in response to each of my prompts. "It's my fault what happened. I did it."

"You know what I think, kids? I think it hurt your dad's heart too when he touched Leia and when he hit you all. I think it hurt him inside too. Because when a person does something that terrible it *has* to hurt them inside."

I paused a few moments as Laird struggled with his own pain and Leia continued to weep.

"You know what I want us to do now?" I said, glancing toward Leia who remained well focused through her tears. "Whenever you're ready, we're going to have your dad apologize to you." I nodded to her.

Leia nodded back, wiped her eyes, and instinctively returned to the seat between Laird and me. I motioned for him to get on his knees[3] and he did so.

"Leia," he began. "I . . . " Laird became overwhelmed with emotion and began to cry, his head hanging in shame. The little girl responded with more tears of her own, and we returned once again to the endless moments of agonizing, meaningful silence.

Eventually I prompted him. "You need to tell her that you're sorry for what you did."

Laird gathered himself yet again. "Leia. I'm sorry for touching you. . . ." He stumbled.

"And I bear all the shame . . . " I coached.

"I bear the shame for what happened. It was my fault. I shouldn't have ever done something like that to you, and I'm never going to do anything like that again."

"And I want you to apologize for making Leia grow up too fast," I said, redirecting him from making an improper promise to the girl.[4]

"I'm sorry I made you grow up too fast. You didn't have a chance to be a little kid 'cause, 'cause I asked too much of you."

"And for having hurt the brothers that she loves so much. For hitting them," I added.

"I'm sorry I didn't control my temper, and I'm sorry I hit your brothers. I know that upset you."

"I want you to promise to Leia that as long as you live you're going to do everything possible, no matter what it takes, to make sure that you never hit or touch or hurt any of these children ever again."

"Leia, I'm going to work really hard to never hurt you or your brothers or sisters ever again."[5] Laird paused and reached up to clasp a small pouch tied with a leather strap around his neck. I had never noticed it before. "Leia, do you know what this is?" he asked.

The girl nodded.

"This is my medicine bag. It represents my spirit," he said slowly.

I could see that this was a meaningful gesture, and I utilized it quickly. "And the part of her spirit that you have taken away by hurting her, you give back now from your spirit."

"Yes," Laird said, understanding the direction I was going. "I give to you from my spirit to make up for what I took from you."

Leia leaned forward and embraced her father, sobbing as she did so.[6]

"Thank you, daddy," she said.

"Oh God, I'm really sorry, Leia. I'm so sorry," Laird sobbed, now relying completely on his own words.

"And from now on Leia will know that you will help protect her and not hurt her," I added as they continued the embrace.

"Do you know that I really mean it? That I'm really sorry for hurting you?"

Leia nodded.

We continued around the room with Laird apologizing to each child that he had hurt and pledging to do whatever was necessary never to hurt them again. We then asked Debbie to return and sent Julia with the foster mother. I asked Debbie to begin by apologizing to Leia for not having protected her when Laird touched her and for not having had good enough communication with her so that she could have disclosed his abuse.

Debbie dropped to her knees as the emotion returned to the room. "Leia, you are my special daughter. You were my first child and I love you so much. . . ." She began to cry deeply and could not go on. Leia embraced her mother, and they sobbed in each other's arms for several minutes, symbolizing another poignant hierarchy reversal—Leia took the superior position, holding her crying mother like a baby. Yet, as her own mother had done several weeks before, Debbie struggled desperately to continue. She pulled away and looked straight into her daughter's eyes. "I am so sorry that I didn't protect you when your dad touched you and that I didn't have the kind of relationship with you that you could come to me and tell me what had happened. I am so sorry Leia. I am so sorry. Oh God! . . ."

"And you're sorry that you let her grow up too soon . . . " I coached.

"Yes. I'm sorry I made you grown up too soon. I shouldn't have left you in charge when I was gone. You were just a little girl and I made you grow up . . . oh my baby . . . I'm so sorry."

"And from this point on you're always going to make the kind of relationship where your daughter can come to you with things that bother her," I offered.

"Leia, I want you to come to me and talk with me about anything. I want it so you can tell me things. . . ."

"And *you're* going to make it so she can," I said, emphasizing the hierarchy of mother over daughter.

"Yes, *I'm* going to make it so you can come to mommy."

And with this, the two embraced again, this time with a noticeable difference—Debbie was in the superior position, holding her daughter in her arms. The hierarchy had begun to correct. It would take many more iterations to be finished, but the work had begun.

We continued with an apology by Debbie to each child and then some spontaneous play with the toys I had brought to the room. Among them was a doctor's bag, which little Julia, who had now returned to the session, had chosen for her play.

The 2-year-old sat on her mother's lap and played with the stethoscope.

"Mommy, listen to Tara's heart," Julia giggled.

"Okay, mama can do that," Debbie said.

"Now listen to your heart," she said. "And now listen to my heart."

I smiled at Debbie who looked more relaxed and natural as a mother than I had ever seen her. "Nothing like a nice consistent little metaphor there, huh?"

Debbie chuckled. "Oh, you want me to listen to your heart through your back . . . okay," she said responding to Julia.

"Are you listening mommy?" Julia asked.

"Yes," Debbie said.

"From now on, mommy," I said, catching Debbie's eye, "you'll be checking everyone's heart more often . . . okay?"

"Yeah." She smiled.

The Humungous Box

I worked with the Larson family for the next 6 months. We had occasional meetings of the whole family, but most of my work focused on various combinations of Debbie and the children working toward reunification and processing all of the themes discussed earlier. I also continued with Laird on his tasks of reparation, which were difficult as he now was virtually homeless. I asked that he make for Leia a bank into which she could put change he might find on the street, along with earnings he would receive when he finally got a job. He used his skills as a craftsman to make a nice bank from a tin can and even found some change to get started on his reparations. This was all symbolic, but it fit the situation. I spent my sessions with Leia encouraging her to talk about her abuse and associated feelings of pain and fear. However, she was only able to discuss these experiences after I engaged Debbie to talk with her about her own abuse.[7]

Much was learned from this case, but the most salient point is also the most bittersweet—in the end, only the offender has the real power to free the victim. To believe otherwise is to hold the narcissistic view that therapists are more powerful than we are. Compared to the family, we are trivial. We can create in our child clients and their adult counterparts an *illusion* of health based on reframes and cognitive restructuring, but we can never have in our possession a fraction of the power of the parent who committed the original injustice. Our job, like a good martial arts master, is to take the energy of violence already deep in the spirit of the offender and transform it into repentance and humility before the victim. With that in place, there is no need for illusion. This is best illustrated by my final session with Leia. Reflecting back many months, I asked if she remembered the two boxes in her life—one for good things and the other for bad. She indicated that she did remember. I asked which box was now bigger.

Leia giggled as she replied, "The box with the happy things! It's humungous!" She spread her arms wider than her normal reach, just as she had done that first day. But this time, she was symbolizing the breadth of joy in her life and not the oppressing pain she had known. Leia had done what so many abused and afflicted people have never been allowed to do. With the help of her family, she had experienced complete contrition and begun to put her abuse into a greater life context. And in doing so she had become free.

TO HEAL ME ALSO: JUSTIN'S CASE

Gwen was nervously trying to convince her 15-year-old son, Justin,[8] that he needed to remove his hat if therapy was to be effective. Her efforts seemed out of place, given this was only her second session in a family therapy begun several months ago. Her mother, Helen, was aligned with her futile attempt at discipline, intuitively trying to restore some hierarchy between mother and son.

Neither woman was having much success.

The therapist, Greg Tangari, struggled to sidestep this amusing conflict. "A lot of times when Justin gets nervous in these sessions he expresses that by using his hat to kinda shield or protect himself."

"Actually, I wanna go to sleep," Justin said. "*That's* why I have my hat in my eyes. I was just deep thinking. My cap of wisdom needs washed 'cause it smells pretty bad."

Clean or dirty, the "cap of wisdom" had become a treatment metaphor. Justin had a superior IQ, achieved without interest in his psychologist's test. Though he conducted himself more as a hoodlum, we'd reframed him "a deep thinker." In each session we'd ask Justin to look into his cap of wisdom for the answer to his latest dilemma—always a problem of conduct.

A colleague from another agency was departing the community and had referred the boy to Greg, noting that he was "a maintenance case" requiring little in-depth psychotherapy. To curb Justin's history of antisocial behavior, this individually oriented therapist had visited, played, and counseled with him as had others in the past, trying to change his internalized sadness and externalized anger and misconduct. They had a wonderful rapport, and Justin spoke fondly of the fellow for many months thereafter. He described how they had played a lot of chess in their sessions, and Justin had become quite good at the game. His behavior, however, remained poor. The young therapist had not seen the elephant in the living room: an underlying family history of abuse, alcoholism, and eventual outplacement with grandma Helen. The therapist knew about all these circumstances, but lacked the necessary theory to understand how everything fit together to explain Justin's increasingly oppositional behavior. Greg took a different tack, setting out to change Justin's life context. He began by bringing Helen to the intake session and getting to know her alongside Justin. She had never been invited to therapy before, but was happy to come and quickly became an active participant.[9]

Contrary to the referral, Helen was actually growing *more* concerned with Justin's conduct at home and school. He was constantly angry and noncompliant, had begun to steal money and small objects, had been adjudicated on truancy charges, and was now threatened with placement in a detention home. A few weeks before, he was transferred from his home school to the "last ditch" day school for unruly youth who had failed the highly restrictive environment of a behavior-disordered classroom. There were clearly more pieces to this game of chess than the one Justin had been playing with his previous therapist. Not surprisingly, it was Helen who explained things before Greg was halfway through his intake.

"He's mad at his mother," she told Greg during the portion of the intake in which he asked Justin to step out of the room. "Gwen is my daughter . . . but I can't say that I blame him any. She's all but abandoned him to carry on like she does. I don't know what to do with her." Her heart obviously heavy, Helen went on to describe a history of drug and alcohol addiction so severe that Gwen was now legally remanded to an inpatient treatment program, following several arrests for driving under the influence. Gwen had also been involved with a series of abusive men, exposing Justin to all manner of violence, neglect, and sociopathy.

In the next session, Greg confirmed with Justin his ill feelings for his mother. In fact, Justin seethed as he described Gwen as the person who had failed to protect him from abuse, left him with dangerous people on numerous occasions, and had repeatedly chosen her addiction over her children.

Greg initially considered Justin's misbehavior to be a metaphorical representation of his mother's own poor conduct, as well as a desparate attempt to love and protect her by demonstrating that he needed her to become healthy. Sadly, the boy's attempts had been futile thus far, as Gwen simply wouldn't or couldn't take the hint or the lead. Greg hoped her early-stage recovery might offer a chance to set things right between mother and son. He wanted to put her back in some form of hierarchy with the boy, allowing him to have the kind of respect he needed for his mother.

But Greg had missed something, which would become all too clear during an abortive attempt at conjoint therapy with mother and son. At one point Gwen had spontaneously apologized for the life she had given Justin, followed by an admonishment for his poor conduct. Justin became enraged and verbally attacked Gwen with extraordinary ferocity. Greg's well-intentioned but errant countermove was to demand that the boy show Gwen the respect she deserved as his mother.

To this, the boy literally screamed his response: "You have no idea what you're talking about! I *have* to talk to my mother this way. I don't know any other way to talk to her. If I can't talk to her this way I can't talk to her at all. You don't know how she's treated me. She doesn't deserve my respect!" And with this, Justin stood up and stormed out of the session, stating that he would never return.

While probably correct, Greg's initial hypothesis was premature. Justin did want to protect and redeem his mother, but first he needed to forgive her. Therapy would need to help Gwen take responsibility for her own actions and *earn* Justin's respect. We staffed the case, and I asked Greg to apologize to Justin for his error, which was itself therapeutic and saved their working relationship. Greg was then to propose that Gwen be permitted to apologize more appropriately for what she had done, allowing Justin to make an informed decision about whether he wanted to have a relationship with her. We knew he would never choose isolation, but his decision had to be authentic and based on free will; giving up his relationship with his mother had to be an option.[10] Justin agreed, and over the next 4 months Greg worked with Helen and the boy under my supervision behind the one-way mirror.

The Puppetmaster

We all felt well prepared for the second conjoint session with Gwen, but as the team watched the first clumsy minutes of "hat therapy," we worried that a repeat performance of Justin versus his mother was about to go into production.

"When Justin does his deep thinking it's truly an inspiring thing to see," Greg continued, turning to Gwen. "He can have such great insight and wisdom that it impresses everyone. And I'm assuming that he gets a lot of that from you." There was an collective groan in the packed observation room behind the mirror. It was no less an error to pronounce Gwen wise than to finagle her son's respect.

Justin was a step ahead of the supervision team, ready to attack his mother on the slightest nuance. "Oh yeah right!" he said bitterly. "I get *all* my wisdom from my mother who doesn't know jack about how to take care of kids."

"Uh . . . that's right," Greg stumbled.

"Where's that wisdom come from, mom? Your butt?" An all-out fracas was one misstep away.

I punched the transmitter button. "You'll have to back out of that one. You have to be gracious to the mom, not deify her."

Greg nodded a subtle acknowledgment and tried to get back in the game. "Your mom and I had a conversation earlier today. We were talking about how we can use what has happened in the past to free you from the strings of the puppetmaster."

"Oh god." Justin feigned a sigh of frustration. "Here we go again. The puppetmaster."

Justin knew the drill, having engaged in endless discourse with Greg about his deterministic view of a life outside his control. He had admitted early in therapy that the very people he most despised, a series of violent adults from his past, were still pulling those strings. Greg kept pushing the boy, almost taunting him, to describe the puppetmasters and to explain the strange hold they had over him. We were, of course, drawing him to identify the host of nefarious men his mother had foisted upon him. And finally, in the best tradition of confrontational therapy, Justin did break down, confessing the identity of the one true puppetmaster.

It was his mother.

Gwen was not a client of Greg's and was in treatment 200 miles away. Thus, we did not know how she felt about her previous conduct and whether she was really sorry, despite her weak apology in the first session. We did know that she had begun placing Justin with Helen before her worst spirals downward, suggesting some sense of caution on her part. Though it had been ordered by the court, she had willingly attended her treatment program and was said to be doing well. We typically find in such cases that the will to be a good parent is often present long after human frailty seems to have prevailed. Even if Gwen couldn't become a competent mother for Justin right now, she could free him from the puppetmaster—his angry preoccupation with her, and his replication of her lifestyle.

According to our usual protocol, Greg first met with Gwen for an individual session to determine how best to proceed. He explained his view of Justin's situation, revealing with as much empathy as possible how Gwen's problems interacted with Justin's. Though he openly acknowledged that Gwen also might gain something from the experience, he emphasized her role as one of helping her son to change, rather than necessarily changing herself. Not only was Gwen willing to participate, but she was rather enthusiastic. As is typical in such cases, she seemed to understand better than we did the role of sorrow and forgiveness. She was living it out. We were at best guides on a path she already wanted to travel.

Satisfied from this session that Gwen really did feel meaningful contrition for her errors, Greg began to work with her to focus and clarify the things she felt most sorry for in her raising of Justin. Utilizing the language of her treatment program, Greg helped Gwen construct a "searching and fearless moral inventory" of ways in which she had wronged her son. She was well positioned in her 12-step Alcoholics Anonymous program to do this task, but the painful list did not come easily. Greg patiently spent an hour helping Gwen collect her thoughts and her concurrent emotions, and put them on paper before taking a break and then bringing the family together.

No Piece of Cake

"Justin," Greg said, trying to wrest some control over the deteriorating session, "the main rule tonight is that you are free to express any anger or anxiety that you have. However, you have to do that without making gross or rude comments."

"Then I'm not going to express my anger against my mother," he shot back, hearing not what Greg had said but what he believed he was saying.

"And that's your choice. But if you do make comments, you need to do so without being gross."

This complex dialog was designed to set the balance between conflict and civility. Things needed to be genuine, without recapitulating the raw confrontation of the first session.

"Do you think you can look me in the eye and say it?" Gwen offered.

"Nope. Not without being foul mouthed or gross or anything."

"So you really feel like that is absolutely necessary," Greg asked, executing the next step in the dialog.

"Yeah."

"Okay, if that's the way it is," Greg turned to Gwen, "then I'd like your permission to let him do it this one time."

"Oh, he can do it and get it out," she said.

"I'm not gonna do it," Justin said with great certitude. The paradox had worked.

"Justin, go ahead and let's get it out," his mother coaxed. "If it's gonna make you feel better, then do it."

"It doesn't even make me feel better. It makes me feel worse. When you say something to hurt someone else, naturally you think you feel good but after awhile you feel bad because it really makes you feel worse than that person."

"That's some of that impressive insight I was talking about," Greg said, genuinely impressed by the level of insight the boy had garnered from this simple exchange. "You know earlier today your mom wrote a personal inventory of things she'd done or allowed to happen that hurt you. I'd like to go over those."

"I don't want to go over them," Justin said in his typical, defiant style. He had been over them enough in life. But it was important for him to hear Gwen acknowledge her wrongdoing, and Greg knew this.

"I understand this is gonna be very difficult for you," Greg said gently.

"Very difficult? It's nowhere near very difficult. It's like out of this world in hardness. It's like no power in the galaxy could like help me through this."

It is not unusual for even the angriest young people to try and protect their parents from such situations, but this cannot be taken as a contraindication to proceed. Such resistance is simply further evidence of the importance of the intervention.

"Well, there is a power in the galaxy," Greg said, attempting to counter Justin's hyperbole. "There is a higher power, and that power is in this room here with you. You have the love and support of your grandmother and you have my support." He paused. "Your mom developed what's known as a fearless and searching moral inventory."

"Oh no," Justin rolled his eyes.

"What she did is . . ."

"I know what it is. Come on, let's start with it." Justin paused, glancing at the list Greg held on his lap. "I know that all of them are not on that paper."

"Then would you please add what's not on the list?" Greg asked. "It would be very helpful."

"Got 5 or 6 more sheets of paper?" Justin scowled, underscoring the extent of his mother's offenses. "What's the first one she wants to talk about?"

Greg handed the list to Gwen, and she began. "Remember the time right after your brother was born that you were left in your room in the dark and Phil pulled the plug on your nightlight and shut your door?"

"Yes, I do," Justin said decisively.

"I shouldn't have let that happen." It was a deceptively small thing. The stepfather of the day had taken Justin's nightlight and put it in his newborn's room. Justin was afraid of the dark and protested. At a moment when he needed to know that he was wanted as a member of a growing family, he was relegated to the dark.

Greg did not miss the metaphor. "It's a terrible thing to let a little child stay in the dark alone . . . to take his light away."

"Plus all the people I allowed to hurt you in your life," Gwen continued.

"What about them?" Justin demanded.

"I'm sorry that I let them hurt you in the ways that they did."

"I just wish I could get a hold of the bastards and strangle 'em." There was a remarkable depth of emotion in his voice.

"Gwen, can you talk more about those people and what they did?" Greg asked. "But not beyond the level where Justin gets real uncomfortable."

"I'm very close," Justin warned. Everything in an apology session is geared toward maximizing the accountability of the offender and minimizing the pressure on the victim. Greg selected his words carefully to keep from overwhelming Justin and escalating him to another storm-out.

"The boyfriends . . . " Gwen continued.

"The dumbfucks," Justin corrected her.

"The hitting abuse," she added. "Bein' thrown in the closet. Bein' slapped."

"There are so many things you don't know about that happened to me from all those punks, and I don't care to express them right now. I'm not ready for that yet."

"I'm sure I don't know everything," Gwen sighed. "And not bein' there for you when you needed me. That was wrong."

"That's what really hurt the most," Justin paused several seconds. "Knowin' that I didn't have a mother to talk to when I needed to say things only a woman would understand. Half the time you were passed out drunk. Geez, one time I thought you was dead 'cause you was passed out for 3 days. . . . I was scared to death I'd lost my mother." Tears began to roll from his eyes, though he tried desperately to cover them with his cap. Beyond the anger, this boy was terribly frightened that his mother would abandon him once and for all—that she would die. Given her lifestyle, this was not an irrational fear.

Gwen also became quietly tearful. "I left you with people you didn't want to be left with. . . ."

"Quite a few of 'em hurt me," Justin said, between tears. "They'd make fun of me. They'd make me do things I didn't want to do . . . god."

"Things you didn't want to do," Greg reflected. We were both concerned about sexual abuse, and this abstruse comment demanded our attention.

"Like when I wasn't hungry, they'd throw food at me or shove it down my throat. They'd pick me up and swing me around like a doll. Slap me. Use me like a toy."

"The only thing I can say is that I'm sorry that I let them people into our lives." Gwen's apology was hollow and weak, a point not lost on the boy.

"I don't mean to be reachin' back into the past to make you feel bad or anything," Justin said in a surprisingly gentle tone. "But every time somebody hurt me and you'd get away from them, you'd tell me you were sorry. To tell you the honest to god truth, I'm at the point where I can't take an apology from you any more."

Justin's wisdom was apparent as he cited his own experience of the "cycle of violence." This is exactly the sort of situation that a proper application of the apology process is designed to address. Gwen would have to go much farther than a simple "I'm sorry" to reach her son, and we would do what it took to get her there.

"I don't blame you, Justin," Gwen said weakly. "I wouldn't accept an apology either. . . . I know you have a lot of hurt. And if I could turn back the clock and put myself in your shoes and take away all that pain, I would. But I can't."

"It's not helping me not living with you. It's makin' it all the much harder."

"That's why we're moving in the direction we are," Greg interrupted, not wanting to let the emotion of the moment bond the pair around Gwen's pathology. "Your mom has been working on it her way, and we've been working on it in ours. Now we're beginning to work together. And you know, Justin, you don't have to accept your mom's apology right now." Following the model, Greg reassured the boy that he was not obligated to forgive his mother, stressing instead that *she* needed to be contrite. It was an inadvertent paradox, as the boy moved to resist Greg in defense of his relationship with his mother and to assert his desperation to find a path to forgiveness and the freedom it offered.

"But I want to accept it," Justin said tearfully, as he turned to his mother. "But it's so hard when so many times you've said it just to make me feel that you was really sorry."

"And I'm not kidding you when I say you don't ever have to accept your mom's apology." Greg attempted to neutralize the unintentional paradox. "But it's something that we will hopefully work towards and then you may choose to accept her apology at some point in time. But it's not required of you."

Justin followed Greg's lead. "Til she can prove to me that I can accept an apology of hers, I won't. A lot of people may think that's cold-blooded, but if I'm hurt, then that's too bad, because all the other times you've lied."

"It doesn't sound cold-blooded to me," Greg said. "It sounds to me like you need your mom to *prove* her sorrow. Really, this is the beginning of that process tonight, not the end." He turned to Gwen. "Are you ready to start?"

"Yeah," she said weakly as she attempted to manage her tears. "I'm willing . . . will you help me, Justin?" The hierarchy reversal was intractable as the offender begged the child victim for help.

And true to family tradition, Justin accepted his role with only slight protest and a great deal of insight. "I will try to help mom, but it's not gonna be no piece of cake. It's gonna be a lot of bullshit along the way . . . but in the end, it's all for the better."

What Really Hurt

Greg returned to the still unresolved issue of what had been done to Justin. "We were talking about the fact that people did things to you that you didn't want them to do. So, should we continue on that?"

The boy nodded. "A lot of times when my mom would leave me with people I didn't want to be left with, they would hurt me. If they were pissed off at somebody, they'd just take it out on me. I mean I'm pretty lucky to be in as good a shape today as I am. 'Cause I've got bad knees, bad ankles, I've had back problems . . . I'm lucky to be alive." This was a bit more hyperbole, but whatever his actual physical scars, his emotional pain could not be overestimated. Greg began to examine the issue of sex abuse with a carefully constructed language.

"Can I make a guess or two about some of the things that happened?"

"You can try."

"Would you rather I didn't?" Greg offered the boy full freedom over the direction of the conversation.

"I don't mind. . . . And I'll be honestly truthful with you from here on." It was as if Justin knew what was coming.

"Many times, men . . . these crazy men that are out of control in these situations . . . can become sexually abusive." Greg described sex offenders in this way to exonerate Justin from any complicity, both facilitating disclosure and setting the foundation for further treatment.

A few seconds passed as all in attendance held their breath.

"I was never sexually abused," he said decisively. "I was always physically abused and mentally abused, but not sexually." And then to punctuate the veracity of his statement, he added, "And I can look you in the eye and tell you that I was never sexually abused because it's not a lie."

"I believe you," Greg said. "But you know, one type of abuse is not better than another type. They're all equally terrible."

"I'd rather somebody beat me up than have 'em yell and scream at me." Justin paused for a moment and then spoke as if he'd just come to an epiphany. "Huh. You know bruises and cuts and scratches go away . . . but this kind of abuse never goes away." He pointed at his head.

"The torture of verbal and . . . " Greg waited to be sure we were still on the same page of music.

"Mental," Justin filled in.

"And mental abuse," Greg followed. "They continue on after the physical bruises heal."

"At the time my mom was so drugged-up or drunk that when she would come and get me . . . by lookin' at me she couldn't tell if any shit had happened to me. That's how fucked up she was."

"Can you give me a sense of what that does to you?" Greg asked, departing just slightly from the protocol by asking something of the victim. By now, it was clear that Justin wanted to share these painful experiences with his mother. To prohibit him would have been disrespectful and untoward.

"God, it scared me to stay with any of those people," he said. "But she didn't seem to know any better. She just kept puttin' me back with 'em. I was scared I was gonna get killed." Justin's eyes shifted ever so slightly toward his mother. " 'Cause you didn't give a shit, mom. That's what really hurt."

"But I do now, Justin," Gwen offered as an inadequate reply to an unasked question that had no good answer.

"I know you do," Justin said glumly as if he were reading a minor line from the hundredth production of a play no one wanted to perform. Yet the fact that he was even willing to play out this grim scene told us that Greg could proceed to the next step of the process.

"Helen," Greg said, turning to the grandmother, "why do you think it's wrong what these people did to Justin?"

"To me a boy should have a good male role model in front of him, not somebody that's abusive."

"Yeah, not some bullshit blowjoe from nowhere who doesn't give a fuck," Justin lashed out again at the long-absent men who still haunted him as if they sat in session this very day.

"Because he, in turn, repeats that same pattern," Gwen added. It was her most insightful comment thus far, but a terribly pessimistic view of her son's future. Justin adopted it quickly.

"You know, I'll try very hard, but statistics show that whatever shit a young boy goes through, he'll do ten times worse to his kids. . . ."

"*If* he doesn't seek help," Gwen countered.

"Even if they do seek help, sometimes they do worse to their kids," Justin said with emphatic hopelessness. It was a critical issue—a window into Justin's future. How he imagined it could easily determine how it would come to pass. The puppetmaster was appearing again as a force Justin felt powerless to resist.

"Actually young men who get help almost always succeed," Greg countered, emphasizing the primacy of Justin's free will and commitment to change.

"That's what I meant, Greg. But the way I said it . . . I didn't explain it simple enough for you. I was saying that statistics show that young men who don't get help are more likely to do that to their kids."

"Yes, that's correct," Greg conceded with a slight smile. With Justin's buy-in he was now ready to move to the next step. "Gwen, why do you think it's wrong for a boy to grow up that way and experience those things?"

"No child should have to go through that," Gwen replied.

"Why?"

"Because it shows that the parent is irresponsible. Not only was I irresponsible, I wasn't a very good mother. I tried to be, but I wasn't. You know, Justin, I did care about you all along. I just didn't know how to show it."

Having just admitted his own free will, Justin would not let this comment go unchecked. Gwen *did* know how to be a parent, even as she had let her addiction get the best of her and her family. She had chosen this course. It had not been thrust upon her by her own ignorance. "You know, Greg, a lot of times my mom was drugged up or drunk or high or stoned or whatever you want to call it . . . I had to steal my own food in order to eat. It was malnutrition abuse."

"I understand, Justin," Greg said. "*Why* was it wrong?" They had to make this transition or the session would sink into utter despair. The goal was hope, not hopelessness.

"Why is it wrong?" Justin said. " 'Cause no child should be brought up like that. No child deserves that shit. Nobody deserves it."

"You know, Justin," Greg regrouped, "you're a great thinker and you think about this every day and you ask yourself 'why?' "

"A difficult question," Justin said in his great thinker voice. "An age-old question. Why?"

"Right. But what I want to know today is *why is it wrong*?"

" 'Cause it scars a child for life," Justin said.

"*How* does it scar a child for life?" Such persistence was unusual, but we needed to establish once and for all the connection between Justin's misbehavior, his sense of pain, the accompanying shame he so obviously bore, and the injustice he had faced during his mother's years of addiction and neglect. Justin was the only client in the room able to get us there. He held up beautifully.

"Some kids that went through the stuff I went through have gone crazy when they got older. Others haven't known what to do about it so they just let it keep happenin'. Me? I finally stopped takin' it and started standing up to everybody who did it to me." It was the core statement we'd been looking for. Justin opposed adult authority because he had known only the authority of violent, neglectful adults.

Greg moved to the next step. "I think all those things are right, and there is even more. I think what it did is cause a spiritual pain in Justin's heart . . . in the place where he loves people. It damaged that."

Helen nodded. Tears returned to Gwen's eyes.

Justin brought his hands to his nose in a praying position, as if to block his own tears. "Some kids that have that happen to them," he offered. "When they become adults, that place in their heart no longer exists."

"It takes the innocence from your soul, huh?" Greg said, drawing from the words of another client in a previous apology session.

Justin nodded as the words resonated with him, reminding us again of the consistency of experience among those who have been so abused. "It makes you feel like . . . like nobody cares for you any more. Do what you want to do. Its not like anybody's gonna help you or anything. Basically what it felt like . . . what it feels like, is that I was raised up on the street."

"You know," Greg said, "I think it must have hurt your mother's heart too, to know that she was so out of control. . . ." He was building a conceptual structure for Justin to transform the confusing sense of anger and bitterness he felt toward his mother into the possibility of forgiveness.

"When mom was drunk or high," Justin continued, "naturally she didn't give a fuck. I could get hurt, I could get shot. I coulda had a broken bone. She was like 'forget you, I'm gonna just keep chuggin' beers and smokin' pot.'"

"I'm not defending your mother," Greg said, validating the boy's dissonant experience of Gwen. "But for anybody to allow that to occur, they must have a pain in their heart that. . . ."

"Anybody who doesn't feel bad after they do it," Justin interrupted with a mix of anger and sadness, "they have a stone-cold blooded heart. They don't even have a heart."

"Well, I do have a heart, Justin," Gwen said unconvincingly.

"Gwen, did the alcohol and drugs cause a lot of pain for you?" Greg asked.

"Yeah, they did. A big pain."

"Do you feel it today as you see what's happened to your son?"

"Yes. Very much so."

"Gwen, how serious are you about beginning the process of mending his wounded spirit?"

"Very serious," she said. "Serious enough to go to any lengths to do it."

"Justin, how serious are you about allowing your mom to apologize? Not to have to accept it . . . "

"But I want to be able to accept it," Justin interrupted. There was a pleading tone in his voice. "I don't want to just keep having to reject it and not believe her. I want to be able to accept it in order for . . . for it to heal me also."

"The beginning step would be to hear it," Greg said gently. "And then the acceptance is something that may come . . . eventually."

"Anybody can say they're sorry or 'I apologize' or 'I didn't mean to,'" Justin said sadly. "But most people who say it don't even know the meaning of the word."

"Maybe its important for your mom to *show* how much she means it," Greg said.

"I can do that," Gwen said. "If you'll let me."

Justin paused a few moments. "I will let her," he said solemnly.

A Sign of Meaningfulness

"Gwen," Greg said, "what I would like you to do is come over here in front of Justin and kneel down in front of him."

Without hesitation nor even surprise, Gwen moved to the floor. Justin did not object, but quickly returned to his prayer-like position, squeezing his tear-ducts to the point that they must have hurt.

"Justin," Greg said. "In our society and in almost all cultures in our world, when somebody kneels in front of somebody else, that is a sign of . . . respect and of . . . sorrow, and humility. It's a sign of . . ."

"Meaningfulness," Justin managed. "And seriousness."

"Yes, it's not something that is done lightly." There was a long pause before Greg continued. "Gwen, would you tell Justin what it is that you're sorry for?"

"Everything that I've put you through that's caused you pain or hurt and for all the people that have done it to you . . ."

Justin began to sob.

"And for not being there to protect him. . . ." Greg coached.

Gwen also began weeping as she repeated Greg's words. Overcome with emotion, she fell into a raw interminable silence. But these quiet moments were far from dead. There was a lot more going on in the finite space between her words than could be measured. It was as if all that needed to be said had been said, but until now it had never been enacted in a way that was deep enough to have real meaning and substance for a boy so deeply hurt. Gwen's willingness to take the position of sorrow, to kneel at her son's feet, was a powerful enactment of her words. If she was not truly sorry this time, she never would be. Though time would be the final judge of her sincerity, this was something Justin needed to witness and feel at a level that went beyond the verbal.

"All I want is for you to be happy. . . . Will you let me back into your life?" Gwen was moving away from the task at hand, but not very far. After a few moments and before he could respond, she spontaneously returned to the apology: "When you needed me and I wasn't there. I'm sorry for that."

"And for leaving him in the dark, both figuratively and in the real sense," Greg directed.

Gwen added this to her apology as Justin gasped every few seconds for breath between his tears.

Respecting the power of the moment, Greg waited a bit before continuing. "Gwen, would you pledge to Justin that you will take this one day at a time and do everything that you can to make sure that he's not hurt again. Will you take his hand and promise him that?"

"I can do that," Gwen said, taking both of Justin's hands and making the pledge, then adding, "Will you work with me on it?"

"Yes, mom, I will," he said with conviction.

After yet another long powerful pause, Gwen punctuated her own inadequacy. "You just don't know how much of a failure I feel like, Justin," She wept. "But I am trying."

"I know you are, mom."

"Gwen," Greg said, "it seems to me that tonight as you kneel in front of your son, and in being humble, that you are more successful than you've ever been in your life."

Gwen nodded slightly. "I don't know about you, Justin, but I'm tired of being sad and depressed and hurt."

"I'm tired of bein' pissed off and angry," he responded.

"If anything's gonna kill us, it's this anger that we carry," Gwen said wisely. "Justin, do you still love me?"

"I'll always love you, mom. It's just that it gets so hard at times to show it." He was speaking about his mother's absence, not his own capacity for love.

"I know."

"And love and forgiveness are very separate things," Greg noted, making clear once again that apology was only an invitation, not a command to forgive. "One does not necessarily make the other occur. But it is the road that we travel to get there."

"You know, Justin," Gwen said, "you don't ever have to forgive me for what I've put you through."

"I know you don't expect me to, mom . . . but I'm gonna try."

A Long, Winding, Bumpy Road

When we first published this case in the *Family Therapy Networker* (Crenshaw & Tangari, 1998), we admitted that it did not have a fairy tale ending. As had happened so many times before, Gwen's recovery stalled and then reversed while the boy remained securely with his grandmother. Even so, the robustness of the intervention became even more apparent. For once, Justin did not follow his mother's deteriorating course. In fact, he continued to improve, albeit with the foibles and misbehavior so often found in bright teen boys. Most notable was the session in which Justin learned that his mother had relapsed into her alcoholic lifestyle yet again with a new man she had met in recovery. Instead of enacting our worst fear that the boy would instantly deteriorate as he had in the past, Justin calmly advised Greg, "I care about my mom and I wish she'd make it, but I'm going to have to let her do that on her own. Right now I have to get my life together."

And over the next year, as therapy ebbed and flowed, Justin went on making slow but significant progress in that direction until the road took yet another twist. Gwen went back into recovery, left her problematic boyfriend, and, for a period of about a year, maintained solid sobriety. In that time she was able to work with Justin in a most consistent way, though none of us counted on her exclusively for his support. She even provided reparation in the form of a computer, which greatly aided the boy in doing his schoolwork (and playing video games). In a remarkable follow-up session some 2 years after the original apology, Gwen brought a letter she had written as a part of her 12-step program. It revised her moral inventory with far greater reflection and depth. As she read it aloud in session, we found her actually returning to the original apology session, this time embellishing the process for which she had, at that time, so few words. Now she was able to say what she needed and wanted to say back then. Reflecting on a letter Justin had written to her recently, she tearfully read:

> Dear Justin:
>
> I am glad you are my son. I love you. Isn't it funny how mom keeps you in line and you keep mom in line? The letter you wrote me made me cry, and so did this one. Please try to be patient with me. I will try to do the same with you.
>
> Everything I write to you in this letter I am very sincere about. I am sorry I haven't always been there for you. I have a disease and when I was lost in it I didn't care about anything except to get my next drink or drug. All I want is for us to be a family. It is so hard for me to live my life without my kids. I've been a terrible mother to you. Before I came home, I couldn't take care of myself. I didn't want anyone to see me that way because I've hurt you too much. I'm so sorry. I know that sometimes I treat you like a three year old, and you're not, but that is the age you were when things in our life starting going real bad. It wasn't your fault it was my fault. I made a bad choice and went down the wrong roads. I don't want you to go down those same roads. You'll have a terrible life . . . and a hard one at that.

> You're a handsome, smart, strong-willed, and independent young man. And you are growing up so fast. I haven't been there in the past and I carry so much guilt inside for that. Think positive all the time. You will be somebody. Because you are my son you are somebody. In life you must always have two plans. If Plan A fails, go with Plan B. You are changing every day of your life. I don't know if you can feel it or see it, but I do. Thanks for sharing your life with me. I love you and care about you more than you know.

Gwen sat for several long moments. "So that's how I started my fourth step," she murmured beneath her tears.

"And I think you started beautifully," Greg offered.

As Gwen had begun to cry early in the reading, Greg had passed a box of tissues to Justin, assuming he would hand them to his mother as a comforting gesture. He did not. Instead he patiently held them on his lap until his mother finished her letter. Only then did he pass the box on to her. It was an unexpected and unmistakable metaphor. The boy would not rescue his mother from her tears or disrupt her process of contrition. He waited until she had gone through the pain appropriate to the moment and only then did he comfort her. It was a sign of how far the hierarchy had corrected. Justin no longer felt responsible for his mother's satisfaction or well-being. He was in the end, however, a gentleman. For months to come we would refer to those tissues with equal parts humor and reverence as the Kleenex of Justice.

There was a long pause as Gwen dried her tears and Justin sat quietly. His posture, sunk down in the armchair in Greg's office, seemed to indicate indifference. But this was not so. He was closely attending to the session and had become a bit tearful himself, though it was nothing like his painful outpouring in the apology session. Nor were there any signs of his historic anger. The original session had worked. Those days were gone and would not be revisited. He was now a remarkably thoughtful and reflective young man.

"I don't want to keep hurtin' people I love," Gwen said, "especially my kids."

"Gwen," Greg said, "I think you've taken more steps in correcting that in the last few months than you ever have before." He turned to the boy. "Justin, what are you finding in your heart today?"

He sighed. "I'm at a loss for words," he said quietly. It was a first for Justin. In over 28 months, we'd never known him lacking in something to say, and with several more years in follow-up, verbosity remained one of his strengths. Yet there he sat, speechless.

"It must have been difficult to hear all of the pain your mom has felt," said Greg.

"I don't know what to say," he reiterated pensively. "The only thing I can say is that I still love her and I'll always love her and I'll be there for her even though sometimes she hasn't been there for me." He wiped a tear from his eye. "That's all I can say."

"Justin, how has it been for you for the last 2 years, while you've been trying to accept her apology as she's been trying to make good on it?" Greg asked, unaccustomed to having work so hard to generate dialog with the boy.

"Hm." Justin thought for a moment. "Well . . . it's been kind of . . . it's kind of a bumpy road."

"A bumpy road?"

"Yeah," he said drawing an invisible graph in the air to illustrate his point as he spoke. "There are hard times and then real rocky times, and then there's high times and really low times. It's the only thing I can think of to express it. It's a long, winding, bumpy road. And sure to come are more high times and sure to come are more low times." It was a remarkable description of the process of forgiveness, particularly for a speechless boy.

"So it's been kind of a journey for you?"

"Yeah, pretty much," he nodded.

Things would remain much this way over the next several years. As was evident in the follow-up session, Justin had released his mother as an object of hatred and pathogenesis, without turning her into one of false security. He could see her for who she was, appreciate her accomplishments, and let her failures be her own. In doing so, he had illustrated an important point in the contrition process. True forgiveness is not about idealization and illusion—it is about reconciliation and release. The sincere apology is the offender's offering of release. Forgiveness is the victim's acceptance, and, ultimately, the relegation of his or her abuse to a small space within a greater life context. For this reason, as Madanes (1990) notes, the therapeutic apology is both an effective strategy and the morally correct thing to do.

NOTES

1. I am indebted to David Eddy, Ph.D., former training director of the Family Therapy Institute of Washington, DC, for the calendar portion of this intervention. I recommend it for such clients, though not before an apology session as this case illustrates.
2. Of note, 2-year old Julia could not manage this lengthy session and Debbie tended to her in the other room. Normally I would have had the mother in session, but in this situation it was simply not possible until later in the nearly two-hour session. Fortunately, the foster mother did an exceptional job of standing in for Debbie and offering support during the process.
3. Before we began to use an invitation to kneel, we had simply directed the offender into this position. Additionally, Laird complained of chronic back problems, so I had taken the unusual step of warning him in advance that he would be expected to apologize on his knees to avoid any question at the moment of impact.
4. Instead of this, the offender should only pledge to do everything necessary to

prevent the offense from happening again, rather than saying he will never do it again. The former is a promise to continue to engage in a process, the latter a promise of a specific outcome, which can lull the victim into a sense of complacency that is dangerous in her future protection.

5. Laird's statement "I'm going to work hard . . ." is an excellent response to this prompt.
6. We do not allow any adult in the room to embrace the offender in response to an apology, a point made to all adults in attendance beforehand. Offenders are also told not to embrace anyone. However, the child victims are not told this as they are free to express themselves as they wish, within safe parameters. Leia chose to embrace Laird, and it would have been inappropriate and disrespectful to stop her, as well as a violation of proper utilization.
7. Of course, Debbie did not give much detail about her own experiences, and at this point it would have been inappropriate to encourage her to do so. Once Leia understood that her mother had been mistreated as a child, she was much more able to share her own experiences. A mother's role modeling can be used for both good and ill, and in this case it made the difference between Leia being able to share or keeping her pain inside her, as had Debbie for so many years.
8. A short version of this case study and some of the conceptualizations in chapter 4 was published in *The Family Therapy Networker* (November–December 1998) under the title "The Apology." It was coauthored by Greg Tangari, LSCSW, the therapist on the case. I supervised the therapy behind the one-way mirror.
9. Justin's father's identity and whereabouts were unknown. His grandfather was in the home but refused to attend therapy until well after the session described herein. Justin had a younger sister and brother who were also placed with grandma Helen, and they also attended later in the process.
10. Unlike Debbie's therapist in the previous case, we were very clear with Justin that he was in control of this situation, while urging him to at least hear his mother's apology before rendering any decisions.

CHAPTER 6

I Never Heard You Cry Before

Please tell me why it had to be me.
I've been screaming this question.
And nobody can answer me.
I have all these problems.
I don't know why.
Was I born like this or is it 'cuz of my past?
I don't know but I wish I did.
Please someone take the stand.
Tell me what you know.
Then maybe I would understand.
When am I going to get my wish?
All I want to know is why.
Why it had to be me.
Can you please answer that question for me?
—A 14-year-old girl

Incest carries a dynamic apart from sexual abuse committed by a non-blood relative and quite unlike that wrought by a stranger. Strangers are untested and untrusted. Their betrayal is explicable more easily than betrayal by those charged to care for the child. Everyone is dismayed when a stranger assaults a child, but when a family member commits sexual abuse the injustice is unparalleled, and that is not lost on children. It leaves them more puzzled and angry than any other form of mistreatment. With all the prospects for sexual outlet in our modern world, how can a parent transform a child into a sexual object acting from the basest of impulses? How can parents betray their own progeny? Worse, the "why question" that so haunts all victims of sexual abuse is especially difficult for incest survivors as they ponder not only their own shame, but that of their own birthparent. Considering for themselves that they were born from one so evil or sick, they may question the propriety of their very existence, or as the client who wrote the opening passage put it, "if my father is a pervert, what . . . who does that make me?"

September, whose case was introduced in chapter 1, had answered this terrible question by retreating toward suicide. Her CPS case worker, Hanna Winthrow, hadn't done anything for the girl in intervening months, leaving her stuck in a psychiatric group home well past her discharge date. In hopeful desperation and with the support of the home itself, I imposed upon a therapeutic foster mother I had worked with on another case, and Connie Dixon immediately expressed interest in the girl. Confronted with an easy move, Hanna acquiesced, though she was none too happy with me for leveraging the placement after she had already given up. Our strained relationship was close to snapping.

Those trials and tribulations notwithstanding, 15-year-old September once again sat in my office on a cold January evening, some 9 months after the bleach incident on her birthday night. She looked plump and angry and terrible. If anything, she had gotten much worse. I was glad to see her out of the group home, but I was amazed they would have released her in such a state.

WHAT HURT WORSE

"So what's up?" I asked in a tone intentionally too light for the moment.

"Oh nothing . . . just everything sucks," she mumbled sullenly. "What can I say?"

"So what happened today?" I asked. Connie had warned me of an incident involving September's little brother while she was visiting them at her stepmother's house.

"My little brother came running out to the car," she said. "Billy comes right up to me and says ''Tember, you know what you did? Well now we can't see our dad. . . .' And I was sitting there thinking 'what am I supposed to do?' " The girl felt maternal to both boys, having been left to raise them during her stepmother Barbara's runaway. It was a catastrophe.

"So what did you do?" I asked, clumsily dodging the impact of the moment.

"I just sat there."

"You know it isn't true," I offered.

"I mean I went through all this crap when I was 5. I should've known better."

"What do you mean?"

"You know, with Rick." Rick was September's former stepfather and first offender. She had put him in prison. "I should've known better so I shouldn't have done it in the first place. I should've just left. But then, you know . . . Billy and Bobby were there. And then . . . you know . . . " Her train of thought shifted and she looked me straight in the eye. "When *can* my dad see Billy and Bobby again?"

"That's for me to work on. That's not your problem." It was a lousy answer, but it was all I had. Tommy had been issued a no-contact order on all his children, though he had offended only against September. I could try and dissuade her, but I knew she wouldn't budge on the issue of her responsibility for their predicament.

"But if I have to take all this shit from them. . . ." September cut herself short with a mix of anger and sadness.

"I will need to work on that," I said emphatically. "You are correct . . . that is wrong for them to believe that it's your fault."

"He's only 6 though, and. . . ."

"And he feels that it's your fault."

"Well it is." September closed the deal.

Just minutes into the session and I was beginning to feel trapped. "Obviously that's a conclusion they've come to on their own," I said. "Because Barbara has been very kind to you and has been very concerned about you and she doesn't blame you for it . . . and your dad doesn't blame you for it. In fact, I talked with him today about the fact that you blame yourself for it."

"What did he say?" September immediately perked up. I thought back to her poem "Life of Gold." Communication from her father was an event of the highest importance to her. I knew she was waiting for the moment when he would put the "gold" back in her life. It was the most valuable aspect of knowing everyone in the case and being able to manage their communication.

"He was astonished," I said.

"Wow." Her surprise was hollow.

I tried to add some enthusiasm. "Actually he said 'why would she blame herself?' "

"I haven't been able to talk to him on the phone for the past 3 weeks. How am I supposed to feel?"

"I don't know. . . . I don't have any idea." I desperately stalled for time, grasping for the straws that might turn the girl back from the dark place where I knew she was heading. "How *did* you feel?"

"Like . . . well, part of me liked him and part of me hated him."

"That's normal." It was a pathetically inadequate response, and it generated a long pause as we each pondered the significance of her words. "Pretty soon we're going to have him in here. How are you going to be with that?"

"I dunno."

"Well, we're not going to do this until you're ready." I needed to understand her uncertainty and accept her pacing. I would not rush her.

"He can sit with Barb, and I'll sit clear over there." September pointed to opposite sides of the room. It is an issue that comes up before every apology session.

"You can sit anywhere you want to. You can sit right here in this chair if you like." I extended this privilege to victims in apology sessions to transfer my power to them and strengthen their position in the family. "I wonder why you'd want to sit across the room from him?"

" 'Cause I'm scared of him," she said tentatively.

"I've never heard you say that before." It was true. Surprisingly, before her father's conviction 6 months after the disclosure, CPS had allowed structured contact. September had expressed no worry about her father, even scoffing at the idea of supervised visitation. He had even brought her to therapy from the psychiatric hospital on one occasion, and no one seemed to have any objection. Upon his conviction, however, the state's attorney demanded an order barring all face-to-face contact. Coming as it did so late in the game, the order actually served to increase the girl's anxiety about her father.

"I wonder what you'll be afraid of?" I asked, relaxing a bit. We were on familiar ground now, and I felt a bit safer.

"I don't know. . . ." She gazed past me toward something distant, unseen. "You know what hurt worse? Not that he . . . like, did. . . ." She stumbled for the words to describe sexual abuse. "Him hitting me, that's what hurt worse."

"Worse than what?" I asked.

"Than, you know, what he did. . . ." She would not say it, and out of respect I would not make her. Yet I knew we were closing in quickly on the ultimate question: Why?

"Why is it worse?" I asked, gently guiding her. "I don't understand. . . . you've not said it that way before."

"I don't know why," she said quite seriously, her thinking still beyond me. "It just is."

"Maybe the being hit is easier . . ." I offered slowly, "easier to understand that kind of pain."

"Probably," she nodded.

"It's hard to understand the pain you get from being sexually abused." I spoke the words hesitantly to her for the first time in many months. "I think you've been trying to understand that pain for a long long time. . . . I think it's very very hard, if not impossible, to understand why someone would do that. . . . I think he hurt you very bad because he took away a lot." I paused, but she gave no response. "You know what he took away from you?"

September shook her head slightly.

"You don't think he took anything away from you?" My voice became gruff as I tried to annoy her back to reality.

She would not come. Instead, she grew more sullen and unresponsive, shrugging just enough to be noticed. September was leaving me, dissociating under her pain and isolation.

"I think he took your father away from you," I said quietly.

Her eyebrows suddenly raised just enough to provide a minimal cue, and nothing more. I could see the point had hit home, perhaps more deeply than I had anticipated.

"Where are you today, girl?" I said.

"Same place I always am," she quietly raged.

"No you're not," I protested, still trying to rouse the feisty girl I'd known so many months before.

"Yes, I am."

"You've never looked this way before." I could hear in my own voice a sort of pleading.

"Well, then *you don't know me,*" she said firmly, leaning forward a bit in her chair as her irritation turned to genuine anger and she began to reengage. "*This* is the way I look."

The moment sent chills up my back. I knew this girl better than any client I had worked with in years, and we shared a deep connection. She had entrusted me with her horrible secrets, highest hopes, and most painful memories, and she was disconnecting from me at what was rapidly becoming her moment of deepest despair. I knew without question that this distancing, this declaration of alienation was as much a goodbye as the hug she'd given me on the evening of her 15th birthday.

TO FAIL AT FAILING

We sat for many minutes in that rare and uncomfortable silence when two highly verbal people with much to say can't find the right words. "I feel like you're slipping away," I finally said in a voice barely audible.

"You know something," she said, suddenly snapping out of her trance, "I guess I'm just so used to failing that I'm just looking for ways to fail. I tried to explain this to Connie the other day, but she didn't understand and then she said 'whatever' or something."

"I think she probably understood." In my desperation for Connie and September to find a connection, I made an assertion I could not support.

"No . . . she didn't," September corrected.

"Then we should try to explain it to her," I offered.

"No, I'm not gonna bother her."

"Finding another way to fail?"

"She goes, 'well whatever you do, if you say 'oh shit, I shouldn't of done that, then you shouldn't have done it.' That's what she said." It was a complex and rambling statement leaving me little to grab on to. I returned to the previous subject.

"How is it that you try to find ways to fail?" I was afraid I knew where she was headed, and she didn't hesitate to confirm my fears.

"You know, the way I think is just weird. It's like the worst thing that could happen to you is that you die and nobody can do anything to you. If something bad happens you can just die . . . you can kill yourself. And whatever the result is, you can die. It isn't a big deal. If you look at it, the worst thing that can ever happen is that you can die . . . and that ain't bad . . . so what's it worth? You know, I just want to give up, 'cause. . . ." It was an intense, battering, subtle tirade offered as casually as a treatise on a new but not very interesting boyfriend. I began to take countermeasures to pull her back from the brink, going first to the girl's strength, her love of argument. If I could get September into a good enough fight, she would come back to finish it the next week.

" 'Cause . . . why?" I asked provocatively.

" 'Cause there's nothing left to live for."

"There's nothing left to live for?" I asked with a measure of sarcasm.

"I understand that all these people are trying to help me, but my life is . . . trash."

"Because . . . ?"

"Of me." It was a chilling assessment. Like one who had been colonized, she was taking on the perception of the oppressor. September was blaming herself.

"You're life is trash because of you?" I fought back.

"Yeah."

"Okay . . . tell me about that, 'cause I'm lost." By mocking her, I hoped to create an illusion of pure absurdity. "How'd your life become trash . . . what have *you* done to trash your life?"

"I've ran, I've been in a Level D group home, I've been in the psychiatric ward, I've been in a girl's home, I've been at the lockup, I've been in a foster home, and another foster home. . . ."

"I would call that having made poor decisions . . . not trashing your life."

"I'd call it freaking up your life."

"I think you made some pretty bad choices."

"And then I go to another Level D and then to another foster home with a 12-year-old foster brother that makes your life like hell. . . ." As she rambled on, a horrible realization came over me. I had successfully gotten September into an argument, one in which the stakes were her very existence. And she was winning.

"Everywhere there are problems," I countered. "Everywhere there are 12-year-olds."

"No! The 12-year-old isn't my problem!" September shot back. "My problem is my result is that . . . my . . . I don't know what I'm thinking here . . . I'm just talking." She chuckled nervously.

"Go for it," I said, encouraging her to let go in the safety of my office.

"Its just that . . . the worst thing that could happen is that you die, so you might as well just give up and fail because . . . it seems like everything I do someone can just prove me wrong. Everything I do, I fail at . . . so why don't I just make myself fail so I can't fail at failing."

"Now I understand . . . thank you." I quickly changed my tack, realizing the girl was as desperate as I to make sense of a senseless situation. Her pain was quietly consuming her, as my own impotence was consuming me. I pressed on, hoping I could find something meaningful to say in the midst of such meaninglessness, but I was unsuccessful.

"Maybe because without failure there isn't the possibility of success," I offered foolishly. "There have to be some failures in order to see what success is."

"So, should I slit my wrists a couple more times and just. . .?" she countered mercilessly.

"That wasn't on my top-five list of things to do, no," I said. "You know, I can't remember if we've talked about this before . . . but when you make a decision, you don't just make a decision for you. You make a decision for everyone."

"No, I don't!" She said angrily.

"Bullshit. Yes, you do."

"So you're telling me if I say I'm going to jump off a bridge, then I make a decision for everyone to jump off a bridge?"

"You make a decision that impacts me, you make a decision that impacts your father, you make a decision that impacts. . . ."

"My father did ten times worse than me dying!" She leaned forward and looked me straight in the eye. She was locked, loaded, and had found her range. "I'd rather be dead than go through that again!"

"I can understand that," I said trying to match her.

"I wish I had died."

"I can understand that."

"I wish I *was* dead."

"That I can't understand," I paused to catch my breath and direction. "'Cause we're on the other side now." I felt a momentary surge of energy, imagining in that split second that I was finally close to putting her in check, defeating her by breaking her self-loathing argument and thereby freeing her from it.

"No, we're not," she demanded.

"You're not going to get hurt anymore," I said.

"Oh? How do you know? I thought that after Rick got put in jail, and then here comes that foster guy." September had also been molested in a foster home when she was removed from her mother at age 5, and this fact seemed to appear at the most inopportune times. "And then here comes my dad.

Who's next? Here's September Dupree, everybody can just fuck with her. She can just sit there and take it all."

"Because now you're going to be protected," I said with as much authority as I could muster. "You're old enough to protect yourself now—and because you have people around you . . . ."

"I was old enough then," she said.

"You were a little kid."

"I was old enough," she insisted, refusing release from the shame of her own abuse.

"No," I said. "No."

"Yes I was."

"You're barely old enough now."

"I was old enough."

"You've got lots of people around who are going to help you be protected. I do understand wishing you were dead . . . I'm not missing that."

"I *do* wish I was dead. I wish I'd die right now. I wish lightning would come strike me." Her attack was withering, wearing me down, and with me her last hope of freedom. I could see a hospital screening just around the corner, perhaps tonight. After 9 months in psychiatric placements, September had been out for 1 week. I couldn't bear the thought of sending her back, but neither could I risk her life to another lethal cleaning solution. To my horror, it was now me slipping into check.

"Listen to me," I said emphatically. "All I'm saying is that for you to die or be taken right now would change a lot of lives—and not for the better."

"Yeah, it would," she slumped back in her chair. "My dad would be happy, and he wouldn't have to go through this shit." It was a stunning moment of déjà vu. She would now sacrifice her life for her father's comfort, just as she had sacrificed for him a year before with her long silence.

LOOKING INTO THE EYES OF YOUR DAUGHTER

A terrible thought crept beyond the back of my mind. In her desperate hunger for salvation, September was consuming me in a way I could not understand or defend against. She was gobbling up my spirit, knowing and yet not knowing that there was a last bite yet to be taken. She was coming dangerously close to that final morsel of me—and when that was gone there would be no more. I was alone. There was no one else. Yet she was compelled to continue, incapable of satisfying her hunger. I had to win and she could not let me win, and thus we were in a perfect, dangerous stasis.

And in that moment I came to the sort of epiphany reached by relearning that which you always knew—lost in this moment only to have it find you instead. I suddenly knew that I *was* powerless. Only in accepting that could I go to my strength. Much as I cared about this lonely, lost girl, and as much as she admired and respected me, I would never be the one to fill her terrible void. As she had said in her poem "Life of Gold," only her father had that power. I had reestablished contact with him that morning in anticipation of an apology session somewhere down the road, and I knew he was heartsick over the pain he'd caused his daughter. I knew he could convince her to live in ways that I could not.

"Well," I said, "I promise to pose that question to your father the next time I see him . . . if you would like me to . . . whether or not he wishes you were dead."

And then in a moment of therapeutic synchronicity, September saw my bid and raised me two. "Will you call him right now and ask him?"

I am surprised in retrospect, but I did not hesitate. Not for a moment did I consider any consequence of this decision other than keeping September alive and out of lockup. I knew even as she said it that it was my only choice, that this phone call could be the single therapeutic moment that would change the course of September's treatment and her very life story. As I dialed, I reflected on my good fortune in getting Tommy's lawyer on the phone that morning to discuss the court order in which phone contact was not prohibited. I had asked him to look into what it would take to get therapeutic contact, and he and Tommy had set an appointment to discuss it. But the moment was here and now. September in her infinite impatience for justice would not wait.

The phone rang twice before I heard a voice on the other end.

"Tommy?"

"Yeah."

"This is Wes."

He acknowledged me.

"I have your daughter here, and she has come to the conclusion after a great deal of thought . . . that she would be better off dead and that you would wish her to be so. Am I correct on that, September?"

The girl nodded.

"She's nodding. I thought you might want to tell her whether or not that's true."

"Well, no that's not true at all," Tommy said. "Um, I love her very much and I'm looking forward to the time when we can put everything back together."

"That sounds a lot like what we talked about today," I said, reminding him of our morning session.

"That sounds exactly like what we talked about today," he agreed.

I continued, "It seems that despite the fact that you and I are making progress, September feels like her life is a piece of shit. Can I tell him what Billy said or Bobby—which one was it?"

"Billy," she said.

"Billy, as a little boy who doesn't know better, said to September that it was her fault that they couldn't see their dad."

"Well I think she knows that it's not her fault," Tommy said.

"Tom," I said forcefully, "she *doesn't know.* She needs you to talk to her about it."

"It's very much all my fault," he said, following my lead. "Billy's a 6-year-old. Billy looks at it like a 6-year-old boy who doesn't know what's going on, 'Tember."

September was a completely different girl. She was glued to the speakerphone as if her life depended upon it, and in many ways it did. She sat silently, considering whether her father might actually be taking her side, not knowing what to think or where to go with it.

"She's thinking," I said to Tommy. "What do you say, September?"

She didn't respond.

"All Billy knows is that he's mad because he can't see his dad," Tommy continued. "He has no idea what's behind that . . . what's causing that. . . ."

"You're actually talking," September said sarcastically.

"What?" Tommy asked.

"She's saying you're actually talking to her," I was as taken aback by the comment as Tommy, and was trying to make sense of it even as I spoke. "She feels like you don't talk to her when you guys talk on the phone. I told her you talked pretty good to me today, and I know you told me you wanted to talk with her as soon as possible in therapy. . . . You want to talk loud so he can hear you and say something to your dad, September?"

"Hi," she said tentatively

"Hi."

"Um, how was your Christmas present?"

"Doin' just fine."

"Did you like it?"

"Yeah."

"Do you ever play with it?"

"I played with it quite a bit there for a while. I haven't played with it much lately." From this odd exchange I realized why the girl had been so desperate for us to call, and at the same time surprised by her father's candor. For months after the disclosure, she had had unlimited phone contact with Tommy and the two of them had never gotten anything said. I had considered conjoint therapy during that period but feared reprisal, though no order had been issued. My tack was to keep on the good side of the state's attorney and CPS so that, when things in court were sorted out, we could proceed with treatment. Unfortunately, this left father and daughter to have these odd conversations in private that apparently went right over Tommy's head. Rather than simply get to the point of what she wanted to know, September would discuss Tommy's work, his leisure time, and in this case his Christmas gift. In this particular instance, the girl was not simply asking if he enjoyed her gift, she was asking if he ever thought of her.

"I bought him a poker game," she explained, letting me in on the discussion.

"Well, that's very nice," I said with a gentle sarcasm. "So why don't you tell him why you wish you were dead?"

"I dunno."

"Well, you're telling me all about it," I said with the harsh tone that matched her own and always seemed to get her on task. "I want you to tell him, 'cause I'm not gonna be defending him anymore. I'm not gonna tell you what he says. He needs to tell you if that's what he wants . . . I wanna know why you want to give up." I knew I could push harder. I was no longer alone.

" 'Cause I don't have anything to live for," she mumbled.

"Tryin' to put this all back together isn't worth living for?" Tommy said with a genuine note of surprise in his voice.

"No."

"No?" I shot back. "How do you figure?"

"It just isn't. My life's all screwed up."

"So there's no hope," I said. "It doesn't matter whether your dad's gonna do his best effort. Do you ever wonder if your dad wishes he was dead?" To this day I do not know what part of my unconscious this came from, but it was exactly the right question.

"Yeah," she said so quickly that I almost missed her response.

"Ever feel that way, Tom?" I asked.

"Uh, I haven't had those thoughts in the past month or so, but yeah, for a while there I was seriously thinking about it."

"Have you ever tried it?" September said with the first hint of anger I'd heard since placing the call.

"No, I haven't."

"Well, it hurts." The anger fell into sadness.

"Well, you wanna tell him about how much it hurts?" I asked.

"It hurts a lot." September paused. "Actually it kinda feels good."

"How does it kinda feel good to hurt yourself?"

" 'Cause the pain feels good," she said slowly, dropping into a light trance. " 'Cause you're so used to getting it . . . that you just expect it, and when its not there, it's like . . . it just hurts. So when you put pain on yourself or somebody puts pain on you it feels good. . . . Did you hear that?" She had shared a crucial detail, and she would not rest until her father had come to fully appreciate it.

"I heard it, but I don't understand it," Tommy said.

"You never understood anything I said." September's gaze fell to the carpet. Once again Tommy was struggling to keep up with this thoughtful girl, and his inadequacies sounded too much like rejection. I felt impelled to protect him in that moment, to spare his daughter the illusion that he didn't care enough to understand her.

"September, that's kinda deep," I said. "I don't blame him for not understanding it. It takes a lot for me to understand it. . . ."

"So what happened to you when you were a kid, Dad?" She interrupted sharply, taking us both by surprise. She had taken a shot at the ultimate question—why had he done this to her.

"As far as what?" he asked.

"I don't know." She was not asking difficult questions only to give away the answers.

We were in too deep. Tommy and I had just started discussing these issues in our morning session. I wanted to consolidate our gains and cut our losses. "I think that's something we want to talk about," I said. "But over the phone it may not be that easy. It's kind of an emotional thing to talk about to somebody on the phone. Maybe we should wait until he can come in."

"I'm just curious," September persisted.

"Do you want to ask him a specific question or a specific. . . . ?"

"Sure," she said. "Why did you call your dad a butthole? What did he do to you that was so bad?" I was losing control of the session to a wild young girl. Yet September was far more skilled than I at managing this situation and infinitely more motivated. She was approaching the summit, and she would not go back down. I could not stop her even if she was exceeding the speed limit of my therapy with Tommy. I could only hold on.

"I think I've told you what he done to me," Tommy said hesitantly.

"No, you told me you had to feed a lot of dogs, and that he always changed the channel when you were watchin' TV."

"Well, I don't remember changing the channels on the TV . . ."

"Well that's what you told me before. Every time you wanted to watch something he'd change the channel."

"Well . . . maybe that."

"Tom," I said, hoping to thwart this strange role reversal before the girl drove her father from the phone with her blistering interrogation. "Will you be willing to talk with September about these things when you two get together . . . if she has questions about your life so that she can understand. . . ."

"I'll be more than willing to talk," he said.

"Why are you talking now?" September reasserted an issue we'd apparently not yet resolved. "Why wouldn't you talk earlier?"

"Earlier?" Tommy said, still puzzled. "What are you talking about earlier?"

"Like when I could talk to you on the phone."

"You didn't bring any of this up when we were talking on the phone, 'Tember."

" 'Cause you'd always be like 'wul . . . wul,' really tired and never talkative." It was the perpetual stance of the victim combining both contempt and sympathy. She mocked him even as she was protecting him.

"September," I said sternly. "You're looking for every possibility of failure in the eyes of success here. You're lookin' for a way to tell your dad he's not trying when he's sitting here trying."

"I know he's trying," she shot back with an annoyed tone.

"Oh . . . okay," I pulled back with surprise.

"I'll be more than willing to talk to you, 'Tember, about anything," Tommy said, almost pleading.

"What reason does she have to go on living, Tom?" I said, still not satisfied that we had come to a resolution of this core issue.

"She's got the rest of her life ahead of her." His words carried so much more power than mine had.

"Do you think that, knowing your daughter as you do, that it could be a wonderful life, or is it gonna continue to suck?"

"Well, it's gonna be better than it has been," Tommy said. "I mean there will be bad days and there'll be good days. A lot of that is what we make of it ourselves."

"Because from this point on, she's not gonna be victimized any more," I said. I was beginning to think we might actually pull September together well enough to get through another week.

"No," Tommy said slowly, "no, she's not."

"And somehow you're gonna have to convince her that you're gonna go back to being a dad and a protector, instead of a person who hurts her. That's gonna be tough, huh?"

"Its gonna be a big job."

"Are you up to it?"

"Yes, I am."

"So how's work?" September said, suddenly breaking the tension we all felt so keenly.

I allowed the girl and her father to discuss his dissatisfaction with third shift work before returning to the subject at hand. "Tom, September is gonna promise you tonight that she isn't gonna hurt herself or kill herself and that she'll continue to talk with us about these feelings. Are you kinda wondering about that too?"

"Honestly, what I'm wondering about is why all of sudden we're gonna stop trying again," Tommy said. "I mean, what happened to make everything go back?"

"Now she didn't say everything had gone back," I cautioned. "She's just saying that she's been stuck for a long time."

"I can understand what Billy said hurtin'. But you got to look at Billy is 6 years old. Billy doesn't understand what's goin' on."

"Well, he's got a good point," I said. "Are you going to respond? He says he wants to know why we're not gonna go on . . . why we're not gonna fight."

"'Cause I've been fighting for a year when nobody else was fighting," September said with a mix of bitterness and sorrow. "And then when everybody else starts fighting, I stop fighting."

"I've been fightin' for the last 9 months, 'Tember," Tommy said. "I'm finally startin' to get ahead. I'm finally starting to get my head above water again. I'm not gonna quit now."

"I'm not gonna quit now," I said with growing confidence.

"But you've been so depressed lately," September said. "Even Barbara said it. . . ."

"Who's not depressed?" I interrupted forcefully, before the unhealthy sequence could be completed. "September, this is a terrible. . . ."

"I mean he was miserable," she said. "Barbara said that he was so depressed he wouldn't never even talk to her either."

"It's a miserable situation," I argued. "What he did was a *terrible* thing. Anyone who did this to his daughter would feel terrible. Right, Tom?"

"I feel pretty bad."

September shook her head with a slight but noticeable incredulity.

"You don't believe him?" I said. "Why do you think he's depressed?"

"Because he had to go to jail."

"Oh, she thinks you're depressed because you got caught, Tommy. Well, let me ask you, which is worse, goin' to jail or looking into the eyes of your daughter and knowing what you've done to her?" It was a devastating confrontation that relied on nothing but my voice over a phone line.

Tommy's response was subtly remarkable: "Wes, you saw what shape I was in when I first came in."

"What did he say?" September looked up at me. She was astonished in a way that I could not interpret at the moment, but which she later explained to me. It wasn't what Tommy was saying, it was how he was saying it—something only his daughter could hear in his voice. Tommy had begun to cry.

"That wasn't any fun . . . keeping that inside. It was like a weight off my shoulders . . . I mean just the fact that somebody else finally knew . . . it was a better feeling than I was having."

"So you were glad I told?" Her amazement grew.

"At the time I wasn't," he confessed. "But now I'm very glad. If you hadn't have . . . I don't know what kind of shape I'd be in now. I wouldn't be sittin' here talking to you, though. I can guarantee that."

"True," she said, appearing at first to understand the superficial meaning of his words and then hearing something much deeper. "You would have been dead?"

"What?"

"She wonders if you'd have been dead if you'd have had to continue to carry this terrible secret," I said.

"I don't think I have the strength to kill myself." Tommy wept.

"But you'd have been dying inside," I said.

"I tore myself up inside pretty bad."

"So in a lot of ways, September saved your emotional life."

"By coming across, she did . . . yeah."

"I've never heard you. . . ." September's voice trailed off. The sentence might have had numerous conclusions, but I later learned the correct one. September had never heard her father cry before, and now he was crying for the terrible things he had done to her. Until that moment, this had been unimaginable for her.

"I would have lost everything by now," Tommy continued. "Instead of having a chance now, everything would have been gone for sure."

"Were you mad at me when I told?"

"No, I wasn't mad at you, because I knew you were going to tell. I told Wes as soon as you told Wes, and I knew he knew."

"It's true," I confirmed.

"I knew it was coming, 'Tember."

"But how?" she asked, her voice pleading for her father's exoneration of her disclosure.

"Because I know you . . . and I knew Wes knew."

"And what do you know about her?" I asked rhetorically. "You know in the end she does the right thing?"

"Well, I knew there was no way she was going to be able to keep it inside of her."

"And you know when she's gotta do something, she does the right thing?" I reiterated.

"Yeah, she does the right thing," Tommy agreed.

I moved quickly to link this with a future apology session. "So how do you think it's gonna be when you two come in here together?"

"I'm sure there are gonna be some heated moments," Tommy said.

"How are you gonna be, September?" I asked.

The girl shrugged, but as she did so a little smile crossed her face.

"You wanna tell him what you told me?" I asked. "Or do you want me to tell him—or not at all?"

September mouthed "you tell him."

"September told me for the first time something that'd I'd never heard her say before. In talking about having you come in, she said she was gonna sit at opposite ends of the room from you."

"I was being sarcastic," she whispered to me, her faint smile growing.

"I thought you were serious," I said, wanting Tommy to hear a bit more of his daughter's pain. "And I asked you why, and you said 'because I'm scared of him.' And I've never heard her say that about her father before."

"I was just being sarcastic." She smirked.

"No, I don't believe you. I think you were serious."

"I *was* serious," she whispered as an aside to me.

"Were you?" I whispered back.

"Yes." She nodded with a smile.

"Okay." I said. "That kinda hurts doesn't it, Tommy?"

"Oh yeah . . . yeah it does."

"Well, you know what hurt worse?" September turned angry again as she felt herself gaining a foothold. "When you hit me. I mean it hurt worse . . . hurt worse most of all."

"See now, I don't understand because you were just talking about hurt and how pain felt good. . . ." Tommy was more confused than combative.

"It did," she said. "I mean I got used to it because you always hit me, and now it feels good."

"What she's saying is that you trained your daughter to seek pain," I said. "We gotta untrain her."

"What are you talking about?!" September said looking at me quizzically.

"I'm just repeating what you said."

"Big words!" she mocked me, still well in control of the session.

"He taught his daughter to look for pain," I said to her as an aside. "To accept pain when she shouldn't accept pain in her life. Now we have to untrain you."

"Oh." She nodded and smiled.

"You've got a wonderful daughter here, Tom," I offered, smiling back at September.

"I know that, Wes."

"What can you say that would make her want to live a little bit longer?"

"I'm sorry and I do want to work this out," Tommy said spontaneously. "I do want life to be different."

"You wanna have a daughter again someday?" I asked.

"Very much so."

"You gonna help her to have her father back?" I asked. "You know I told you today I think you took her father away from her."

"Yes, that caught me totally off guard because I didn't see it like that. I didn't see it at all. . . . I see it now. I didn't see it. That's probably one of the last things that I would have came up with myself."

"Well, there's always the possibility of change, huh?" I said, convinced that September would now live.

"That's what we're working for," Tommy said.

"So, September, are you gonna agree to work with us or are you gonna give up?" I asked. "I wanna know."

There was a long pause as the girl fiddled with the paperclip chain she'd strung together across my desk throughout the conversation. We were at the most critical moment of her therapy. She lifted her eyes to meet mine and whispered in a voice barely audible. "I guess I'll go to work."

It was a bittersweet thing for a defiant young girl to let her beleaguered therapist win, even when the prize was her life. I pushed her a bit harder to get a full commitment. "You're gonna have to say it louder so everyone can hear."

"There's only two people in the room." She smirked.

"And a telephone. What are you gonna do?"

"I said I guess I can work," she said more loudly. Then as an aside to me she added, "But I can still think about it."

"You bet you can," I agreed. "You can talk about it and you can think about it. But you're gonna be in here fightin'. Did you hear her, Tom?"

"No," Tommy said.

"Say it louder," I pushed.

"I said 'yep.'" She tried hard, but she could not prevent her small smile from erupting into a broad grin.

"Yep, we're gonna keep trying?" I asked.

She nodded.

"There are no problems that cannot be overcome," I said optimistically. "If people have love, then even the worst problems can be overcome."

September shook her head.

"September, is it not possible?" I asked as an aside. "You don't have to believe it right now, but can you believe that I believe it?"

"Yeah, you can believe it," she conceded.

"Tom, do you believe that if people have enough love in their hearts, they can overcome any problem?"

There was a brief silence.

"I think he hung up," the girl said, still not convinced that her father would really be there until the end.

"Tom? Did you hear me?"

"Yes . . . I was just thinking. I was honestly trying to think of a problem you couldn't overcome. I can't think of one."

September laughed out loud, something she hadn't done in many months. "How about getting over your third shift job?"

I laughed with her. "She thinks that a third shift job might be insurmountable even if you had love in your heart!"

"There's ways around it though!" Tommy said hopefully.

I could scarcely contain my excitement as I reviewed the videotape of the session. Though I had thought I understood it before, it was only then that I realized the full importance of this deeply flawed man in the life of his daughter. The session had purged me of the illusion that I was capable of healing September's broken spirit alone and in isolation from her offender. It was Tommy's job to undo what he had done, and no matter how long September and I worked together and how much she consumed of my waning resources, I could be nothing more than a catalyst for the contextual change she needed. We'd gotten very close to collapse that evening, but I was now confident that September's prolonged brush with bad behavior, bad fortune, and bad social service would finally come to an end. She could begin her process of contrition toward healing.

But within days, the larger system that engulfed and controlled her would turn whimsical yet again, casting the fragile girl deeper into a realm so inexplicable and surreal that it eclipsed everything that had been done to her before. And given her history, that was no small feat.

We will return to September's story in chapter 11.

CHAPTER 7

Navigating the Child Protective System

> And I looked and saw a whirling banner which ran so fast that it seemed as if it could never make a stand, and behind it came so long a train of people that I should never have believed death had undone so many. After I had recognized some of them I saw and knew the shade of him who from cowardice made the great refusal, and at once and with certainty I perceived that this was the worthless crew that is hateful to God and to His enemies. Those wretches, who were never alive. . . .
>
> —Dante Alighieri, "Canto III," *The Inferno* (1971/1948)

When the private injustice of a given family triggers the attention of the child protective system (CPS) and the state asserts its vested interest in the safety of minor children, a whole new production emerges on the family's life stage. All at once, they experience a loss of control and an increase in complexity as they encounter a new cast of characters and a very different script. These include CPS, a foster family or residential facility, a judge, a *guardian ad litem* (GAL) and several other attorneys, and sometimes a court-appointed special advocate (CASA) and/or a review board. In some states CPS has subcontracted much of its work to private corporations adding yet another chorus line to an already brimming stage. In cases involving formal criminal charges, the team will also include a court services officer. If the therapist was involved before the entry of CPS, she has heretofore been operating virtually unencumbered. Hereafter, she will be a part of this larger system of social control, which has an entirely different set of rules, many of them dynamic and poorly defined. She will also find a manifold increase in what must be utilized in treatment, which can itself wither even an experienced clinician.

Because this chapter opened with a citation from *The Inferno*, one may gather that I have concerns about how this drama routinely plays out and our therapeutic role in it. Yet my critique, which is shared by many others (see chapter 3), should not be construed simply as antagonism toward the system nor self-righteous outrage at its intrigues. Such a reductive and overly personal interpretation does not foster the debate necessary to improve the system, but instead reflects the reluctance we all feel in the disquieting thought that our society is failing its most vulnerable members. My goal is not to complain about how bad our child protective systems are or how corrupt their participants, but to propose how good they could be if reorganized around a critically optimistic and family-friendly model. In doing so, I will offer a map of the territory and some advice on how to navigate it, noting some of the obstacles one can expect along the way.

OFFICERS OF THE COURT

Court systems become involved in two ways that affect children in cases of family injustice. The first occurs when family members have been charged with a crime, usually sexual or physical abuse, or, in the case of younger offenders, any sort of juvenile misconduct. These courts impact cases of family injustice most often by regulating the contact between victim and offender through court order or incarceration. However, in this section we shall focus more on the court that oversees children who have been taken into custody to protect them from any form of family injustice.

Attorneys

Attorneys may function in several key roles, including in many states that of *guardians ad litem* (GALs). In this capacity they are practicing outside the tradition of their discipline, because GALs represent not the client but the abstract concept known as "the child's best interests." In practice, this means they can find themselves in direct opposition to their own clients, especially older children and adolescents who are more able to articulate dissent from the GAL. For example, a child may demand contact with biological parents or even a more aggressive reunification plan. The GAL may disagree, deciding to cut off visitation or terminate parental rights. For any other attorney such disagreement must end with acquiescence or resignation. For the GAL, the child's input may have a great deal of impact on her recommendation or none at all, but it will always be weighed against the best interests standard as interpreted by the GAL. This can be a blessing or a curse, depending on the quality of the attorney and the relationship she has with her client. It is good form, and in some states required, that the GAL make the court aware of differences of opinion. Unfortunately, most children in custody and their families do not know this, and client input is often suppressed in favor of expediency. Of note, some states appoint both an attorney to advocate for the child's wishes and a GAL who may or may not be an attorney.

Of course, this work pays very poorly and requires more time than most attorneys are willing or able to give. Many children are lucky to consult their GAL for 20 minutes a year, and even this usually comes just before the court hearing. Yet the GAL's power is immense as he is one of the few people who can at any point bring information to the attention of the judge. However, because they are required to conduct independent investigations of the child's best interests and because this almost never happens in a systematic way, the GAL tends to base his tack on a cursory overview of volumes of data and a quick consultation with the client. These data are usually summarized in reports and recommendation from CPS, which may downplay input inconsistent with its position. In short, months of treatment, reams of reports, and endless discussions may sum to a 2- to 3-minute presentation by the GAL in court. Moreover, the vast majority of case planning goes on without input from the GAL, who cannot afford to attend most meetings. Because of poor funding, such work often falls into the purview of new attorneys or a part-time quasi-pro-bono operation of more established practices. Few GALs would quibble with the supposition that this overburdened and underfunded scheme questions the extent to which our society values due process in determining the best interests of vulnerable children.

The state's attorney is usually connected with the district attorney's (DA) office, or in some states with CPS. Though I have met many fine exceptions, many of these attorneys do not consider the family court a high priority. In cases when the attorney is a DA, it is important to remember that most DAs are elected, and the greatest emphasis in that process is placed on the record of criminal prosecution. Most voters do not even realize the role of the DA in child placement cases, particularly if these tasks are delegated to assistant district attorneys (ADAs). The turnover rate is often high, as ADAs either leave or are promoted out of the family court within a few months of arriving. Thus, it is not surprising that the typical DA or ADA does not get much involved with the churning of the system.

The third attorney is appointed to represent the family. If ever there existed a disparity in the justice of rich and poor, it is in the appointment of counsel for indigent families in the system. Though statistics on abuse and neglect show no racial or economic stratification among the general population, those who can afford legal representation are rarely involved with CPS for long. Those who cannot are further marginalized because their rights rely on a system of attorneys who are again underpaid for their services. Exceptions are found in cities that have created an assignment system where such cases rotate between many participant firms so that they represent only a small portion of the attorney's general practice. In theory, this can reduce burnout and allow the attorney to focus on a smaller number of cases.

Also notable in many family courts is a distinct lack of advocacy and adversarial process, which would normally serve to protect client rights and due process but is often subsumed in a sort of "team within a team" approach. Here, the attorneys essentially caucus and decide what to do, and then present it to the judge. In no other situation can one find three attorneys in the same room putting forth such a concerted effort to agree.

The Judge

Attorneys are fond of saying "the courtroom is the judge's kingdom." For therapists trained in a spirit of free will and valueless caring, this kingdom is rather unsettling. Family court is not the most prestigious bench, and the biggest problem facing these judges is once again a lack of time and resources. Out of necessity, most attempt to review the data at hand and make a quick decision so that they can keep the docket moving, lest they face a pile up of cases from which they will never emerge. To make a dent in this docket, judges must rely on GALs for relevant information, who in turn rely on CPS, which in turn is notorious for spinning information to match its view of the case. Concerned about this, some judges have instituted a system of asking for input from all key players during the court hearing. Although this is good for attaining a breadth of information that might otherwise be suppressed, in some courts it comes without benefit of oath, allowing anyone to state any opinion they wish without being held accountable for it. For those who have not been through it this seems unbelievable, yet some child and family courts operate this way as a matter of course, considering hearsay as if it were real evidence. At best, this sometimes tends to work. At worst, it results in a great deal of invalid and unreliable input.

Another approach is the use of review boards consisting of volunteers drawn from the community who sift through volumes of information, meet at least once a year with all the players in the case, and make recommendations to the judge, which he can then implement or ignore. Most boards are drawn from the ranks of well-educated professional people who have attained a fair degree of critical thinking skills. This has the dual attribute of making them fairly good at getting business done and making decisions, but not particularly reflective of the clients whose cases they review. Although it would require recruitment, we suggest having at least one member on each panel who has successfully made it through a bout with the system, perhaps a former foster child or a biological family member of one. Beyond this, the greatest strength of review boards is also their greatest weakness. Some members may be drawn from the ranks of mental or social service providers, but most are not. This leaves them to consider a great deal of fairly technical information without much training. We have found the most effective panels include one professional member who is not involved in the system and can thus render some advice on more technical matters. We have also found the most beneficial boards do not try to micro-manage cases, but instead gather data and make recommendations based on that data.

A final problem we have seen with review boards is their selective use. Some jurisdictions have organized themselves so that only CPS can call for review of a case. In others, the judge selects the cases. Either represents an error in design, because they create a self-selection bias. CPS referrals are invariably made to gather more support for their position and to avoid scrutiny of the CPS system. Judicial referrals are often made because a case has become very difficult to manage and perhaps a bit beyond the point of successful intervention by the board. Instead, we recommend that all cases be reviewed at least twice a year, creating a system of accountability and enhancing due process. In short, a properly implemented system of review is one of the best ways to compensate for the shortcomings of an overburdened court, especially with regard to control and decision making that would otherwise be more than a court docket could bear.

A final role of the judge is more indirect. Because she has the power to write court orders, the judge sets a certain tone for how families are approached and treated in her jurisdiction. We know a judge who is greatly revered for her advocacy for the rights of families and children. She wisely balances child welfare and family integrity and forces the rest of the system to do likewise. She also uses a carefully executed system of citizen boards to sift through information and make recommendations. We do not always see eye to eye with this judge, but we appreciate her strength of character and the tone of due process she sets; her jurisdiction runs more smoothly for it.

CASAs

According to the National CASA Association (www.nationalcasa.org), the CASA movement came into being after courts began realizing that decisions were being made about abused and neglected children without sufficient information. A judge in Seattle conceived the idea of using trained community volunteers to speak for the best interests of children in court. CASA states that this experiment was so successful that judges across the country began using the same system. In 1990 Congress passed the Victims of Child Abuse Act, which among other things encouraged the expansion of CASA. There are currently 900 CASA offices in the United States and some 42,400 volunteers. The organization boasts "numerous evaluations and scores of endorsements from the US Advisory Board on Child Abuse and Neglect, the National Council of Juvenile and Family Court Judges, the American Bar

Association and the Office of Juvenile Justice and Delinquency Prevention of the U.S. Department of Justice."

From the name and credentials alone one might wonder what role the CASA serves, particularly given that the child's legal advocate should be the GAL. In fact, the association claims that the CASA programs are also known as Volunteer Guardian Ad Litem Programs, though this would be a misnomer in most jurisdictions with which we are familiar. In our experience, CASAs have a far more ambiguous role than the GAL. In some states, the judge appoints a CASA to investigate when he becomes concerned that the child may be at some risk from the system. In one state, CASAs serve as evaluators in domestic and family court, though we would question that practice based on issues of expertise. In other cases, we have been unable to discern the CASA's role from that of big brother or sister or case manager.

With very little reading between the lines, it is clear that the CASA system came into being because of the failure of GALs to adequately investigate and advocate for the best interests of the child and because CPS had overplayed its hand at information management. Rather than spend the money to correct the problems of the underpaid GAL, the system used CASA as a way to attach a volunteer to a child to gather information for the judge and to advocate for the child outside the highly political and bureaucratic structure of the system itself. As a privately funded charity wholly reliant on volunteer labor, the program is also cost-free to the court.

CASAs should be the therapist's natural allies in working with family injustice, and many times they are. However, in cases of open conflict, a CASA often becomes yet another adult in conflict in the life of a child. In highly amicable cases, the CASA simply adds another layer of agreement. September's case (chapter 11) included an unfortunate example of the former, even as the CASA herself was exceptional. When she disagreed with the state's attorney and GAL, they simply demanded that her report be ignored. A case from a different jurisdiction turned out quite the opposite. There the CASA so overidentified with an addicted mother that she actually introduced herself to us as "Mrs. Jones' CASA." When asked what change in CASA policy had allowed her to switch from advocating for the Jones children to advocating for the mother, she became flustered and explained that the children belonged with their mother and she needed to *advocate for the family.* Normally we would have welcomed her enthusiasm for rectifying the injustice of the girls' outplacement and would have worked to reintegrate them in the 30-day window she was proposing. However, in this case the teenagers in the family had stated in no uncertain terms that they would not return to a mother they saw as a hopeless heroin addict. In fact, they stated that any attempt to send them home would result in their running away, regardless of the consequences. We asked the CASA to join therapy and to listen closely to the girls, who initially refused because they had "been over this with her a million times," but they eventually gave in. When she actually heard the girls' horrible stories of their mother's addiction, abuse, and her numerous relapses, the CASA changed her recommendation to allow the girls to go to adoption. Before the mother could learn of this change, she was taken to the hospital after another heroin overdose and thereafter ran away. To her credit, the CASA apologized to the girls for losing her sense of priority, which I believe was itself quite healing.

Like review boards, CASAs benefit from and are hampered by their role as lay advocates. They come from all walks of life with a common desire to help children. They receive introductory training and are then thrust into a truly brutal world of family dysfunction, child abuse, and systemic chaos. Realizing this, most CASAs keep their advocacy within the parameters of a layperson; others take on the mantle of trained professionals even without the background to do so, making sweeping assertions about the child's best interests that are beyond their capabilities. CASAs should be afforded the respect they deserve as advocates for due process, but should never expected to serve an evaluative function that is beyond this scope.

Summarizing this all-too-brief synopsis of the family court system in cases of child protection, we find in the best of circumstances a system of overworked professionals highly dependent on volunteer or near-volunteer labor that attempts to disperse justice based on limited deliberation over whatever data happen to be available, in the least time possible. Making this system function requires unusual dedication to the idea of due process by each court officer. It is greatly aided by an affinity for restorative justice. Those qualities notwithstanding, the court's shortcomings are no secret, and the need for improvement inarguable, because it has the greatest power to make matters better for all involved, as well as significantly worse.

THE CHILD PROTECTIVE SYSTEM (CPS)

Caseworkers

Where court officers have studied the law, CPS workers have usually studied social work,[1] a product of the same social liberalism that later generated the New Deal and the Great Society. Social work originated in Jane Addam's "friendly visitor" coming into the home to help the socially oppressed and underprivileged become better citizens and access services useful in raising their socioeconomic class. Some movements, most notably "family preservation," have remained consistent with this origin, but there is considerable disparity between this ideal and the typical practice of social work. Outside of the welfare system, most families will encounter a nonclinical social worker only when they have been reported for child abuse and neglect, which renders an experience more of hostile intruder than friendly visitor. Thereafter, social work becomes an integral part of the family's life as it struggles to regain control over its own destiny and in many cases an obstacle to that goal.

No strangers to poor funding, undertrained, underpaid, and overworked social workers may carry two or three times the recommended caseload. The work tends to be thankless, unpleasant, low in prestige, high in responsibility, and lacking in support or supervision, making for high turnover. This in turn leads to an even greater overload as staff struggle to cross-transfer cases to compensate and maintain coverage. Not infrequently we have seen a child with three or four caseworkers over the course of his contact with CPS and sometimes many more. Recently, I had a pair of sisters who had three caseworkers in less than a month, leading them to trust no one to remain long enough to be of service.

Given this inhospitable environment, the system generally does not work very well, leading to a raw cynicism among many line-staff, which is reinforced daily as they process their cases in a sort of in-house support group. This in turn creates a family-phobic groupthink, which begets more of the same environment in which new ideas are rarely welcomed and often are tenaciously opposed. At times CPS even seems to avoid serving children in the greatest need and removes children from families who could have been treated with much less severe interventions. We have seen ageism, racism, sexism, and classism in these cases as well as a surprising number of workers vicariously processing their countertransference and problematic family histories through their cases.

The Power of Information

The court has the most explicit legitimate power, but no entity has more implicit power than CPS, most of which comes from controlling the flow and use of information to the court. Depending on local convention, several methods are used to accomplish this. First and foremost, CPS controls the *source* of information by directing referrals to certain mental health providers for evaluation and treatment, and away from others. Needless to say, these professionals tend to be handpicked by CPS for their malleability to the CPS position. Just as a good attorney knows which experts to pick to support her case, so does a CPS worker know where to send a case for maximum support. Thus, if a given CPS office is highly focused on keeping families together, it will send clients to professionals known to be family friendly. If CPS tends to favor family disintegration, it will send cases to individually focused, family-phobic providers to gather data for the termination of parental rights. Still other CPS offices are more strategic in referring cases, sending those they see fit for reintegration and reunification to family-friendly professionals and the rest to individual therapists.

Regardless of their typical stance, these practices are inherently flawed because they place *far too much clinical control in the hands of CPS workers*, most of whom have little or no training to make predictions about treatment success. In fact, we find that, despite our collective experience in this area, *we* cannot predict who will succeed and who will fail with any degree of certainty. A comprehensive evaluation greatly helps, but even so we prefer to enter every case with the aforementioned sense of critical optimism, expecting the best and preparing for the worst. Allowing CPS to determine a priori whether a family goes to a family-friend or family-phobe will invariably change the course of the case for its duration by stacking information sources either for or against the family. Instead we propose that all therapists interested in working with such cases become specialized in both child protection and family reunification, and balance each with critical optimism. CPS workers should base referrals on the flexibility and breadth of the therapist and his history of success at finding and implementing the right plan to bring about permanency for the child. Finally, we would advise attorneys and judges to be ever vigilant for "ringer" assessments from therapists or evaluators known to favor one approach over another (chapter 8).

The second way CPS controls information is to function as the clearinghouse for data submitted by all other sources. In some jurisdictions CPS will contract evaluations or request reports from its various sources and then choose what it wants to include in its recommendations. In other jurisdictions the overt suppression or exclusion of data is likely to cause a serious backlash from an angry judge, so CPS instead submits all written materials, along with its own position paper. An experienced CPS worker can fashion a report that takes into account the input from all sources, but highlights only agreeable information and recommendations. This has the appearance of being less biased and more informed, when it is not. In high-agreement cases there is little spin and more disclosure. The more heated the disagreement about a case, the less likely it is that information will flow freely and without bias.

In some of our worst cases, CPS has overtly suppressed evidence that is exculpatory to the family and asserted information that is exaggerated or blatantly false in open court, even when based on complete hearsay. Bobbi's case in chapter 10 is a prime example. If no rules of evidence are enforced, no one is sworn to testify, and little advocacy is shown by the family's court-appointed attorney, the judge often accepts the CPS position without further scrutiny. Although judges and CPS officials rarely have a friendly alliance, judges may feel compelled to side with CPS workers simply because the system cannot continue on a daily basis if they do not. Unfortunately, the system is only as strong as its weakest links, and in many cases the central link of CPS is very weak indeed.

Foster Homes

As a young family therapist I was trained by Haley and Madanes to involve the child's context in his treatment. In cases of foster placement, I assumed the logical extension of this perspective would be to involve foster parents in the therapy of their charges. After failing at this several times, I consulted Cloe Madanes who admonished me for "expecting too much from people who are not the family of your client." For 10 years hence, I have struggled to reject this sobering advice, but almost always have found it to be true. To understand how such homes exist as the norm, one must understand the fundamental economic reality that guides CPS in its management of foster and adoptive homes and that will constantly influence how the therapist works with these families while attempting to bring about reunification.

Supply and Demand

In every jurisdiction there are far from enough foster parents to meet the current need and even fewer adoptive resources. Using a capitalist economic metaphor, this means we have inflation—too many foster children chasing too few homes. However, because the price of a bed is carefully regulated without consideration for demand, the supply of homes is not free to expand and contract in alignment with that demand. This problem is typically lost on a state bureaucracy that has no background in macroeconomics and very limited motivation to spend more money on foster care. Thus, rather than allow the market to generate new beds through expensive price incentives, the system instead goes begging for additional homes. This excess demand makes the retention of foster parents far too important, forcing the system to cater to them even when this conflicts with the interests of the child or his biological family. It is like a tight labor market where retention of employees is placed above productivity, simply because replacements cannot be found. Even in my critical stance, I am not immune to the resulting process of coddling poorly behaved foster parents. Unless they were overtly abusive, I have actually fought to keep clients in fairly disturbed homes until something better opens. This is one of the most joyless experiences I have ever undertaken in working in the system, but it is necessary for three reasons. First, even disrupted placements from very poor homes can reflect badly on the child, making him harder to place down the road. Second, disruptions can just as easily lead to even worse, more restrictive, or distant placements, any of which may set reunification back months. I have pressed for a move only to regret it later when things turned out to be even uglier. Third, except in cases of abuse or neglect, moving a child from a foster home rarely shuts the home down, and more often than not the problems are inherited by the next child and the ones thereafter.

I encourage CPS behind the scenes to look for a *more appropriate* (not just different) placement for the child, but I also work with them, the biological family, and the client to soothe the foster parent and minimize her reactivity to child behaviors for which she is often partially responsible. In this process I try to avoid any pretense or demand that the foster parent change in any way. Although this certainly enables bad behavior in the foster care system and creates a dubious role for the therapist, it is at times a necessary charade in the overall process of reintegration and reunification.

When things do become flagrantly inappropriate or abusive, I strategize with CPS on how to move the child quickly to safety in the manner least damaging to her mental health or "reputation" in the system. There are too many examples to mention over 10 years, but they include the foster parent who made his charges drink vinegar as a punishment for bad homework, or the middle-aged man who was in competition with his 16-year-old foster son for the affections of the man's 21-year-old girlfriend. Of note, the boy won, but had to move to continue the relationship. The vinegar kids were not moved until some time later. Both homes were sanctioned but continued to take foster children due to the problem of inflation.

Like other entities in the system, foster homes are quite subject to countertransference and tend either to be family-friendly or family-phobic. But because they are so diverse, they must be subcategorized under a different taxonomy. We turn now to the specific types of homes one will encounter in the system, realizing that there is always great variance among cases within any typology.

Missionaries

People become foster parents for a number of reasons, though the one most commonly stated is a sense of "mission" or "calling." Families functioning under this rubric are often highly religious, spiritual, or socially conscious, seeing themselves as missionaries to the poor and downtrodden. Indeed, to do selfless good for needy children seems an ideal motivation to foster, and a true execution of this rubric does make for the best homes. Unfortunately, most missionary foster parents we have seen over the years struggle to achieve this necessary selflessness, leaving them disappointed with a situation that offers little short-term gratification.

It is important to note that *this is not at all due to malevolence or ill intent.* Instead, such foster parents are like real missionaries. They like to be recognized for their sacrifice. And like most targets of missionary intervention, precious few foster children are appreciative of their efforts. In fact, they often blame the foster parents as part of the process that keeps them from their real family. Conversely, most foster parents have unrealistic expectations for their own reinforcement; no matter how well you train them to manage their countertransference, they are invariably hurt and angry when the foster child is loyal to her parent. I know this not only from countless interactions with foster parents in my own practice and that of my students, but because I constantly battled the same feelings and experiences in my own role as a "missionary" foster parent.

A missionary family must have a mission. The best of these families conceptualize their mission as working to reunify the child and biological family. Failing that, they accept, with respect for the biological family, the long-term placement of the child and/or help the child toward permanency. Unfortunately, family-friendly placements are exceptional and most instead define their mission as one of saving children from inadequate families and raising them in their own image. Not surprisingly, this is most apparent in states where long-term foster care is still the norm, though it appears covertly elsewhere. At best, these family-phobic placements look disapprovingly upon a child's connection to her biological family. At worst, they actively undermine it. When this rescuer stance brings on resentment rather than gratitude, the foster home tends to discharge the child to look for one who will give them a greater sense of satisfaction.

To help missionary homes work, therapists must resort to constructivism, offering a great deal of reframing and normalizing as well as accommodation and utilization of the culture of the home. In some cases, the therapist can offer some of the "strokes" missionaries need to keep on their mission. Certainly, with some intervention and management, missionary homes are by far preferable to others, even if they take a great deal of patience. In fact, there are few reasons other than a genuine sense of mission for anyone to open their home to a child caught up in a history of family injustice. One of the most prevalent is money.

The Innkeeper

Some foster parents are motivated not by altruism, but by economics. Although a single placement could never sustain a home, taking several children can generate over $2,200 a month of tax-free income, depending on jurisdiction. Placement of one very difficult youth can generate between $1,000 and $1,500. If a couple establishes and staffs a group home, they can generate even more revenue, and with business deductions they will pay little or no taxes.

Before the reader reacts in anger—either at me or at the type of foster parent I am describing—it should be noted that most of us entrust our own children to similarly motivated people via daycare, for which we pay between 3.0 and 4.5 times as much per child/hour as the state pays foster parents. Our own provider was a wonderful caregiver who truly liked small children and made her home open to their growth and development. However, she was also a member of a capitalist economy and expected to be paid on time each week. Most of the readers of this book have or will get paid to care for others. Why should foster parents be any different?

The answer is simple—making a profit to parent a child or to act *in loco parentis* is antithetical to the selfless act of loving a child without condition. This incongruity may be arguable between the adults in the foster care system, but it is inarguable among the children. They know the difference between a deeply flawed biological parent with no other motivation to keep them than a bond of love, and the paid care of a foster parent who, based on the child's experience, can evict her with 24-hours' notice. Such foster parents are more like innkeepers than parents, providing shelter and rules for the child and little more.

Signs of the innkeeper are manifold. One may be a lack of other gainful employment or primary income from disability payments or alimony, which is supplemented by taking several children. Others have actually quit their jobs, citing their vocation as the care of youth, and they now rely exclusively on foster care payments or in some cases adoption subsidy. Like the far more mythical "welfare mother," they take in more children to raise their monthly benefits. We have routinely seen homes licensed for three children taking six, and I once had an adoptive home that took 10 kids and was making about $6,000 a month in adoption subsidy. Not only is this done without argument from CPS, it may be *encouraged* as a way to place a growing number of kids. Another mark of the innkeeper is the requirement of the child to have a job. Although this might seem a fine way to occupy the time of a mischievous youth, it may really be a way to defer the cost of necessities. I once knew of a group home where working children were required to contribute a portion of their earnings to the foster parents. No one complained because the home took teenage boys who were difficult to place. Another key indicator is the innkeeper's unwillingness to spend money on his foster children, aside from a small weekly allowance that is often tied to a system of chores. The innkeeper typically cites high overhead as the reason for this policy, and if he has no other job this may be a serious concern.

Foster care was never designed to be a career, and a good portion of the monthly stipend (usually at least 25%) was intended to go for the child's personal needs. We routinely spent 50% to 100% *more* per month on our foster daughter than we received, because we treated her no differently than our biological daughter. In fact, a profit motive can only work in foster care if one skimps on the child's upkeep. Yet until the middle-class and upper-middle-class more readily open their doors to these children, some of their care will fall to families who are inclined more to profit than mission.

Innkeepers do have one key role to play in the larger system. They actually work fairly well for children who are on short-term reunification plans, specifically because they do not make an emotional investment and are always ready to replace their current child with a new one. However, for long-term care an innkeeper can be a very hopeless and demeaning placement option. For these children it is usually best to reframe the family as having a different style of parenting, which is more like school or daycare, professional not personal. Of course, this is a stretch in describing innkeepers, and the homes usually do little to support this frame. Whenever possible, the therapist should negotiate with the system to move long-term children to a more missionary-style of placement, though this usually requires a level of influence few therapists can command without retaliation from CPS. More often a very skilled therapist must help "life raft" the child through such homes, allowing her to invest her trust in the therapist and not the home while holding out for reunification or permanency. It is especially important in these cases for CPS to understand that the therapist's client is the *child and biological family, not the system,* as the therapist must be allowed to show unquestioned benevolence and tolerance for the child rather than defending the system and the innkeeper. Beyond this, the best strategy is to keep the peace and, as Madanes suggested, not expect too much.

The Professional

When one does find a higher-income family taking foster children, they often fall into a third category that is somewhat a combination of the missionary and the innkeeper. These individuals do not need the income from foster care, nor are they particularly moved by spiritual conviction to care deeply for the children. Theirs is not so much a mission as a sort of social obligation. Many are professional people, including teachers, therapists, and social service providers who found they could not do enough in their 9-to-5 job to satisfy their sense of duty, so they have taken up the cause in their homes.

This would seem an inviting situation, a professional parent bringing a good education, financial resources, and honed parenting skills to bear upon the plight of a needy child. In theory, such parents are more able to take input, balance their role against that of the other providers and the natural family, and avoid excessive countertransference. The professional relies on skill and thought rather than spirit and heart, believing that he can guide a child toward adulthood and still keep a safe distance. However, the practice of professional parenting is no panacea, as he is as out of place in the role of substitute parent as the innkeeper. He simply has more humanistic motives. To be successful, foster parents must live the role of a real parent, even for a short time, while avoiding conflict with the biological parent. Accomplishing this by professionalizing the relationship is illusory at best, and rather cold and indifferent at worst. Even experienced parents who have raised many children may not realize that they cannot simply sign on to play a role.

Like the innkeeper, professional parents have their advantages. They move kids through their homes with ease—whether through placement disruption or reunification. Sometimes they even present themselves as a short-term solution and offer great support for returning children to their birth home. In the best of cases I have even seen them willing to mentor biological families, but more often they leave that task to another professional. CPS sees them as having "good boundaries" with their charges, but they are often considered by children to be aloof and disinterested. From our perspective, one who considers the raising of children a kind of vocation risk maximizing the pain and minimizing the gain inherent to a system that attempts an institutionalized alternative to our waning sense of community responsibility.

Where missionary families often try to dominate treatment, it is sometimes hard to get professional families to attend. Many professional parents refuse even to transport the children—a task that is increasingly handled by CPS, its subcontractors, or most strikingly taxi and bus drivers. We have even lost placements because we insisted on including professional parents in treatment, largely because they consider themselves above the fray of systemic discourse and prefer to allow the children to "deal with their own issues." The exceptions are therapeutic homes, which are usually required to be involved in treatment. These, designed for short-term placement of more disturbed youth, are rarely more effective than regular professional homes. Moreover, therapeutic parents are trained to consider themselves agents of change, even if that means they have completed just 30 or 40 clock hours of training in behavior management and crisis intervention. This can lead them to take a quasi-expert stance that often adds to the cacophony of opinion already present in the system.

Professional homes work best if the therapist can access the parents themselves and draw them into the team with as little time imposition as possible. Again, in the spirit of utilization such parents must be acknowledged for their skill and expertise and given a sort of peer-supervision, rather than therapy. In terms of self-utilization, it has helped to share that I have fostered, giving me an expertise that exceeds my Ph.D. When all else fails, the therapist may need to put the onus on the caseworker to execute some of the roles the foster parent considers out of her purview, while helping the biological family pick up the rest. This tends to enable poor fostering, but may be the only way to save the placement and guard the child from feeling abandoned. Few CPS workers will ignore such requests from a therapist who is obviously trying to prevent a disruption. Again, the best remedy is to make the overall tenure in professional homes as short as possible. Beyond this one should use them respectfully, carefully, and once again with no expectation of follow-through.

The Civilians

At first encounter, civilian foster parents are as different from professional parents as one can imagine. In fact, they would be missionaries by category if not for one major difference: They come from outside the traditional system and always in response to the needs or pleas of a given child or sibling set. Rather than beginning with a mission to save children and then finding children to save, they stumble upon a single child in need, usually a neighbor, a friend of the family, or someone they have met in their work. This seems a wonderful placement option, drawn as they are from the natural environment of the child. And as the system has become short on homes and a bit more flexible, such volunteers are often welcomed.

We have at times supported civilian recruitment on theory alone. But on the whole, this practice has not lived up to its promise, with most ending as the once-beloved child is ejected from the civilian's home, often without being given the standard 7-day notice. In 1 year I had two such placements open and then close for this reason, and I was required to report a third for neglect, leading it to close. This is because civilians are by definition untested and inexperienced as foster parents, and they rarely have any concept of what they are really facing. Some have not even experienced raising children in the age range of the placed child. Lacking the normal hazing process of placement and disruption, civilians come to foster care with a very rosy perspective.

Not infrequently overzealous civilians actually express an initial willingness to take the child *without compensation.* This is particularly true for older teens, who in some states can go to "approved homes" that have not met foster care requirements and cannot be reimbursed. In this, the civilian is expressing a naïveté in excess of the most adamant missionary, imagining that she can sustain the placement with little more than love and shelter. This usually dissipates quickly when the child begins needing and wanting things, both emotional and material, that the civilian does not have the will or budget to purchase. This leads to resentment and hostility, which in turn leads to a request for subsidy, which requires the civilian to attend training and get licensed. In response, some families comply and some simply disrupt the placement. Those who persevere enter the formal foster care system and find themselves surrounded by the "regular army" discussed herein, struggling with its strange language, customs, and procedures just as biological families do. Usually the new inductee is utterly astonished by the system's machinations, as was my wife in her civilian phase as a foster parent. Even if a civilian family survives placement of the child it originally sought, they rarely go on to take additional children. We did not.

Finally, civilians are even more likely than other placement families to expect reciprocity from the child. Because they have taken time away from their daily world to care for the child, they feel entitled to frequent adoration, which they get as often as most parents do and perhaps a bit less. Thus, despite their auspicious beginnings, we find civilian homes less likely than others to succeed. When they do work they are usually ideal, allowing a child to live with a family they already know and that knows them. Unfortunately, this rare ideal tempts caseworkers and therapists into embracing these homes when they rarely succeed. And when they fail, they hurt the hearts of children more than a standard foster home. It is one thing to have a stranger disrupt a child's placement and life. It is another when a trusted friend does it. The worst of these cases have occurred when the civilian solicits the child *before* she is even in the system, helps her to report her family's unjust behavior, and facilitates her movement into custody and then into the civilian home, only to disrupt the placement a few weeks later when the dream is over.

Civilians offer the therapist one advantage over other foster homes: They are usually more willing at the start to be involved in therapy. Sometimes they even request it. At this point the therapist must align with the family as quickly as possible, thank them profusely for their sacrifice, and offer a crash course in how the system works and how to work it. I have done this many times; most families were a bit shell-shocked in the process, but they later expressed appreciation at my candor. If the therapist makes a strong connection, the civilian will come to him first as a source of guidance and information when things get difficult, and he can troubleshoot problems before they get out of hand. It is also vital to dissuade civilians from offering their homes for free, *before* they become resentful. As critical as I am about attempts to profit in fostering, subsidy is a reinforcement to continue after a child begins to overstay her welcome.

Kinship Placements

Based on the power and natural bond of the extended family, kinship placements are often considered preferable to the standard foster home. In fact, the 1997 Adoptions and Safe Families Act (PL 105–89) encourages kinship placement for children in custody and establishes a "kinship care advisory panel" to investigate the efficacy of this approach. Kinship placements have most of the assets and liabilities of the civilian home, to which we add a sense of indebtedness, duty, obligation, and emotional baggage common to extended families. Where civilian placements volunteer in a spirit of beneficence, kinship homes are draftees of their own conscience and family ledger, and not infrequently are reluctant ones.

The second problem with kinship placements is the multigenerational transmission of psychopathology, particularly when addiction is involved. Although this can be greatly exaggerated by family-phobes, one may find varying levels of dysfunction among the placement family. Some kinship placements we've worked with are only *slightly* better compensated carbon copies of the family from which the child was removed and may lack that family's commitment to the child. Alternatively, the placement family may compete for the child, undermining the birth family's reintegration plan.

Kinship homes can certainly work, especially if the extended family assists appropriately in the improvement of the biological parents and reunification of the family. We have been very impressed with more than one grandparent who rose to this duty with grace and dignity after 25 years of parenting. Occasionally, we have seen aunts and uncles assume this role on top of their own families and succeed brilliantly. Yet, on average, very few kinship placements we have worked with over the years have survived to the point of reunification. And in each that failed, the children experienced a tragic loss of connection with family members. If a child is hurt by the failure of a friendly civilian placement, they are devastated at the loss of a blood relative.

For the therapist, the same "quick-connect" strategy used in working with civilians is also useful for kinship homes. Beyond this, things get more complicated than in any other foster setting, especially when the therapist must negotiate multiple family generations to resolve entanglements. Often the therapist must either keep poorly bounded families from allowing improper contact of parent and child, or draw together disengaged families to resolve past conflicts that are playing out in reunification. This can keep the therapist very busy and a bit confused. In some kinship placements it is often a good idea to schedule a comprehensive assessment at several levels of the family before attempting to intervene. This is expensive, time consuming, and rare, but it can greatly reduce errors and misplaced children. Given the sway of multigenerational family dynamics in such cases, failure to do so begs disruption.

Group Homes

Aside from a nod to the many dedicated workers who try to staff and run group homes, I can think of nothing good to say about them. Evolved from orphanages, group homes are *total institutions* for kids. With the notable exception of programs like the venerable Boys Town, most are poorly staffed by very young and underpaid workers who turn over quickly. Many have a lack of discipline that can make juvenile detention a safer bet to weaker residents. Routinely, I have had young and vulnerable teens enter these facilities with all their possessions in the world, only to have them stolen by older youth who intimidate them into silence. Sometimes these children are even punished for "losing" their belongings. The conditions in some group homes are so objectionable that I know some very good CPS workers who always weigh the detrimental effects of residential living against retaining the child at home, and except in the most severe circumstances determine that the biological family is safer. I have seen others actually threaten oppositional foster children with group home placement. Although this harsh strategy is risky, I admit to using it myself when I believe it might prevent that very outcome.

Every other category of foster home *can* work; even if they often don't, however, I have little optimism for any group home model I have seen.

Group homes violate every known tenet of human interplay. They put radically different youths into an aversive, angry, poorly disciplined but highly punitive setting, with a staff who are often 4 to 8 years older than their charges, and expect a tolerable outcome. This is why many states have begun a deliberate movement away from group home living except as temporary shelter or high-level lockdown. Others still cling to antiquated systems of private residential placements, with literally hundreds of charity-funded homes remaining in service. Many are actually housed in old orphanages that have been retrofitted as separate "cottages."

At the risk of proffering an upsetting hyperbole, the group home concept has more in common with a refugee camp than family foster care, both of which exist to feed, house, and control groups of people. Unfortunately, when we create such camps to relocate and protect the population in time of strife, it is all too easy to continue the war without attention to the human consequences. The institutional and concentrating nature of group homes insulate the rest of the system from having to deal with children and families as individuals. In the final analysis, this may be their greatest shortcoming.

Adoptive Homes

In general, CPS or "special needs" adoption has been considered the great panacea for resolving the foster care crisis in the direction of permanency for the child, but it has generally fallen short. First of all, adoptive parents[2] share many of the same characteristics as missionary parents in terms of motivation, and the problem of supply and demand is even more severe. Adoptive parents generally (but not always) have a higher level of long-term commitment to the child, even as this generates a new set of issues for the therapist to grapple with. We have found that a good model for considering *problematic* adoptive placements is the sociological study of the colonizer and the colonized (Memmi, 1965). All adoptions and long-term foster placements have some degree of colonization, the difference being in the extent to which the family accepts and attempts to mitigate these countertransference-based tendencies.

Highly colonial families evidence a deliberate, possessive, authoritarian, and dogmatic enculturation process even if they are otherwise quite benevolent. Once the pre-adoptive agreement is signed and adoption is imminent, they begin to exert dominion over their children. In fact, their likeness to real colonizers is astounding, including the conversion of the child to the parent's preferred religion, the changing of his name, and the total disconnection from all previous family ties and traditions, even the healthy ones (e.g., grandparents, aunts, and uncles).

Sometimes this is very obvious and rather offensive. A young mother whose children were in foster care appeared to us to have serious issues with her own mother, who happened to be a prominent social worker. We asked the mother to therapy and she gladly came, expecting only to be asked about the young woman's adoption from Korea. In fact, at every turn the Anglo mother deflected the therapist's attempt to intervene in their relationship, projecting the problem onto "Sue's Korean mother." She went on about how the "Korean mother" had beat Sue, and how the "Korean mother" had rejected Sue and cast her aside. The fact that the adopted mother had done these same things also was explained as a reaction to how "Sue's Korean mother had made her unlovable." Not only had this sort of language damaged their relationship for over 20 years, it was racist, serving to deny the young woman's very cultural and racial heritage and thereby the young woman herself. The problem was summed well when the daughter grew indignant with these insults, jumped up, and yelled, "Mother, my name is *Insoo*, not Sue! I've never been Sue and you've never accepted that." Though this is the most blatant example of colonization I have ever seen, more subtle versions are common and often quite stress inducing.

One happened as I was finishing this book. I began with a family who was quite interested in their teenager's problems of "attachment" and quite unwilling to face their own in the same vein. The girl at 15 did not use drugs or alcohol, did not have sex, and only once had smoked part of a cigarette. She was loud, but rarely violent. She was very smart but had poor grades due to a lack of effort and, I suspected, attention deficit disorder. As the only adopted child in a family of four siblings, Jenna was rarely prone to crying, fearlessly claiming that she was afflicted by a family of three perfect children and "me, the bad one, the black sheep." Yet when I asked her to say a true word to her mother, and cut out all the whining and bickering, Jenna wept openly on my couch until her head was between her legs and she was gasping for air. Her mother sat idly by and missed every cue I offered to get her to hold the girl, even as she admitted she had never seen Jenna so genuine and emotional. "God," the girl said, choking, "can't you see? You treat me like I'm some kind of third-world country. Can't you just see *me*?" It was as heartbreaking as anything I have ever witnessed, and her mother's face did not change until she also began to cry—and to complain about how badly the girl had treated *her*. Jenna had never heard about my colonial theory of adoption, but she had lived it. I am happy to report great progress in resolving this case as the family has worked hard to adapt themselves, as has Jenna, to her uniqueness. In a recent email her mother wrote the words I had been hoping to hear over several months of therapy design to reorganize this family away from its focus on Jenna's pathology. In good humor and much welcome self-deprication, the mother wrote, "Isn't this a turn of events . . . we ALL need therapy, not just Jenna! Ha ha ha."

In sharp contrast, less-colonial families realize that a healthy adult is the product of all his life experiences, both good and bad. They strive to accommodate and assimilate aspects of the child's background, while setting limits and guidelines for his current life. Most of all, they have respect for the child's biological family, building a profound connection to their adoptees without expecting them to disconnect psychologically from their families of origin.[3] This may or may not include actual openness in the adoption,[4] but it always includes an acceptance of the biological family as a relevant concept in the child's life. They follow what I consider the cardinal rule of adoption—they look first to themselves before assuming that the child or her attachment problems are the source of pathogenesis, just as Jenna's family has learned to do.

Because of the missionary need for reinforcement present in adoptive families, these are difficult issues to overcome. There is a profound unfairness in the biological parent getting to show off on occasion (or being imagined in this way if there is no contact) while the adoptive parent must deal with the day-to-day struggle of raising the child. The biological parent has all of the joy and none of the responsibility in such situations, making for an immutable jealousy on the part of the true caregivers. To mitigate these feelings, the less-colonial family undertakes a careful process of self-awareness and self-management to avoid inappropriately expressing or acting on them. They know that the needs of the child far outweigh their need for gratification. Highly colonial families, like Insoo's adoptive mother, simply vent their anger in the belief that it will eventually become obvious to the child how terrible her birth family really was and how heroic the adoptive family is. Others, like Jenna's mother, become cold and distant to deflect attention on the present family relationships, and protect their own hearts from the child's anger and rebellion.

Less-colonial families also avoid forcing their own culture into the life of the child, especially with older children and teens. They prefer instead to make offerings of religion, values, morals, and goals that are always open to accommodation as a part of the child's natural growth. They are experts at authoritative parenting, expressing neither the carelessness of a laissez-faire parent nor the control of an authoritarian one. These adoptive families recognize themselves as part of a dialectical process in which the biological parent forms the thesis and they the antithesis. Out of this process emerges a completely different entity, which is like both families and neither. I recently had an adoptive mother carefully restrain her new daughter's urge to convert to the mother's faith of Judaism, reminding her daughter of what she would give up as well as what she would gain. Of course, this openness and offering of free will only served to excite the girl more about the conversion process and the way it would help her join with her new parent.

A truly astonishing example of the noncolonial parent was an older fostermother who later adopted a sibling set. I have never seen a group of children more bonded with a nonbiological parent than these teens were with Loraine. They would do anything she asked of them, even as they were quite oppositional with other adults. Privately, I asked the 16-year-old girl what Loraine had done to make such a connection. She explained the entire story in one sentence: "She took our mom off the street and tried to get her straight." A veteran of the system and savvy in the ways of foster care, Loraine first took the two oldest boys and then scoured the state for the younger sisters, and the youngest boy. Working with CPS she brought them all under one roof and, on completing this reunion, she did the unthinkable. She went out on the streets of Denver, found their mother stripping for tips and drugs, brought this woman into her home and tried for 6 weeks to rehabilitate her. When the mother reached her fourth step of Narcotics Anonymous (NA), she offered the children an apology for how she had harmed them and subsequently disappeared back to the streets from which she'd come. The siblings promptly disconnected from their mother and placed all their stock in "grandma" Loraine, who continued to express nothing but sadness that she had failed with their mother. She encouraged them to visit their mom whenever she was in jail.

I certainly do not recommend that foster or adoptive parents conduct guerrilla rehabilitation of wayward mothers as a matter of course, but the point is still clear. Loraine went above and beyond to accommodate and assimilate the children's culture into her own. She knew that when you take in a child, you also take in the child's family, though she took this more literally than anyone I have known. Even after the mother had broken her children's hearts by relapsing, Loraine urged them toward forgiveness and tolerance.

As with everything else in the system, these ideas are very contentious due in part to the natural tension that forms in the adoptive or long-term foster family as it takes a necessary and inescapable position counter to the birth family. But regardless of the ongoing level of contact, which can vary greatly with each case, it is vital to a successful adoption for children to have reconciliation with the biological family in order to be released from the disturbed relationship of the offending parents and to move on with their lives in their new families. A successful reconciliation that improves placement success requires great skill by the therapist and a good relationship with both biological and adoptive families, not to mention with the children. It is certainly no easier than it sounds, but it is a special type of contrition process we have found to be of great import.

THE FUNDAMENTAL FLAW

As I said at the beginning of this chapter, it is not my goal to complain about CPS or foster care, but to map its rugged territory and discuss how to navigate it. In doing so, I have purposely avoided the long litany of horror stories about children who were more mistreated in custody than they were in their own homes (Scott, 1994; Toth, 1997; Wexler, 1995). Elsewhere in this book I have documented a few disasters to illustrate a number of problems in treating these cases, but I am quick to admit that the system does not *routinely* generate horrific abuse of its own. Although any mistreatment in foster care is intolerably unjust, a focus on these extremes draws us away from the core reason that foster care is inherently flawed. Even if all foster parents were ideal missionaries trained to be perfect in motive and deed and properly remunerated, all the systemic and funding problems were resolved, and family foster care completely replaced group homes, the concept of foster care would remain an inadequate and potentially iatrogenic response to family injustice. This is because the fundamental shortcoming of foster care is much more basic than the sum of its many flaws: *In the minds of most children, it is better to be abused and loved by your parent than not to be loved at all.* The typical child will tolerate a great deal of injustice from the family before taking a self-protective stance because he sees a flawed family as better than no family at all. This tolerance increases if the child knows other children who have been placed in the system, accounting for the high levels of recantation during sex abuse investigations. Even neglected children, who by definition receive very little attention from their parents, are hungry for this familial connection. Except when placed in good adoptive or quasi-adoptive long-term homes, they will not get this in the system, and even in good placements it will not be an easy process to achieve.

If you study its etymology, the word *discipline* comes from the word *disciple*, meaning "to follow." Children *almost always* follow those with whom they feel connected. In place of discipleship, foster care emphasizes rules without love, consequences without compassion, interaction without connection, and dependency without bond. This is not due to the character of the foster parent but is the nature of the system by design. Theoretically, one might remedy this by encouraging foster families to expand their hearts to show love to their young charges and invite them to reciprocate, thereby gaining discipleship. In fact, this is the missionary foster parent's main tool. Unfortunately, it is all too prone to the romantically reductive notion that no matter what a child's problem it can be overcome with love, which has created a number of excruciating problems all its own. This sort of love may be necessary, but it is *never* sufficient. That is true for all children, and it is tenfold so for the heartbroken children of abuse and neglect, who struggle to form healthy attachments when they have no one to serve as a pattern. Working with any style of foster family, the therapist must instead help them *lovingly accommodate and assimilate* a troubled young person in an atmosphere of authority, while maintaining good boundaries and enforcing natural limits and consequences. This is no easier than it sounds.

There is also the issue of love's durability and duration in a given foster home. Early in my career, a foster family attended therapy on Tuesday, expressing "love" for a 12-year-old boy placed with them for just over 2 weeks and pledging to keep him until he was 18. As a novice, I was pleased because the boy had no other options than a distant group home. Upon further reflection I realized that the bond was too sudden and too early in the placement. My anxiety was validated that Friday when the family disrupted the placement after the boy began banging his head on the side of the house in a silent fit of anger. They called me right after they called the sheriff, who took the boy to the emergency shelter before I arrived. This scene has been repeated all too often over the years. With several iterations in a given case, it forms an excellent foundation for a borderline personality as the child's fears of abandonment are repeatedly reinforced by one empty love after another.

A TALE OF TWO PLACEMENTS

A few years ago I had an extraordinary opportunity to observe a naturally occurring experiment that illustrates quite simply what I have suggested in this chapter, setting the stage for the next. A caseworker referred two children to our institute, a boy and girl ages 7 and 9, respectively. The mother had done nearly everything to fulfill her case plan, except applying for the Medicaid benefits to which she was entitled. The worker, a former student and strong family-friend, wanted the children home and was frustrated that the mother seemed reluctant to take this final simple step. She worried that the mother was delaying reintegration out of fear or guilt. In discussing the case with me the worker mentioned what she termed the "dueling placements."

The boy was with a professional family who saw their goal as reunification of biological families. They were staunch advocates for this position but refused to bring the child to therapy; on some occasions they did not even have him ready when the caseworker came to transport him. At least twice a week they would call the worker to complain that the biological mother was not working hard enough to get the children home. They were happy to keep the little boy as long as necessary to accomplish this goal, but stated a concern that "the longer he is in the system, the more he is going to deteriorate." They noted that, after every unsupervised visit with his mother, the little boy spent 2 or 3 days feeling sad and lonely. They attributed this to feelings of loss and grief and pressed for a speedy reunification to address the problem. The worker agreed and sent the family to us.

The little girl was with a strong missionary family who saw as its goal the salvation of abused and neglected children from negative and dysfunctional families. They called the worker at least twice a week to report that the girl was terribly afflicted by any thought of "sending her back with that woman."

They complained that the worker should not be pushing reunification, as "the longer this girl is in the system the better chance she has to be safe and happy." They reported each week after her unsupervised visitations with her mother (held conjointly with the boy) that she would spend 2 or 3 days appearing sad, lonely, and distant from their family. They attributed this to the mother's "inappropriate conduct during the visits," which they felt made the girl more depressed, and claimed that the mother was "just playing those kids off of each other." When queried about how they had deduced this, having not attended the visits, they noted, "Well, something really bad must be going on there because of how long it takes to get her back on track when she comes *home*" (meaning their house). They asked to adopt the little girl and pressured the caseworker to move toward termination of rights. They even started calling the boy's foster home to get them to join in this plan. That family refused.

Because I did not attend the visitations, I did not know who was right—nor did the foster parents in question. I do know that the accuracy of their accounts was less relevant than the perceptions and theories implicit in them.

And so it is with most aspects of the child protective system.

CONCLUSION: THE BABY AND THE BATHWATER

Suggesting that some of the players in the greater child protective system bear too much resemblance to the neutrals in a Dante-like inferno of injustice creates an understandable defensiveness against critique. Moreover, taking such a position does not make for an easy relationship with that system. I once gave a workshop on foster care based on this chapter and was quoted the next day in the local newspaper as saying that children were so afflicted in custody that they were better off not reporting child abuse. I checked with the agency that hired me, and they agreed I had not said this, nor am I proposing it herein. To be quite clear in summary, these are my positions on the child protective system as a method of responding to family injustice:

- Children must be protected from all forms of family severe injustice.
- There are many ways to do this, the most radical of which is to put them in foster care.
- Foster care is flawed in many ways, including some that cannot be overcome, limiting its effectiveness and at times rendering it iatrogenic.
- Foster care must still exist, though it should be used sparingly under a family-friendly model as discussed herein that promotes reunification and the least detrimental alternative.
- The system is made up of people. Each of us can choose to be neutrals, or active participants in change. We favor the latter.

Where others have come close to ejecting the baby of child protection with the bathwater of CPS, we recognize the need to balance both in the service of family justice. Clinically, this produces a very difficult experience for the therapist, who must walk the tightest of wires in servicing the needs of the family and child in the larger context of a powerful and capricious system. My brief presentation of that system may compel the reader to feel even more like Dante at the gates of hell, reading its famous inscription "Abandon every hope, ye who enter here." If so, I have perhaps made my point too well. With all their difficulties, we have evolved ways of thinking and working in these cases that we will discuss and illustrate in the remaining chapters, which provide a strategic advantage to therapists as they guide their clients through and out of the system.

NOTES

1. In some jurisdictions this is not a requirement, and anyone with some sort of human services training or experience can serve in this capacity. Unfortunately, this means there is no regulation of the practice of social work, and the title of "social worker" is not legally protected in those states. This is especially troubling given the power these workers, some straight out of college, hold over the lives of children and families.
2. Consistent with the theme of this book I am referring to families who adopt children from CPS, not those seeking private adoptions.
3. Conceptually this is true across the life span. Practically it is more important for children adopted at ages greater than 7 or 8 to have actual, well-regulated contact with appropriate members of their biological family.
4. Based on our own experience, we tend to favor openness whenever possible. In CPS adoptive cases, we find that the choice is not if a child will seek reconciliation with biological relatives, but when and how. To the extent possible, we see the adoptive family as the stable platform from which to launch such exploration.

CHAPTER 8

Family-Friendly Therapy and Evaluation

Priorities and Process

In spite of everything, I still believe that people are really good at heart.
—Anne Frank, *The Diary of a Young Girl* (1952)

Mental health providers have usually been trained at the masters or doctoral level in some form of psychology, counseling, family therapy, or clinical social work. However, knowing these rather arbitrary distinctions says very little about what the clinician actually does in session, as the practice has become so eclectic. As with everyone in the complex tapestry of the system, mental health providers may be family-friends or family-phobes. Beyond this, they usually fill two roles, which should be but rarely are clear and distinct.

THERAPIST OR EVALUATOR

The roles of evaluator and therapist are not only different, they are typically incompatible. I raise this point because nowhere are these boundaries less clear than in child protective cases and rarely will anyone tend to them, leaving the clinician to develop and assert the correct position. We first examine the basic distinction between these roles and then study their obfuscation, much of which is integral to the system. The rest comes from mental health provider error.

The therapist's client is the child and/or the family. The evaluator's client is the court. Where the evaluator should be disinterested and unbiased, the therapist should be vested in the child and family, advocating for their mental health and well-being. The therapist is free to use a wide variety of strategies with the goal of invoking change. Although it is useful to be creative and flexible in evaluation, the structure of the process takes precedent and is usually narrower and more focused than therapy. The therapist is an ally, while the evaluator is a natural adversary of the family even if he is a family-friend, because he is trying to root out information they are motivated not to share. When I am serving as an evaluator, my search for family strengths is not readily apparent as a function of the evaluative process, and the family may even perceive the process as a bit malign. Where the therapist wants the clients to succeed, the evaluator wants only to perceive them as accurately as possible. This is generally where the clarity ends.

Almost always, evaluators are called upon to provide data on parental fitness. If they are unbiased by family-phobia, they will speak to the viability of reunification and the optimal services necessary to restore the family to minimally adequate functioning. This is the expected outcome of any evaluation and thus no surprise to the expert involved. What is astounding to the uninitiated is how this also holds true for the *therapist treating the family or child.* The court and CPS expect with no qualification that any therapist serving in this capacity, regardless of pay or referral source, will testify as an expert regarding parental competency and potential reunification. In fact, this role is actually written into service contracts offered to many therapists. Because this expectation combines the very different roles of unbiased evaluator and client-centered therapist/advocate, it is a very uncomfortable position indeed. The therapist can attempt to avoid it by asserting confidentiality and privileged communication or state clearly that he was not hired for the role of expert witness, but most judges have the statutory authority to override the privilege and any other protestation one might offer in cases of child welfare. Before protesting, the reader should remember that it is this very expectation that gives the therapist the credential to advocate directly for the child's best interests within the context of the family, and thus it becomes an important tool in treating family injustice.

There are three hedges against inadvertent multiple relationship in such cases, all of which involve repeated and emphatic attempts to educate everyone, including the court, on (1) the differences among an expert witness, a fact witness, and an "expert treater" and which role the therapist can legitimately fulfill; (2) the limits of confidentiality and privileged communication in such cases; and (3) where one's loyalties lie—the therapist with the client and family, and the evaluator with the court.

Witnesses: Fact, Expert, and Expert Treater

The *expert witness* does nothing but evaluate and render clinical recommendations. She has no stake in the outcome of the case, advocating only for the data she has collected and the process she used to collect it.[1] The most significant characteristic of the true expert is the power of her opinion in court, an exception to the rule of evidence that prohibits the common person from proffering her viewpoint as reliable testimony. For example, an expert in a sex abuse case could speak not only to the child's disclosure (a fact), but also to the nature of child disclosure in general, his believability, the concept of repressed memory, the degree to which the described behavior parallels typical offender behavior, and any other issue for which he has been qualified on the stand.

The *fact witness* is at the opposite end of the spectrum. She can only state what she perceives with her five senses, and is specifically barred from interpretation, conjecture, and opinion. An example is the neighbor who testifies "on Tuesday I saw Amy's stepdad spank her with a belt." The neighbor cannot render an opinion as to whether this constitutes abuse or reasonable discipline or whether Amy was harmed or upset by the situation, only that it happened.

The *expert treater* falls into a strange limbo between the expert and fact witness. If a therapist is properly qualified during voir dire, she can speak her opinion but only on the case of interest. For example, she can discuss the disclosure of the child and speak to her opinion on its veracity, but she should not discuss sex abuse disclosure in general. More important, while she may offer an opinion on this case, she should not be expected or allowed to proffer it as if it were objective or unbiased. Being neutral, or worse an adversary of the family, is not a good basis for treatment, and any therapist who says she is unbiased is either being less than helpful to the family or disingenuous. This puts the expert treater in a very odd role, having an opinion that is inherently tainted for all the right reasons (e.g., empathy, positive regard, benevolence), and she should never claim otherwise as a matter of ethics and good therapy.

Unfortunately, many professionals in the system do not know and honor these critical distinctions, and many family-court judges do not recognize them in qualifying witnesses. This makes for a confusing hodge-podge of opinion, often giving the independent testimony of a disinterested evaluator the same weight as the subjective advocacy of a CASA or the policy-tainted critique of a CPS worker. To help clarify these roles, we recommend that the first few reports that one writes as an expert treater explain this difference without a trace of condescension, and clarify the role one has properly assumed.

A HIERARCHY OF PRIORITIES

I recall professors in my graduate programs being quite insistent on asking us in practicum "who is the client?" It took me several years of working in family therapy and CPS cases to realize how key this issue really is, especially in complex cases of family injustice. Given the multiple influences bearing down upon them, both the evaluator and therapist must assertively manage a well-defined hierarchy of priorities with specific goals at each level of this hierarchy, which help manage countertransference and allow a balanced, critically optimistic stance. They also allow the child's therapist to be family oriented, a leader of both the child protective team and any therapeutic intervention, without losing sight of the child's best interests. The therapist and evaluator must assert and adhere to this hierarchy in each and every decision and make all parties aware of this stance in the initial interviews and case conferences. Starting with the child victim and ending with the larger society, this particular hierarchy has the property of moving from the most to least vulnerable parties in a given case.

The Child

Without question, the welfare and best interests of the child should be the top priority in therapy and evaluation. Although this should be obvious, it often is not, as exemplified by the "Mrs. Jones' CASA" case described earlier. The goal here is to protect vulnerable youth at the micro-level from physical, emotional, and psychic injury, which is of course the stated purpose of any CPS intervention. However, keenly aware of contextual issues in the life of the child, the therapist and evaluator recognize that such injury can come from many sources, including the intervention of CPS. Further, while we know that in some cases children must be prevented from having any contact with their parents, in the majority of cases such prohibition is quite damaging. For the evaluator, the goal is to recommend a "least detrimental alternative" for the child based on an analysis of all factors in the child, family, and larger system.

Unfortunately, this is where many dogmatic family therapists and family preservationists get into trouble by prioritizing the family's needs above the child's. Their intentions are good, as they know the staggering failure rate of foster care previously cited, but they have lost sight of their obligation to keep children at the forefront of their thinking, even if they conceptualize the family as the client. In their zeal, those who go beyond family friend to "family worshipper" put the child at risk. True family friends are first and foremost therapists of the child. They just work differently.

The Family

The welfare of the biological family should be the second priority, with the goal of preserving it as much as possible as the primary context for the child. For the evaluator, the goal is to assess the viability of this tack. We believe that although some improvement has occurred in the last 10 years many children are still unnecessarily outplaced without adequate attempts at family preservation. Another portion of children is necessarily removed, but held in the system well beyond the time that it takes to reconcile the family. In each of these conditions, the therapist should advocate for a safe but expedient reunification. A smaller portion is necessarily removed and taken through a failed reunification only to remain in perpetual limbo. Despite the problems inherent to adoption or long-term care of CPS cases, the therapist must recognize the need for permanency planning, and work to help children adjust to this new family context and that context to adjust to them.

In any reintegration case the biological family is important for a second reason—as a deterrent to future abuse by the offender. The law is not a sufficient deterrent to reoffense in cases of abuse or neglect, because offenders do not carefully consider the consequences of their actions before committing them. Thus, the legal system is virtually incapable of protecting society from such offenders without a powerful ally: the family and natural community. As noted in chapter 12, the best hedge against reoffense is establishment of a family and community that defends victims against offense and uses the system as a way to back it up.

Just as dogmatic family therapists may become caught up in the family to the detriment of the child, child-focused therapists are most likely to diminish the priority of family rehabilitation and reconciliation. They focus instead on their exclusive, one-to-one relationship with the child, combined with a misplaced faith in outplacement. Except under the worst-case conditions discussed in chapter 9, this is a severe error and rarely brings about a just outcome.

The Nonoffending Family Members

The third priority is the nonoffending parent or family members. In most sex abuse cases this is usually the mother, or with teen offenders, both parents. In physical abuse cases it can routinely be either parent. In some families it may include grandparents who were heavily involved in the care of the child. In any case, the nonoffending family members are crucial because their response to the disclosure is a good predictor of the victim's ultimate recovery. The goal of treatment is to restore the nonoffending members to respectability in the eyes of the child, to help them become protectors of the child, and to establish open communication with the child. For the evaluator, the goal is to determine the extent to which this is reasonably possible. Unfortunately, as anyone who has worked with such cases knows, nonoffending parents are often the most difficult to work with, particularly in the more severe cases. In fact, our experience has been that nonoffending mothers in cases of sex abuse are far more difficult clients than the offenders themselves, due in part to their tendency to distance themselves from any impropriety. "I couldn't have known," is a typical response, even if the mother has been in a series of violent or sexually abusive relationships herself, or if she was treated violently by the person who abused the child.

Individually oriented therapists working with nonoffenders tend to mismanage them by agreeing that they bear no accountability for failing to protect the victim, thus exonerating them before they have even entered the contrition process. Child therapists err by vilifying them as if they were the substantial equivalent of the offender himself, particularly if the therapist takes an unnecessarily paternal role in working with a child. Instead of giving into parent bashing, we recognize the difficulties of treating nonoffenders but also the fact that they will be one of the most powerful curative factors in the life of the child. Thus, whether difficult or not, the nonoffending members must be elevated to a high priority in the life of the child and their welfare and mental health taken very seriously in the process of contextual change.

The Offender

The goal in treating the offender of physical or sexual abuse is rehabilitation with the concomitant creation of a supportive safety net that will maintain scrutiny of his conduct and help him avoid reoffending. Unfortunately, as noted earlier, the traditional approach is to completely exclude offenders (particularly sex offenders) from the hierarchy, isolating them both physically and metaphorically from the family treatment process. I will not reiterate the reasons why this is a poor decision, but will simply note that the family-friendly therapist must recognize the importance of the offender's role in the contrition process, which transfers the guilt and shame of the offense away from the victim. Evaluation at this level is of critical importance because it must assess as accurately as possible the amenability of the client not only for accepting treatment, but for benefiting from it. Of course this is a very difficult prediction to make, and many times the evaluator's recommendations are designed to create more methods of evaluation over the course of reintegration than to reach a definitive conclusion. What we attempt to do is generate the best hypotheses for the court as to the client's future behavior and then suggest valid and reliable ways of testing them.

Opposition to the offender having a priority in this hierarchy (especially sex offenders) is widespread, because those who work with offenders rarely work with victims and vice versa. As Bruce Laflen notes (chapter 12), there is also a tendency for offender therapists to be a very static in-group, and to be interested in sexual deviance as an intrapsychic dysfunction rather than an interactional process. All this leads to the offender being extricated from the hierarchy by his victim's therapist as well as his own. Bringing these two groups of professionals together, as we did in Laflen's Kansas City program, is crucial in correcting and broadening their treatment goals and restoring justice to the disturbed relationship foisted upon the victim by the offender.

Society

The fifth priority for the therapist or evaluator is society, with the goal of protecting the lives of children at the macro level by reducing the probability of a reoffense. We might lament our role as agents of social control, but anyone working with family injustice, abuse, and neglect is expected to work diligently to prevent reoffenses in both the specific family and beyond. Unfortunately, this priority is frequently elevated above the welfare of the family, and even the victim, and both therapists and evaluators should call attention to this condition when they encounter it. Under any theory of legal, social, or therapeutic justice, the legitimate needs and rights of a given family or victim should never be sacrificed for a perceived greater social good without very careful reflection and due process. From our perspective, there are few cases in which such an exchange would be just, sensible, or even necessary, and we would again refer the reader to the restorative justice literature for a broader account of this issue.

The Mental Health Provider

The sixth priority is the therapist or evaluator himself, with the goal of trying to survive without doing harm. This work is not for the faint-hearted, requiring discipline, courage, and resolve as well as a good system of professional and social support and supervision. Many simply give up after being battered by the system a few times, and I am at times surprised that our institute has been working with this population as long as we have. Another risk for the therapist in such cases is prioritizing his own emotional or financial needs above the client's. In the former case, therapists are attempting to vicariously work through their own countertransference issues. In the latter, they can continue to bill clients for years and years if they justify their existence to the client and to the insurance company. Both victims and offenders may be subjected to this sort of treatment when courts aggressively order such overinvolvement. A therapist who has the correct hierarchy of priorities never places himself above the needs of the family, child, or society. In fact, the ethical codes of our various professions demand no less. Simply put, we must remain healthy enough in our work to stay at the bottom of this list of priorities and still live to tell the tale.

For the evaluator, even state contracts can be lucrative and there is a constant pressure by CPS for the evaluator to come up with the "right answers," even though this is blatantly unethical. It is commonplace for CPS to blacklist evaluators and therapists who do not meet their demands, and internal politics nearly always overtake good clinical judgment within CPS. Therapists and evaluators who survive both ethically and practically are usually extraordinarily good at working at the lowest levels of the system, just as Minuchin and colleagues (1998) suggest. Interestingly, more than one of our students has noted that this process is more like a strategic therapy of the workers and system than a collegial discourse.

LEVELS OF FAMILY RECONSTRUCTION

In attending to issues of family injustice, evaluators and therapists must also recognize and assert the difference among reconciliation, reintegration, and reunification in their discussions with CPS. As with the hierarchy of priorities, one would expect everyone to adhere to these concepts, yet it is common for case plans to fail precisely because the language and practice around these issues becomes murky. We have identified three levels of reconstruction in our work and offer them in an attempt to create a more standardized language:

Reconciliation

According to the *Encarta World English Dictionary* (Microsoft Corporation, 1999), reconciliation can mean:

- The ending of conflict or renewing of a friendly relationship between people after a dispute or estrangement.
- The making of two or more apparently conflicting things consistent or compatible.
- A religious sacrament whereby an individual's sins are absolved through confession and penance.
- Causing two or more apparently conflicting things to be consistent or compatible.

In cases of family injustice the idea of reconciliation encompasses all of these concepts in one form or another. In our taxonomy reconciliation exists at the *lowest* level of family reconstruction, representing a process by which the family encounters one another in therapy and perhaps nowhere else. The goal of such reconciliation is not to make everyone feel positive and loving, or to settle every dispute among family members. It is more analogous to the reconciliation of a checkbook, where everything is put where it belongs and things add up. In other words, the "why" and "who" questions are answered and the family's history begins to exist in a larger context beyond the offense. In practice, reconciliation should begin as soon as practically and safely possible, taking into account the victim's needs and wishes, regardless of plans for unification or termination. As noted earlier, we have learned that most therapists and child protective systems err on the side of delaying reconciliation, usually from countertransference and family-phobia.

When the parents do not appear good candidates for reintegration or reunification, they may remain indefinitely at this level. However, missing the importance of reconciliation, many court and CPS workers give up on family contact as soon as the reintegration plan has failed. This is almost always a mistake. As noted earlier, we have had numerous cases where biological parents remain in some managed contact with their children even after they have been adopted. Only when this has been tried and proven in error should reconciliation therapy be ended. Further, for permanently outplaced children, reconciliation can and often does take years to accomplish as they move through new developmental stages and reflect on their life history once again. It is for precisely this reason that seemingly happy young people adopted at birth suddenly have an uncontrollable yearning to find their biological families in early to middle adolescence. Their emotional checkbook is not reconciled. For both adoptive and long-term foster families, the therapist must normalize this process, as it is often very threatening to the connection adoptive families have established with the child.

Reintegration

When a family has reached a point in the process of reconciliation where they can encounter one another outside of therapy, they generally move to the next stage. Reintegration[2] begins when quasi-normal activities are resumed but before the family returns to living together. Initially, this is likely to include supervised visitation beginning with CPS agents, and eventually moving to supervision by members of the family. There is no way to determine *a priori* how long reintegration will take because the range of family injustice and misconduct is so broad and the rate of recovery so variable. However, the rule of thumb is that it usually takes longer than it needs to. In a family-phobic environment, this is because even the necessary motivation for reintegration is a scarce resource. A colleague consulting from another jurisdiction recently told me that a 15-year-old girl's reintegration was being delayed because the district attorney (DA) and *guardian ad litem* (GAL) thought she was having sex. When asked how they knew this, they said that another fellow in their purview had told them so and even claimed to have impregnated her. Three negative pregnancy tests later, the DA and GAL still stuck to their guns. The colleague expressed concern as to why the girl was more culpable for this than the fellow, who under statute would be considered a sex offender, not a reliable source.

Even in family-friendly or reversed-contingency environments, the wheels of family justice move slowly as systemic determinism grinds much of the process to a halt. Because of poor reimbursement rates in many jurisdictions, competent and unbiased evaluations for parents are difficult to obtain yet are still required by the court. In some jurisdictions it is not uncommon to have a 3- to 6-month wait-list for these evaluations, which must be completed before any movement can be made toward reintegration. Court dockets are often backed up and it may be up to 6 months between hearings. Review boards can improve this situation, but quick reintegration is much more difficult that it appears

Regardless of how long it takes, it is vital that reintegration begin and be completed *partway* through therapy. It should never be its final result, nor should it end just as therapy is beginning. The two must go hand in hand, with reintegration being but one more step in that process. Reintegration may be thought of as a test-bed for reunification, an opportunity to see how family members do in a controlled setting before moving to the final phase. Alternatively, families may remain at this level if the offender and/or nonoffending parent proves safe to be around the children unsupervised but has not been able to correct other areas of life sufficiently to warrant final reunification. The most common and frustrating example of this is in cases of addiction or severe mental illness where the parent is able to remain sober or compensated for visitations, but cannot do so throughout the remainder of the week. We originally termed this the "Dollies on the Shelf" approach to parenting when we encountered it in the state hospital. In this model, parents would put their children "on the shelf" for the week, then take them down to play. When finished, they would return them to the hospital on Sunday. This scheme could go on for years, despite our attempts at deinstitutionalization and community-based services. The hospital even colluded with these families to justify its existence. The practice only ended when the facility was closed.

Initially we held disdain for these families and the systems that supported this practice. However, in later years, as we came to see this same condition in CPS cases, we began to take a more empathic perspective. Having repeatedly failed to reintegrate these children, we found ourselves happy to have *any* contact by the biological parents, even if it was heavily managed. I have seen several young people who spent years living in solid missionary foster homes while maintaining contact with their biological parents through weekend visits and an occasional overnight. Ultimately, we have come to see Dollies on the Shelf as a less-than-perfect strategy for turning a case that cannot move to reunification toward a more acceptable outcome.

Reunification

If reintegration is successfully completed, the family should be deemed ready to live together and resume a normal hierarchy. This marks the ultimate challenge in such a therapy, as the previously disintegrated family must once more begin living as a unit, preferably a more functional one. Next to keeping children in the system too long for their own good, the worst problem we have faced is the reunification of families concurrent with a discontinuation of services. In fact, although it may seem paradoxical, we routinely recommend retaining a full year of custody after a child returns to her biological family, with full therapeutic services in place. This allows for the real work of family therapy and reunification to gel while the state retains some control over the entire process. In family-friendly jurisdictions this power is used wisely. In other jurisdictions such an approach can be disastrous, as family-phobes remain overinvolved with the family and ultimately prevent it from succeeding.

TESTING AND EVALUATION

Nearly every biological family in the foster care system will be exposed to procedures designed to evaluate their fitness, psychological stability, parenting capacity, and intentions toward their own children. The first thing to *forget* about each of these levels of evaluation is the idea that they are objective. I am a psychologist and trained extensively in research and testing. I routinely conduct parenting and custody evaluations for the court. Very little of what I produce is objective. Even if there were a truly objective test of parenting, one could not separate that data from the subjective interpretation of the interviewer. When I am an evaluator, I am impartial in the sense that I do not enter the process with a preconceived idea of its outcome; but I am also aware of and clear about my own personal biases. Every evaluation is subject to the theory and belief system of the person writing it, and evaluators who think otherwise are ignoring their own training and theory of family nature.

As an evaluator, I am still a critically optimistic family friend. This means I will look hard for family strengths, even as I would never suppress evidence of weakness. Sometimes I cannot find enough of what I seek and must recommend an elaborate period of ongoing assessment, including the goals and services necessary to attempt reintegration, and the threshold in a given family that would meet the psychological "good enough" standard. At times I must reluctantly recommend truncation of the parent's rights and custody. In contrast, (ethical) family-phobic evaluators will usually look hard for pathology even as they would never suppress evidence of strength. Sometimes they cannot find enough of what they seek and reluctantly recommend reintegration, hopefully with the sorts of services that would raise the probability of success. They too set a threshold, but it may well exceed that which I would consider "good enough." In short, we are the products of the subtle lenses we use to view the world. This makes our recommendations inherently subjective, which is why expert witnesses with mutually exclusive testimony have become the bane of courtrooms everywhere.

As noted in the section on constructivism, the truth matters in these cases. Thus, we are especially obligated to get as close to it as possible when evaluating children and families in the system. In making such assessments we must remember and assert vigorously in every case that each procedure of evaluation, formal or informal, meets certain criteria before it is taken seriously in the decision-making process. The first is that of validity, or the extent to which the procedure measures what it is supposed to measure. The second is reliability, or the extent to which the test is correctly applied and consistently measures the variable of interest. It has been our experience that the majority of procedures used in child protective cases are invalid or unreliable, yet are offered as if they were objective fact or at least well-reasoned clinical opinion. This is most apparent in courtrooms where the oath is waived by the judge in favor of free expression. Even in more orderly systems, any attempt to press for the most valid and reliable indicators is rarely welcomed by CPS, specifically because such procedures prevent a level of freedom and flexibility that might be easily confused with capriciousness. The typical procedures used in a case of family injustice can be broken down into three categories.

Category 1. Formal Evaluation

The first level of assessment includes psychometric instruments, clinical interviews, and other techniques applied by psychologists thought to be experts in the field, or at least those with whom CPS often finds agreement. The strength of formal testing is in its reliability. Arguably, when applied correctly, modern testing and normative data provide a consistent picture of psychopathology, cognitive capacity, and personality style across diverse individuals. However, the science of testing has yet to yield a reliable and valid measurement of parenting that generalizes well to these populations and that has an acceptable error rate. For instance, the Minnesota Multiphasic Personality Inventory (MMPI-2) is an empirically derived instrument that produces a fairly objective set of data for psychodiagnosis, but does nothing to predict parenting other than by extrapolation. The same is true for the Millon Clinical Multiaxial Inventory III (MCMI-III). However, psychopathology itself has not been found to have a clear and predictable connection to parenting and there is no "bad parent" profile on these instruments, nor is there any *DSM-IV* diagnosis that reliably predicts it. Both instruments, and especially the MMPI, are very susceptible to self-report bias and thus are easily invalidated by a client facing a forensic parenting evaluation. The Thematic Apperception Test (TAT) has a long tradition of questionable usage, and may reveal as much about the examiner as the subject. Additionally, the House-Tree-Person Test has little utility in such cases as it lacks reliability and validity.

Properly administered, the Rorschach Comprehensive (Exner) System has vastly improved that instrument's objectivity and we recommend it, despite an awareness of its critics who we believe have been challenged quite adequately in recent literature. However, it still has nothing specific to say about parenting. Several protocols are now available that claim to provide objective measurement of parenting, but none are proven or culture-free, particularly for this unusual population. They also tend to measure tangential issues like "parental stress," which may or may not have anything to do with fitness or the viability of reintegration.

In the hands of a skilled evaluator, clinical interviews and structured behavioral observation tend to be more valid than testing (e.g., they are easily tailored to be highly case specific), but are less reliable because they are subject to the theory and perspective of the evaluator as well as his interviewing and observational skills. Using behavioral observation, the family is brought together on several occasions and placed in front of the one-way mirror. The evaluator enters the room and asks the family to perform specific tasks designed to generate increasing levels of stress. Even the length of the session (at least 2 hours) creates a necessary tension to gather data on the client's typical parenting style. This structure increases the objectivity of the observation without leaving the process up to the whim of the family (as with nondirected observation). The observer can give directives and then retire behind the mirror to observe their execution, reducing his presence in the actual milieu.

Well implemented, structured observation places the parent in a valid parenting situation and assesses his or her response set. Problems of inter-rater and test-retest consistency are abundant, though these can be controlled through manualizing the procedure and using it with supervision. However, because it optimally requires several 2-hour sessions, structured observation is a major expense for cash-strapped agencies.

Taken as a whole, formal evaluation is far from perfect, but it has an important role in child protective cases, helping to lay a more empirical foundation for all treatment and case management to come. When things go poorly and reasonable efforts are not sufficient to bring successful reintegration, a well-done parenting evaluation can explain why and offer clarity for the next step. Most important, formal evaluation is far less prone to bias than the other forms of scrutiny discussed next.

Category 2. Semiformal Evaluation

Semiformal evaluation procedures include visits between children and families, reports of therapy contacts, and interviews conducted by the caseworker. There is little one can say about these evaluations as a group, because their validity and reliability are wholly dependent on the method used and the quality of the interviewer—a point that will usually be missed when CPS recommendations are submitted. The most common point of attention is the supervised visit between family and outplaced child, usually held at the CPS office. Under this procedure, a person having little or no training in behavioral observation attends the family visitations and reports her interpretation of what goes on. Occasionally these observers have a college degree, but sometimes they are students. The observer may even be the family's caseworker or CASA, with all the biases built into that role. Yet this unstructured supervised visit is often examined without hesitation in lieu of a formal structured observation, giving it the dual attributes of being both highly influential and completely without validity and reliability. In fact, when discussed in a case plan, the observed visits often sound more like gossip than assessment.

Such data are best incorporated by an unbiased evaluator into a broader assessment of the child and family in the context of the larger system. Far from a novel concept, this is exactly the model used on the better-funded divorce and custody side of family court. The evaluator takes into account relevant data not just from the child and parents but from extended family, friends, therapists, babysitters, teachers, CPS, and any other reasonable source. This is so the evaluator can understand the child's best interests within the context of her life experience, which necessarily includes the divorce and all that has happened hence. On first blush this seems the perfect model for the child and family involved with CPS. The evaluator can take all the data from his category 1 assessment and combine it with category 2 information to decide what is valid and reliable for decision making. This would necessarily involve an assessment of the child in his present social context, which is the world of foster care and CPS. By now, the reader will probably realize why such an assessment never happens: CPS is interested only in the accountability of the family, not the experience CPS has provided the child. Like the divorcing parent who insists that his ex-wife is the only one who needs to be evaluated, CPS is rarely willing to be a subject of the assessment.

For this reason, category 2 information is usually entered into evidence as though it carries the same reliability and validity as any other source. If skilled, family-friendly workers collect it, such data may contribute to the greater service of justice; if family-phobes are in charge, it will not. Without any screening mechanism, only the judge is left to quickly sort out which is which, and what to do in response. As questionable as category 2 data may be, it does not compare to the odd methodology implicit in the informal evaluations discussed next.

Category 3. Informal Evaluation

The informal evaluation is a form of scrutiny that is at times afforded much greater importance than it deserves. It consists of the subjective impressions of the various agencies based on incidental contact with the family. This includes observing clients in the hall prior to the court hearing, seeing them in the CPS or clinic waiting room, bumping into them at the grocery store, or visiting them at home during surprise drop-bys. The worst is rumor. With incredible frequency we have seen entered into the record data based on hearsay and innuendo gathered from friends, neighbors, and even other clients, which is then used in serious decision making. This is wholly inappropriate, and the therapist and evaluator should oppose its every occurrence.

Nearly always conducted without informed consent, these procedures are not only invalid and unreliable, they are also duplicitous, generating data that are as much a projection of observer bias as an indication of family functioning. In some CPS reports, how the family treats the caseworker has been given as much ink as the way they treat their children. In one case, 85% of a CPS court report involved the worker's complaints about the young father and his rudeness and menacing behavior toward her and her staff, including an incident of hostility in the parking lot. We agreed that the fellow's intimidating conduct was reprehensible, and we worked successfully with him to improve his approach to everyone he encountered. However, we did not feel these incidents had anything to do with the initial complaint of medical neglect against his paramour. Because of the parking lot incident, we suggested to CPS that the worker had been compromised and could not be expected to remain objective. She was nonetheless retained on the case.

Though usually abused, category 3 data can be useful for one thing—assessing parental motivation, which is difficult to examine with more formal procedures. We were once embroiled in a case in which a single mother surrendered her children to CPS while serving a brief stint in jail for a nonviolent crime. We took the case, not realizing that we had been selected as ringers, intended to fail so that CPS could make a case for terminating the woman's rights. When we began to succeed, CPS promptly fired us. We were prepared to testify on the mother's behalf, but it was not our place to approach the court. She had to launch the case herself and call us as witnesses. We referred her to the best attorney in town and even asked a case manager from the community mental health center to take her to the first appointment. Unfortunately, when the attorney wanted a $500 retainer (well below his usual fee), the woman balked. We discussed the consequences of inadequate representation—that she would probably lose rights to her children—but the woman said she couldn't afford the attorney. We suggested she take advantage of the 3% unemployment rate and get a job, but she declined.

At this point I recommended closing the case and retracting the therapists from the fray. CPS had behaved very badly, repeatedly violating this woman's rights to due process. Yet she had been just as unmotivated in refusing to spend the money to rescue her children in an easily winnable case. Of course, she should not have had to spend the money to get competent counsel under our judicial system; however, her unwillingness to hire the attorney caused her to fail my category 3 test, which I believe was both reliable and valid in assessing her willingness to sacrifice for her children. It did not help that we later learned from her mother that the woman had bought an expensive gift for her new boyfriend. Rather than hiding any of this, the therapist explained to the woman that we considered her decision an indicator of her motivation to have her children returned to her and that it influenced our decision about her case. We suggested she consider this in any request for future testimony, which of course never came because she did not hire the attorney. I had to compare this woman with Debbie (chapter 5), who sold her blood plasma to get gas money so that she could have more than the minimum visits while her outplaced children, or the young father who walked 3 miles to therapy every week. These individuals passed the category 3 tests with flying colors by showing exceptional motivation to bring their children home.

WORKING WITH THE CPS "TEAM"

CPS is designed to manage a large number of cases in an efficient manner. This will surprise those who have worked for or with the system, as it has rarely been considered adequate in either efficiency or capacity. Nevertheless, when one recognizes the sheer volume of cases it handles, regardless of outcome, process, or responsiveness to need, it is clear that the system transacts an enormous amount of business. These efficiencies can only be maintained if the system is relatively free of obstructions and conflicts between the various players. Given the issues at hand, it is unlikely that these diverse factions could routinely come together in a peaceful way. The resulting conflict is usually addressed in one of three ways, which I shall describe in the order of the least to most typical.

The Cohesive Team

From my experience the least common and most desirable option by far is one of authentic cohesion. Cohesive teams deal with overt conflict by consensus building through accommodation and assimilation, with an eye on the single mission of bringing about the best interests of the child. Therapists concerned with family injustice are pleased when a team will accommodate input different from the zeitgeist, because it allows for a change in perspective and direction of the case. Alternatively, the team may assimilate dissent by making fundamental changes in its own philosophy based on new information. The cohesive team is not just mutually respectful, but generative of a *dialectical tension* within this atmosphere of openness and trust. Ulterior motives are notably absent, political agendas eliminated, and those with power are respectful of those with knowledge. Such a team is worth examining largely because it is uncommon, but the ideal is certainly attainable, as we shall discuss in chapter 12 and briefly in the epilogue. When consensus cannot be reached, the cohesive team may respectfully agree to disagree and let the judge make the ultimate decision, just as she is designated to do.

Overt Suppression of Dissent

Without a cohesive team in a CPS case, the most likely method for dealing with conflict is to eliminate its source. As a rule, the more difficult and contentious the case, the more likely that differences of opinion will be quashed or their proponents eliminated. And it will come as no surprise to those who have struggled with the system that the obstruction most often eliminated is the therapist. I have rarely seen a GAL, caseworker, or court service worker removed or recuse himself from a case, even when a child or family is vehemently objecting to his service. Yet when they take a strong stand on the child's best interests as we recommend herein, therapists commonly come under the CPS gun.

Firing or blacklisting therapists, evaluators, or any other player simply for disagreeing with CPS is coercive, capricious, unethical, and a denial of the client's right to due process and self-determination. While this position may seem a bit extreme, we have had such bad experiences with this situation that we feel wholly justified in taking it (chapter 11). Further, as the therapist has the advantage of knowledge, experience, and relationship with the clients, her firing sacrifices an important resource. Of course, if countertransference is obviously clouding judgment, a different arrangement may need to be made, but we have rarely seen therapist firing used toward the client's best interests or with due attention to its potential iatrogenic outcomes. Firing and blacklisting are present both in privatized systems where the foster care provider pays the therapist on contract, and in state CPS agencies. Courts should pay very careful attention to who is footing the bill in such situations with an eye toward "hired gun arrangements" and act accordingly. This leads us to the next and most common level of conflict resolution.

Pseudomutuality

In the absence of a cohesive team, even a modicum of conflict can be uncomfortable for anyone who fears testifying in open court on recommendations not previously established by consensus or suppression. I discussed one case with CPS all morning and we still did not see eye to eye, though the discussion was cordial and well received on both sides. Just before the hearing I suggested we each present our testimony and let the judge choose, as I was far from certain about my position and knew CPS felt just as unsure. This was obviously the best solution and the workers initially agreed. Then to my astonishment, when the hearing began CPS instead testified *my position* and recommended that the child remain in the home. The judge disagreed with both of us and removed the child. One might wonder why CPS did not retain its initial position, which I (and ultimately the judge) found as tenable as mine. The answer can be found in the concept of *pseudomutuality*—a system's attempt to appear cohesive and harmonious at all costs, when in fact it is not.

Pseudomutual teams are examples of "groupthink" where dissent is systematically categorized as deviance and ended before it begins. On the surface they appear highly efficient and effective because they can move through a caseload with ease. Upon further scrutiny, the flaws of low conflict become apparent. There is no dialectical tension and no antithesis, only thesis. We have also found that such teams have a greater tendency to hone in on the weakest cases and avoid the more complex ones, because this also serves the goal of lowering conflict and tension. Quite commonly, CPS teams are deliberately engineered this way by contracting with therapists and evaluators who are compliant. These are essentially the "ringers" of the system—professionals who are so amiable and predictable that the CPS worker or court service officer knows what he is getting before making the referral. If she ever had it, the ringer has surrendered the ability to take an authentic and unbiased stand, which is only enhanced by the aforementioned problem of blacklisting and firing.

CONCLUSION: BEST INTERESTS, BEST PRACTICES, AND BEST OUTLOOK

Bad therapy and evaluation have no place in the process of restoring justice to families, yet they are all too prevalent for the reasons noted. With great frequency I have interviewed a child or parent who reports that she has accomplished nothing in previous therapy or has been (in my opinion) inadequately evaluated. In fact, I saw 3 youth in 1 month who all separately reported having individually oriented therapists who did little more than listen to their horrible disclosures and then respond empathically. They had not helped them reconcile with their families, with whom two were now living, nor done anything to help them put their abuse in context. One did recommend a book, however. These youth have not had their sense of justice restored or their best interests met. In fact, one young man of 17, without any prompting from me, stated, "I think what I have here is a problem of injustice." When I agreed and explained it to him as I have to the reader of this book, he said, "You know . . . no other counselor has been able to make me understand the things you have." To which I replied, "Maybe it's you who haven't been able to make them understand." He smiled.

Regardless of its quality or quantity, all therapy and evaluation in these cases has *impact* and thus it needs to meet not just the minimum practice standards, but the best. Our decisions and interventions are, as one judge put it, a potential death penalty for the family. As such they must be taken quite seriously. Good therapy can have a positive impact whether it follows this model or not. However, bad therapy of this or any model is not only unhelpful to the client, it *fills a void of client need with unhelpfulness.* Thus, many a family has been directed to treatment by the court or CPS, received bad therapy, and then returned with the edict that they are untreatable—utterly hopeless. In the case of the three young people just mentioned, bad therapy led them to the point of removal from their homes or foster placements. In fact, the parents of each child had cited their previous attempts at therapy as a primary reason that the youth were hopeless and should be placed. "We've tried all that before," said one parent in our initial phone consult. "It hasn't done a bit of good." Having later met with these kids and their families, I understand why. Even worse are poorly conducted evaluations, because they carry the full weight of expert opinion and are much more difficult to recognize by the layperson.

For the therapist, this work is excruciatingly difficult and pays very poorly. My colleagues, who know me from our more profitable ventures, are always surprised to learn that our institute takes Medicaid and private foster care contracts at half of our usual and customary rate. But it is also the most satisfying of any work I have conducted, and thus we continue to have a positive outlook on these cases and our role as evaluators and therapists in them. To do good therapy and see a single child returned to a safer and more just home, free from the intrigue of the system, creates an excitement few experiences can match. To share the very spiritual environment of an apology session, to watch as the contrition process unfolds, is unlike any other therapy. To intervene in the larger system to help it heal families as its default mission is remarkably rewarding. And with that hopeful closing, we turn now to the conceptualization of and intervention in foster care placement.

NOTES

1. For this reason it is improper for CPS ever to have the power of purse string or blacklisting over evaluators, although almost always they do.
2. Throughout this book I have deliberately used this term idiosyncratically. In many social services systems, "reintegration" means going home. We separate this from "reunification" because it works better conceptually as a process and not an outcome and allows us to discuss each separately.

CHAPTER 9

Tracks and Strategies in the Foster Care Crisis

> If you try to give an institution of the state, or of any government, anything like the love one is meant to invest in a family—and if the institution is an orphanage and you succeed in giving it love—then you will create a monster: An orphanage that is not a way-station to a better life, but an orphanage that is the first and last stop, and the only station the orphan will accept.
>
> —John Irving, *The Cider House Rules* (1985)

When we began this work we had no concepts, strategies, or language to describe working with foster children and their families, and thus no way of communicating that work to others. As we struggled for a working model, we found the best analogy of outplacement to be that of a hostage crisis. This is not meant to be sardonic. Foster care is quite simply a situation in which a powerful other takes a child from the parent and then sets up a contract for his return. This particular contract comes in the form of an ordeal in which the clients must attend a series of odd encounters in professional offices where people speak in a strange language, write secret things about them, and invariably point them to a class or therapy so they can learn to parent their children according to ambiguous and ever-changing guidelines. The family and child must go to courtrooms where attorneys they did not hire talk about their case a great deal to each other and far less to them. To meet the ransom, the parent must engage in the evaluation, go to the therapist, attend the classes, endure the secrets, appear in the courtroom, learn the strange language, and allow herself to be talked about long enough and with enough enthusiasm so that the powerful others will let the child go free. As an ordeal, the process is also designed to weed out those who will not endure it.

Before continuing, I must make two things quite explicit:

1. I recognize implicitly that the intended purpose of this abduction is benevolent, and not the base self-interest of political ideology or monetary gain.
2. In many cases the *theory* of foster care is a necessary solution to a difficult problem.

Unfortunately as noted throughout this text and supported in the literature, the practice of foster care is often the problem to the solution, falling far short of its theory in process and outcome. This means that the hostage crisis can easily turn from benevolent to malign before anyone, even those directly involved, realize it. Across hundreds of cases, we have found that when foster care goes bad, it nearly always does so along one of several predictable tracks. And as prediction is the core of intervention, such a model can be invaluable in guiding our practice.

THE PYGMALION COMPLEX

Many cases begin on the first track, going wrong under the guise of doing right—the heartfelt desire for a child to reach her greatest potential. George Bernard Shaw's *Pygmalion* (more famous and far more genial as the 1956 musical adaptation *My Fair Lady*) finds Professor Henry Higgins taking a bet that he can turn "guttersnipe" Eliza Doolittle into a proper lady. Yet in the end it is Higgins who learns real civility, realizing far too late that the measure of a person is in her character, not her social graces. In these cases, the system is Higgins, attempting to externally enhance the lives and social circumstances of children in foster care rather than enhancing their natural homelife. Despite data to the contrary, the system's participants firmly believe the best life for the child is with a family of the system's choosing who will raise the child with the proper middle-class values, usually leading to disinterest in or even hostility to the biological family. It may surprise those who have not seen it first hand, but a major contributor to the Pygmalion complex is the "cuteness factor" of a child, which makes the child more adoptable. Thus, when we have a very cute little child as a client in foster care, we become vigilant for Pygmalion behavior on the part of the caseworker and foster family. This may be as subtle as the search for more serious pathology in the biological family or the tactical placement of a child in a more adoptive home. It may be as overt as sending the child to a far-away placement or restricting unsupervised access even when the problem is not one of violence or sexual abuse. Regardless of the specific behaviors, the therapist can often spot a Pygmalion worker by his attitude regarding the family contrasted with the objective seriousness of the offense.

In any case of outplacement, the therapist must help the biological family to improve their parenting style, set boundaries, invoke structure, adopt nonviolent methods of punishment, and go through a process of apology and repentance for any offenses of omission or commission. However, in Pygmalion cases biological families may be held to a much higher standard, requiring even more of this than seems appropriate. Wexler (1995) offers an appendix that includes a checklist of 99 items purported to be standards for the non-neglectful parent and challenges any parent to meet them at the required 63% level. Though the list is quite outdated (Polansky, 1978), it does make the point of how easy it is to use a seemingly objective instrument sans normative data to unfairly judge a family. This is the lot for families caught up in the system, especially when they are the subject of the Pygmalion complex. In response, the therapist must advocate for realistic goals and fair measures of success, asking the team if the family would have to meet the same expectations if not already involved with the system. This tack invokes the standard of the "good-enough" family, which sets minimum acceptable standards compared with their own culture rather than a less attainable and less appropriate standard. This should be the sole manifesto in such cases.

To the uninitiated, the simple act of setting goals, sticking to them, and measuring the outcome seems obvious. Yet we have seen a distinct lack of interest on the part of child protective services (CPS) for this sort of contractual obligation, preferring instead to maximize its own flexibility while minimizing client leeway. If goals are clear, then goals can be achieved, and all parties can be held accountable for the outcome and the stated response to that outcome. In practice, this means that a family may "pay the ransom" and still not have its children back; one list of goals is reached, only to be replaced by a second list or an extension of time "to see how things go." This is the rationale by which CPS disregards progress it sees as illusory or at least transitory, ignoring the fact that this generates a poorer prognosis by creating hopelessness, disillusionment, and ultimately a self-fulfilling prophecy. Moreover, we have seen numerous cases for which time cannot reasonably make any difference. The family will either succeed or fail when and only when a well-managed reunification finally occurs. If anything, prospects diminish with time and the inevitable crystallization of outplacement on child and family dysfunction.

Even though she may advocate well, the therapist has little choice but to help the family struggle through a Pygmalion complex. If the therapist becomes rebellious and refuses to help the family meet the demands of CPS because they are excessive or coercive, the family may not regain the child for some time, if at all. In the end, however, if they can outlast the system, families in Pygmalion cases actually have a fairly good chance of reunification, because their cute little children usually wear out their welcome in CPS long before they are extricated from their parents. The manner by which they accomplish this brings us to the next section.

THE RANSOM OF RED CHIEF

In the O. Henry short story *The Ransom of Red Chief,* two con men kidnap the son of a rich man, only to find they have taken a turn-of-the-century version of the *Home Alone* kid. Anxious to be rid of him, they go to the spot where they have demanded a $2,000 ransom be placed. Instead, they find a note addressed to "Two Desperate Men," which reads in part:

> In regard to the ransom you ask for the return of my son. I think you are a little high in your demands, and I hereby make you a counter-proposition, which I am inclined to believe you will accept. You bring Johnny home and pay $250 in cash, and I agree to take him off your hands. You had better come at night, for the neighbours believe he is lost, and I couldn't be responsible for what they would do to anybody they saw bringing him back.

The con men scrounge up enough money to meet the father's demand.

There is rarely such wry humor in the real-life Red Chief, though her similar talent for civil disobedience is remarkable. Sometimes starting out as cute and lovable, she has eventually started fires, harmed pets, sexually and physically abused foster-siblings, and been generally disagreeable to the point of frequent and unceremonious ejection from her placements. September remains to this day my best example of a Red Chief, having logged 59 moves between the age of 14 and 18.

Sometimes we recommend sending Red Chief home for a "trial run" with a host of services to assist the parents, noting that she is about to force a placement disruption anyhow. Our hope is to bail out while the system still has some perceived influence over the child and family. Though this has worked on many occasions, such recommendations often go unheeded until the placement is disrupted and the system is forced to implement the recommendations by default. In one Monday case conference, we recommended sending a Red Chief home on Friday because the placement was deteriorating and we felt the mother was ready to handle him with some external support. CPS refused even to consider this—until Friday at 5 P.M. when they lost the foster home and the children's shelter was full. Citing our Monday meeting, they simply sent the child home. Far from a lucky break in the case, such a move etches an indelible impression on Red Chief that he can escape a bad situation through wild and unpredictable conduct. Thus, he becomes an even greater terror, taxing his parents' limited resources and not infrequently reentering the system. We have even had some parents literally replicate O. Henry by asking that the child not be returned home. They claim that he is now too difficult to control after a round of foster care, particularly if outplacement has led to a hospitalization or a restrictive group home for behavior disturbance.

There is also a troubling tendency for caseworkers to implicitly or explicitly blame a Red Chief for her problems, even when she is outplaced for abuse or neglect. Routinely, workers admonish young victims to "quit acting up at the foster home, or the judge won't let you go home," thus faulting the abused child for her retention in the system. Here, the therapist must explain how unhelpful this is and ask to change the entire frame to one in which everyone focuses on "doing his/her job." The therapist calls the family together with the professionals and assigns a job for everyone and what each must do to complete it. The child's job is to be good for the foster parents under the direction of parents, the parents' job is to follow the case plan under the direction of the therapist, and the therapist's job is to help everyone work together under the direction of the court.

Essential in such cases is the enhancement of the biological parent's skills at discipline (i.e., encouragement of discipleship in the children). We coach the parent to implore the child to behave in foster care and to follow the foster parents' directives almost without question. With our best foster parents, we form a team wherein they provide information on how the child behaves in person or over the phone, and the real parents develop interventions to correct the behavior. Our favorite variation of this technique, and one especially suited for young children, is what we call "my mother's voice." In this intervention, we ask the parent to record his voice on a cassette tape recorder instructing the child in proper behavior in the foster home, interspersed with a series of metaphorical stories of Nancy Davis (Davis, Custer, Marcey, & Solarz, 1996; Davis, Custer, & Solarz, 1990) or familiar songs. In cooperation with the foster parents, the child is asked to listen to the tapes each evening and to remember the directives of the parent. While no substitute for an efficient reunification, these techniques are valuable for maintaining fragile placements, which in turn make for more auspicious case plans. Of note, there is considerable support in the literature for involving biological and foster families in such a spirit of cooperation, yet this remains the exception in most CPS agencies, especially family-phobic ones. And nowhere is this more apparent nor the outcome more unfortunate than when Red Chief rears his head.

THE STOCKHOLM SYNDROME

As difficult as they may seem, Pygmalion and Red Chief cases are not as problematic for reunification as the next two tracks, both of which involve countermotivation not within the system but in various elements of the family. The third track parallels the renowned Stockholm syndrome in which the child becomes so infatuated with the foster parents, group home, or custody in general that he simply refuses to go home. This usually appears in the most ideal placement homes, those that have a true sense of mission, incite discipleship, and spend money freely on their charges. Ironically, many of these fine families are actually pressing for reunification, which seems to paradoxically discharge the natural rebelliousness of the child and make her want to stay even more. A variant of this is what I term the "Stockholm illusion" of a child before he has really encountered the system. These children feel their lives would be greatly enhanced, or at least their parents would get a powerful jolt of reason, if they were put into foster care. Unfortunately, this illusion of the grass being greener elsewhere is rarely realized, and more than one child has been horrified at the outcome when they actually get what they have asked for.

In Stockholm cases it is improper for a therapist to request that a foster home become substandard. He can, however, ask that it become more aversive in authoritative ways (e.g., setting strict curfews, chore lists, and properly supervised involvement with friends). In one case I consulted, a family-friendly CPS worker intentionally placed a belligerent girl with a Stockholm illusion into the strictest foster home he could find, expecting that she would get over her tantrum with her family. It worked quite well, in fact, and the girl came out of the experience with a new appreciation of her mother's style of discipline. I have recommended the same thing myself on occasion. Additionally, the therapist should work with the biological family to try and "win back" the child, typically using the contrition model of reconciliation. If, on the other hand, the child was placed for his own bad conduct, authoritative but loving styles of parenting are taught. In this one particular instance, time is actually a useful strategy, because it allows homesickness to set in and novelty to fade. Conversely, rapid reunification plans actually exacerbate these cases, as the child learns quickly how to switch back and forth from this track to Red Chief to derail the case plan.

When the bond of foster child and foster parent is genuine, and the foster parents are exceptional, the therapist may enlist them as a sort of "godparent" to remain in the life of the child after reunification.[1] This can be as simple as sending a note back and forth on occasion, to establishing respite-care visits on weekends. Additionally, such godparents make excellent protectors in the contrition process. While requiring a great deal of creativity, patience, and flexibility on the part of therapist and system, it may well be worth the effort.

THE UNCONDITIONAL SURRENDER

The opposite of the Stockholm syndrome is the "unconditional surrender" wherein the parent becomes so overwhelmed with violence, guilt, stress, anger, substance abuse, psychopathology, personality dysfunction, or simple disinterest that they actively or passively capitulate to the system. Given the gravity of this situation, the first strategy is to carefully discriminate one type of surrender from another, as each requires a different response.

The first type is the most benign, resulting from an errant perception of the child's best interest. The inverse of the Stockholm syndrome, these families believe their children are better off in care. Madanes (1990) referred to these as "containment" cases and suggested that the therapist guide the parent to believe that she and not the system is really the best remedy for her child's situation. Therapy may also help parents to trust the skills they do have (Haley, 1984) or learn those they don't. In more severe containment cases, paradoxical strategies have worked, wherein the therapist simply agrees that raising the child is too difficult and that someone else must do it. However, this must be used very selectively after more direct approaches are exhausted as it can backfire on occasion.

A second type is generated by the system itself. This involves family-phobic caseworkers pressing for surrender intentionally, or in some cases unwittingly. Here, the therapist must challenge the system while simultaneously encouraging the parent to succeed. Sometimes, as in chapter 10, it is necessary to use very confrontational means to dislodge parents who have become submerged in the reality of their situation. In this the therapist takes on a sort of drill-sergeant mentality in which he will not let the parent recruit give up, no matter how agonizing basic training becomes. To those who have never done it, or who feel they could not because of personality, it may seem surprising that a beleaguered parent would serve out this sort of enlistment. But just as the recruit knows his sergeant wants him to graduate, so does the weakened parent realize the benevolence of the therapist who is pushing so hard. This strategy is never appropriate in the next type of surrender, one in which the parents are genuinely disinterested in their children or demonstrably too disturbed to care for them.

A parent may simply abandon the child to the system and depart, sometimes relinquishing her rights and sometimes not. This may be due to the poor character of the parent who overtly abdicates her role in favor of her own self-interest. It is most common in sex abuse cases when a mother sides with the offender, blames her child for lying, and refuses to participate in the reunification process until the child recants. It may also come more benevolently from a parent in the throes of severe mental illness or substance abuse, which renders him incapable of meeting even the minimum requirements of the reunification process. In less obvious cases, the parent presents well for some period of time, only to self-sabotage the case plan again and again, often blaming the system or the child for his or her failings. In one such case, the father was a wonderful participant in therapy, attending at least twice a month and helping his daughter through her bouts of bipolar illness with aplomb. However, he did not feel he could manage her at home, and in assessing the situation I could understand why. This Red Chief girl was so difficult that on occasion I refused to see her in my office. Her foul language and loud demeanor frightened other children and offended the adults in the waiting room. I explained to her the concept of free will and that, bipolar or not, I would only see her in the parking lot until she shaped up. Over the next several months my staff and I made substantial progress, including a psychological evaluation, a complete overhaul of her medication, and a great dose of my drill-sergeant routine. Ultimately, after many individual and family sessions in the office and several in the parking lot, all of which amounted to a test of wills, the girl was indistinguishable from any other. In fact, she was better than most, charming and quite likable. Her drug problem was in remission, her sexual behavior managed, and her temper under control. At the case plan, I suggested we move to the reintegration stage and begin weekend visits. The team agreed.

Her father never returned to therapy, no longer participated in the case plans, and did not even attend court when subpoenaed. The youth deteriorated.

It is not always so easy to spot the surrendering parent. In a flawed system of child protection, they are like a clear radio signal surrounded by static. Thus, it is best to assume nothing in this regard until the static is tuned out, a reasonable evaluation of the entire context of the case has been made, and the locus of the problem is found. In the above case, the system did everything right for this girl and her father, and she was ready to go home. His surrender stood out like a sore thumb.

WHEN ALL ELSE FAILS: AGING OUT

Sometimes it is impossible to reach reunification, adoption, or even long-term foster care, leaving the therapist in a truly unenviable position of being the most important, consistent adult in the life of the foster child. Before discussing this final track of the foster care crisis, which focuses on an individual approach to the treatment of family injustice, I implore the reader to note the operative words "*when all else fails.*" Working with a child sans family or permanency should only be attempted when there is literally no hope of a better solution.

A classic practitioner of self-utilization, the therapist in *Good Will Hunting* (Bender, Van Sant, Damon, & Affleck, 1997) uses stories of his own life and a series of directives, both subtle and wildly overt, to open his client to adulthood and healthy interpersonal relationships. In doing so he provides a parental influence for a boy who was battered by men in his life and ultimately abandoned by his mother. At the same time, the therapist helps Will maintain and enhance his attachments to the only real "family" he has, boys from his neighborhood who are like brothers to him. The therapist guides Will in how to attain a meaningful relationship with his new girlfriend and how to make his love for her the defining factor in his life. In fact, many a therapist has missed the point that this is really a movie about couples and family therapy done through the individual.

The real-life victims of family and systemic failure have become "orphans of the living" (Toth, 1997), finding themselves lost in the system and cast adrift at age 18 without permanency or even a predictable place to finish their adolescence. The data on foster care to adult transitions are generally abysmal. In some states the system must care for children until they are 21. In most, a child can stay in the system voluntarily, though precious few do. Even if they have a foster home that will keep them that long, the need to "leave home" overpowers what better judgment they might have, and they cut the strings as soon as possible. Unfortunately, this almost always leaves them with *nothing*. Despite the vague and limited promise of "independent living" programs, few foster children are ready for life outside the system, and the state rarely funds them adequately to get them on their feet. The worst cases emerge among youth who have been placed in group homes or other institutions, because at age 18 they have undeveloped skills of independence and overdeveloped yearnings for freedom.

The bottom line is the same for these youths as it was for the mythical Will Hunting—someone has to raise them, and this is rarely their foster family at the time they age out. Except for very strong missionary homes with selfless commitment to the children they take, *this job will fall to the therapist.* We can debate the propriety of this from any of a number of standpoints (boundaries, paternalism, directive versus nondirective therapy, enabling a flawed system, countertransference, therapist needs, etc.) but nothing changes the fact that a very skilled therapist is the only person who has a reasonable chance to serve in this role over the long tenure of a lost foster child and after that child's release. Realizing this and not being afraid to express it, we have received an increasing number of these cases over the last 10 years. In response, we have developed an Ericksonian style of psychotherapy that has been successful in "raising" these youths. This sort of therapeutic parenting has proven essential in giving young people somewhere to turn when they have no competent family to listen to their problems, provide intelligent advice, help them learn to network, offer stern lectures, interview and critique their paramours, teach them to budget, express caring, and above all else say the simple words that make the difference to a youth who has rarely heard them—"I'm really proud of you."

In no other form of therapy will issues of personal influence be more at play. Thus, if one chooses to work in this way, she must adhere closely to the following guidelines.

- *Manage countertransference.* Therapists must undergo a careful review of their own issues to be sure of the motivations in taking on such a role. There is nothing wrong with a therapist deriving a sense of emotional gratification from his work, but this must always take a distant back seat to the client's needs. Moreover, an attempt to meet narcissistic needs in doing this sort of therapy is akin to the missionary's desire to be thanked.
- *Maintain consistency.* A therapist must not undertake such a case if she cannot keep it over the long haul. Children who have lost their families are fragile enough when they come in. Therapists are not interchangeable when practicing this way. Unfortunately for those interested in profit, young people who leave the system usually lose their Medicaid benefits and most do not secure jobs with insurance. We are all expected to do a bit of pro bono work, and this is a good place to practice for free.
- *Manage your caseload.* Because these cases take extra time, energy, and raw emotion, and because they accumulate over long periods of time, therapists must be very judicious about how many young people they take into this sort of therapy. I avoid having more than five or six such cases, some of which I have followed now for 10 years. September is one. Additionally, these young people must know that, though they are important, they are not alone in needing access to my time. It is one thing to be consistent, but another to be on-call daily for 5 years.
- *Maintain boundaries.* Because these relationships are so close to that of a parent, the therapist must have good boundaries in balance with therapeutic intimacy. Therapists must remember that, while they are exercising a parent-like influence on these young people, *they are not the child's parent.* This is not a social or reciprocal relationship. It is therapy. This needn't be imprinted onto the youth (or therapist) at every encounter, but it does need to be gently clarified from time to time.
- *Clarify roles.* While the young person is still connected to the system, everyone must understand that *she* is the client and not the system. While necessarily and frequently clarified in any CPS case, it cannot be overstated with lost youth. I have repeatedly had to be very blunt with CPS workers who did not understand that I am not their proxy in getting a late teen to behave in certain ways or to agree to certain things, just because they have contracted my services. If I believe that something is in a child's best interests psychologically and emotionally, I will work on that goal even if the client convincingly objects, just as do real parents in such situations. However, when the system expects to me to meet its needs in the social control of such a youth, it is usually disappointed. Sometimes it is hostile.
- *Seek consultation.* Whenever involved in such a case, one must seek good supervision and consultation to maintain all of the critical elements. Peer consultation with a supervisor trained in this or a similar approach will take note of obstacles to successful therapy and make the therapist aware of them

before they ensnare him in an unproductive track. However, supervisors who see the entire matter as a conceptual boundary violation are likely to urge so much reservation as to make the entire experience useless.

If you do this work well you will receive the same reward all parents and parent-figures do—you will be fired. This is as it should be if we are to complete the most critical phase of the therapeutic parenting—leaving home. Ultimately, I see these young adults perhaps two or three times a year and am rarely involved in their daily life for any period of time. When a crisis erupts, I help to resolve it and then I do what a well-bounded parent would do: I make sure that I am out of the picture until my presence is requested again. In the final scene of *Good Will Hunting* we see a similar phenomenon—Will leaving Boston for a new life with the young woman he has learned how to love. It is no coincidence that the car he is driving was given to him by his "family," the three neighborhood boys he'd grown up with, and that his last act in his hometown is to leave a heartfelt goodbye for his therapist.

CONCLUSION: FOSTER CARE AND THE JOURNEY TOWARD JUSTICE

Children are generally ill-served by any of the tracks discussed in this chapter, and therapists should work alongside families to limit the injustice that foster care may add to what the child has already experienced in his home. There is, of course, an additional track that we all hope and strive for. It is the journey of the child from the injustice of his family to a benevolent system where he remains only long enough to be successfully reunified with a contrite and reconciled family—or, after all attempts have failed, to move on to a loving adoptive home.

In walking the difficult road of foster care with a child in custody and her family, there are usually more twists and turns than the cleverest mystery novel, and it is usually a nerve-racking experience for everyone involved. Recently, in the midst of a particularly difficult case, I had a dream in which a cardboard box was being held in state custody and I had been contracted to take its case and get it out. But no matter what I did, I could not get the box released. I woke up in a state of great anxiety with the vivid image of this cardboard box sitting in front of a judge's bench relying on my precarious skill to guide it through the system.

I should like very much never to have this dream again.

NOTE

1. I am indebted to Cloé Madanes's consultation for this idea of godparents.

CHAPTER 10

You Can't Fight the System

Yes: in six months—in three if she has a good ear and a quick tongue—I'll take her anywhere and pass her off as anything. We'll start today: Now! this moment! Take her away and clean her. . . .
—Henry Higgins in George Bernard Shaw's, *Pygmalion* (1916/1999)

"They're not playing fair in this case," Melissa said. "This kid's being victimized worse in foster care than she ever was in her home, and her little boy . . . where do I even begin? I really need help." Melissa was a very young therapist who had sought our consult after being battered with several very difficult cases. She begged to present first in our supervision group, and was nearly breathless in her description of the case. "This 16-year-old girl, Bobbi, got taken out of her parents' home for truancy. She has a a little boy named Zach, who just turned 3. Both are in custody. Bobbi's caseworker is just a little gung-ho. Cassie is hell-bent on getting Zach away from Bobbi. She even went out to the foster home last week and threatened that if Bobbi didn't give Zach up, then she'd never be allowed to go home to her folks."

At best this was undue influence. At worst it amounted to extortion. Without question, it was a serious ethical violation, a point not lost on the young therapist.

"Cassie told the former therapist that her goal was to 'get this little boy away from *those people*.' That therapist got so uncomfortable with the case that he resigned after seeing Bobbi twice. He didn't want any part of it. When he heard I'd gotten the referral he got a release and called to warn me that Cassie was on this 'mission'."

"How far has she gotten?" I asked.

"Bobbi and Zach aren't even placed together now. When they first went in, Cassie had them sent to a bridge home."

We called bridge homes "shopping homes"—foster families who took a series of children until they found one they wanted to adopt. To have made such a placement for a teen mother and her child signaled Cassie's intent to separate the two from the start. It was an unusually bold move.

Melissa continued. "About 2 months into the placement, they saw what they claimed were bruises on Zach and they pulled Bobbi out. Then Cassie went out to Bobbi's new foster home and delivered the ultimatum. It was just days into the placement, and of course Bobbi was still shaky so she was an easy target. What's really amazing is that when CPS actually investigated the report, the allegations were unfounded. No abuse was confirmed." But the pair remained apart.

Bobbi had been taken from her child, leaving him with highly adoptive parents on an unsubstantiated charge of child abuse. The case certainly warranted attention. However, before we could proceed, it was imperative to know what Bobbi really wanted to do with Zach. If she was genuinely considering giving him up, then the behavior of CPS might turn out to be an inappropriate means to a just end. Cassie's tactics might be unsavory, but we couldn't go against Bobbi's real wishes just to prove that point.

"She wants to keep him," Melissa said firmly. "I've been over it with her very carefully. But she's also scared to death. She says that every time she makes up her mind to keep Zach, somebody from CPS shows up and tries to talk her out of it. Last week when I went to the first case conference, I told them that my understanding was that Bobbi had made her decision and that they should respect it."

I knew this had not gone over well. "What did they say to that?" I asked.

"They tried to fire me," Melissa said. "They were very diplomatic about it. They told me that perhaps they should get her hooked up with a counselor *of her own* who could really work with her on clarifying what was best for her and her child. Her family told them they already had a counselor they were happy with. CPS insisted that she needed *her own counselor.*" It was a typical tack for CPS—trying to divide and conquer a family. Despite Melissa's careful assertion of the priorities of treatment, with Zach and Bobbi at the top, Cassie went on to portray her as singularly an advocate for Bobbi's parents, Jesse and Beth.

Of course, Cassie had much to be concerned about in allowing Melissa to continue the case. Like Henry Higgins in Shaw's play, Cassie chose to see Zach as a child in need of rescue and pressured the young girl to surrender him. Facing Cassie's ultimatum, Bobbi first gave in, then retracted. Melissa had begun to expose this plan and thus became an obstruction to it. To remove the obstruction, Cassie simply stated that Melissa was biased toward Bobbi's parents and thus in a multiple relationship. However, Melissa skillfully restated her priorities and reminded Cassie that under CPS's own rules and regulations, the family was allowed to have a therapist of their choosing. Further, though CPS liked to ignore it, Bobbi and her parents had not lost their rights under the law. If they pushed the issue in court, the judge would side with Melissa and allow her to continue with the girl and her family.

Yet even as this conflict was underway, a new crisis was developing. Following Bobbi's most recent bout of ambivalence, the bridge family had become impatient and asked for Zach to be removed. They wanted a child they could keep and were apparently less concerned about the impact on the little boy.

As CPS allowed no visitation, Zach already missed his grandparents, who had been central caregivers in his life. He was very attached to them. Then his mother had been taken from him, and a few weeks thereafter his foster family sent him away. Not surprisingly, he became deeply depressed and difficult to manage. In fact, when Melissa finally got the family into conjoint sessions, our training staff behind the mirror witnessed one of the most despondent 3-year-olds we'd ever seen. Zach wouldn't play, despite a room full of toys, choosing instead to hang in the arms of his family members like a limp dishrag.

As is common with Pygmalion cases, simple interventions with the family take a peculiar but necessary backseat to the organization of the larger system. Instead of focusing on Bobbi's truancy, her fledgling parenting skills, or the hierarchy failure in her family, Melissa was forced to deal with symptoms related to the placement itself. To get back on track, we decided to attend another case conference with Melissa and CPS shortly after the move to Zach's second foster home. Bobbi and her family were not invited, as CPS felt we needed to get "all the professionals on the same sheet of music." This, of course, meant that CPS wanted to pressure Melissa to support their position on the case and quit being obstreperous.

Cassie and her supervisor made their position very clear—they announced that given Zach's despondency, something truly terrible must have happened to him. They wanted Melissa to find out what Bobbi or her parents had done to Zach to make him "so disturbed." They suggested that it was probably sexual abuse, though Cassie admitted to having no training and little field experience in this area. She also had no evidence. What she did have were "rumors about the family that the father had molested Bobbi and her sisters." When pressed, they admitted that this rumor came from Bobbi's 18-year-old ex-boyfriend who was now trying to get custody of Zach. Apparently Cassie considered him a reliable source on the topic of incest, even as she had successfully petitioned the court to supervise his visitations with Zach. When asked, she admitted she had reported her suspicion to the investigative unit of CPS, and a worker had met with Bobbi at her school to ask if she had been molested. Confused at this turn of events and a bit scared, the girl summoned all her courage and admitted that she *had* been sexually abused. She described the incident that took place when she was 9 years old and laid the blame firmly at the feet of her then 15-year-old cousin Ralph. She had never told anyone this before. The investigator asked if her father had also molested her. He reported she got a strange look in her eye and said as convincingly as any young girl he'd interviewed, "Well . . . of course not . . . he's my dad."

Despite yet another unfounded allegation, Cassie was convinced that Zach was "just not normal," reiterating how badly the child must have been treated to come out this way. In fact, she noted that Zach was the most disturbed 3-year-old she'd ever worked with. With over 6 months of experience since receipt of her bachelor's degree in social work, Cassie could safely make this assertion, though we could almost hear her supervisor groan at the absurdity of her pontification. The supervisor had been at CPS a full 8 months longer, so her specialization was similarly limited.

Against this surreal scene of family phobia, I could not help but pose the obvious questions. Might Zach be depressed because he'd lost his mother and grandparents? Could this be the "terrible thing" that had happened to him? Might the placement disruption with the on-and-off adoptive parents have impacted him adversely? Wouldn't this be consistent with the research on foster care—that it can have a devastating and detaching effect on very young children?

There was no response, though Cassie and her supervisor seemed nervous. They confessed they had not studied this research, but they had read the current laws on foster care and adoption. Cassie mentioned that under permanency planning guidelines, we had a 15-month window before we had to move to termination. "We're getting close to that deadline," she reminded the group.

"What are you talking about?" Melissa countered. "This case has only been in the system for 6 months. Why would we even consider termination at this point? Even if we followed those guidelines to the letter, we're 9 months away from even having to file that petition. Even if the time had elapsed, you can't terminate parental rights without a legitimate attempt at reunification." Melissa also gave them a copy of the report she had written and a release from the family for all videotapes of the sessions, both of which she was submitting at the next court hearing. She explained that the tapes of Bobbi and her parents documented the quality of parenting CPS could be expect from the family, as well as specific areas for improvement. She also mentioned they were very moving films.

This prompted a quick response. The following week, CPS wrote a letter apologizing for any implication that Melissa was not doing a good job with Bobbi and Zach, assuring her that she should continue the case. They also asked to see the videotapes. We invited them to a showing, but before they could come a new crisis arose.

RED CHIEF EMERGES

The second foster home was expressing great displeasure with Zach, and once again they placed the blame squarely on Bobbi and her family. "I don't know what *those people* did to Zach, but he just isn't right," the foster mother told Melissa in a manner too reminiscent of Cassie's language to have been unaffected by her. "He throws tantrums and he won't share with the others. He stands for hours and does nothing. He won't play. We try to engage him, but he just falls out. And then! The other day, he sat there with his legs spread apart, and he just drove this little truck back and forth between his legs—back and forth. There is something wrong with that." There was the distinct hint that the foster mother was looking for sexual abuse in every behavior, no matter how benign. Other than his truck driving, Zach's only activity was fighting with the other foster children in the home.

Apart from their suspicious nature, born of a thorough debriefing from Cassie, it became apparent that Zach's second foster parents were interested in taking children that were easy to parent. Unfortunately, few such children remained in a system beset by escalating severity. Further, with Zach they had now acquired four 3- to 4-year-olds, even though they were not so licensed. To keep order, they had the children on a strict regimen that included very short haircuts to ensure easy grooming and bedtimes of 6:30 P.M. Though Melissa had questioned this treatment, CPS would not challenge such practices nor did they expect foster parents to take any therapeutic advice, no matter how benevolent. Many homes short of demand, they couldn't risk losing any placements. After several weeks, Red Chief Zach continued his isolation, depression, and acting out, and the family began to talk of removal.

At that point we suggested that CPS go ahead and send Zach and Bobbi back home with services in place through Melissa's organization, particularly as Zach was not old enough to overpower his family with his new tools of misbehavior. However, CPS refused this option, believing they could hold the placement and because early childhood homes were comparatively easy to find. Further, they were on record as favoring termination of Bobbi's rights and to retract now would question their judgment and make it difficult to send Zach to adoption.

CAPITULATION AND REDEMPTION

Throughout this period, we guided Bobbi and her family to instruct Zach on how to behave in the foster home to "do his job." This was difficult, of course, as the 3-year-old was really too young to be given instructions once or twice a week, and Bobbi and her parents were notoriously bad at setting limits. Nevertheless, after a few sessions Zach actually began to behave better after his visits than at any other point in the week, suggesting even to a skeptical CPS that such sessions were helpful. We were about to upgrade this plan by adding sessions for Bobbi and Zach in the foster home when we encountered an unexpected reversal of fortune. Focused on the Pygmalion and Red Chief phases of the case, we wholly missed the emergence of Bobbi's unconditional surrender. Cassie's pressure on the girl to give up Zach had taken a greater toll than we realized. Despite a very positive evaluation completed by a third party, Cassie continued to berate the girl's parenting and speak ill of her family. Bobbi had completed her case plan by attending school religiously, even when she came down with a severe case of the flu. Initially her learning disabilities made each day an encounter with embarrassment and failure until Melissa arranged for her to be placed on an individual education plan (IEP). Her school situation improved dramatically at that point. Now all that kept her in custody was Zach, and the standoff with CPS. As her parents were adamant that she not surrender the little boy, she was left in a double bind that made her appear more ambivalent than she was. Melissa had shored up Bobbi, but somewhere along the way the pincer became so tight that Bobbi simply stopped "doing her job" and passively surrendered.

The antecedents of surrender were laid during Zach's second placement, when CPS concocted a system by which Bobbi was to telephone Zach each evening as a form of visitation. It was a deceptively small thing and went almost unnoticed by Melissa and our supervision team as we focused on the larger issues at hand. But before we knew it, Cassie released the surprising data that Bobbi had not made a single phone contact with Zach in 2 weeks, and this became her principal objection to reunification. The requirement was unequivocally set up as a category 3 test of the girl's real motivation. If Bobbi didn't make the calls, CPS would argue that she was not interested enough in her child even to pick up a telephone, the instrument of communication adored by teenage girls throughout the world. The test might have been valid and reliable had it not been initiated while Zach was still in the rigid second placement where suspicion and negativity were well entrenched. Moreover, given the early bedtimes, the home required her call to come during a 45-minute window between dinner and lights-out. Worse, the foster mother made it difficult for Bobbi to get through to Zach even during this window. If Zach was unavailable, Bobbi was, at our direction, to talk to the foster mother about him and document this. Unfortunately, the woman gave only bad reports, laced with unfounded suspicions of sexual abuse and mistreatment. Bobbi's tearful aversion to this experience mounted until she found herself avoiding the phone calls altogether and making excuses to hide her irresponsibility. She knew she could not bring herself to end her relationship with her son, nor could she stand up to CPS and the foster mother, so she decided to blow the case plan and then blame the system for her failing.

We were convinced from extensive private dialog that Bobbi did want to keep Zach. Had we not been so certain, the level of influence necessary to counter the unconditional surrender would have been too severe. Yet at 16, stuck in foster care and facing undue influence, she had very little ego strength. Our best hope was to use the strength of her family to guide her back to the position of mother—something she had been denied for some time. Yet even this tack took careful maneuvering. CPS now reframed the situation as Bobbi's parents forcing her to keep Zach when she didn't really want him. At one point, they had gone so far as stopping visitation to limit the family's influence on the girl, claiming the grandparents were intrusive. Amazingly, in one case conference Cassie wondered aloud why the girl would even need contact with her parents, noting that if she really were ready to keep her child she'd also be ready to be out on her own. Once we protested this untenable position, CPS reluctantly agreed to regular conjoint therapy with all three generations. This had been our format for some time when the problem of telephone calls came up at a case conference.

At our next session, we dismissed Zach to the waiting area and the care of Bobbi's sisters to focus on getting the parents to direct their daughter. This would not be easy, of course, as the family's initial truancy charge emerged from their inability to get their children to obey. Moreover, we had to help them influence their daughter very directly while respecting her as a mother. As the techniques used are straight out of Haley's work with oppositional teens, we will dispense with commentary of the power and hierarchy side of the intervention, focusing instead on how this case exemplifies one approach to an unconditional surrender. In this particular case, the family actually takes the therapist's role in confronting the client, and the therapist simply guides the conversation through modeling and redirection.

Melissa opened the session with Bobbi, Jesse, and Beth. "We need to talk about these phone calls, Bobbi, 'cause I'm concerned. It's just gonna be really bad if you have Zach taken away because you haven't been making these calls. I don't want to see that happen. You've been doing all the work of coming to therapy, and that is the hardest part—to come in, to work on stuff, to show up every week. I just don't want something as minor as a phone call to lead them to saying you can't have Zach." She paused. "So what's going on with that?"

Bobbi had a tendency to underrespond in such situations, so we were unprepared for the sudden and unprecedented wave of emotion that emerged. "It's hard to talk to him on the phone!" she burst into sobs. "I want him to *be* with me. I don't even understand why they took him from me. It's not right." She paused, but could not collect herself. "I see a lot of people out there abusing their kids, and my son gets a bruise on the butt from a foster mom and they believe the foster mom over me."

Bobbi had always claimed that the first foster mother actually bruised

Zach and then blamed Bobbi to have her removed so they could adopt him. We doubted her story, but also knew that whatever mistreatment Zach had received fell far short of CPS's own criteria for removal.[1]

"And nobody can tell me the truth," Bobbi wept. "Everybody was too scared to tell me the truth."

As much as we felt for Bobbi's plight, our best hope was to drag her to her feet. We couldn't afford to join her in a death-spiral of bitterness. "You know, Bobbi, the stupidity of the system is no excuse for you playing this game stupidly," Melissa said with a tone both firm and caring. "It's no reason for you not to play this game right."

"I'm tired of playing the games!" Bobby lashed out. "I've been in custody for 11 months and they done *told* me I should be home—I'm only in custody 'cause of Zach. Why'd they take Zach out of the home in the first place?"

"Bobbi, your job is to call Zach," Melissa said, ignoring the girl's diversion to focus on this simple, but profoundly important issue.

"Nobody even talks to me anymore! I don't have anybody coming by. . . ." Her tears and anger combined to form a dull whine.

"Uh huh," Melissa said. "I see you twice a week and I talk to you."

Bobbi was about to respond when Jesse spoke, his voice insistent but caring, "What Melissa's telling you is you gotta make them phone calls." He then dropped an unexpected bomb on his daughter: "You don't start making them phone calls, dad's gonna stop our house visits."

Bobbi looked up in surprise, and the room fell silent as Melissa tried to determine how to retract Jesse from his ultimatum. To soften his demands would undermine his authority at exactly the moment we most needed it, but his tack was too harsh for the broken girl. Before Melissa could respond, Beth picked up the ball and began to run.

"You need to make up your mind what you want in your life," Beth said forcefully. "Look at your best friend, she abandoned her child and went to Texas—*for a guy!* And her mom is in the same position I was in before CPS walked in and took you both away from me. You have a child to think about. You need to be thinking about that child and what you want in your life. Not about guys, not about something else, worry about getting your education and worry about making a life for you and Zach, if that's what you want."

"First thing you oughta be worryin' about is your son," Jesse continued without pause. "I know you do . . . but you need to make the calls." It was a stunning example of firm parenting that we had never seen from this family before, despite several months of therapy.

"It's hard, daddy," Bobbi's sobbed. "Especially when they tell me he's sleepin' and I know he's in there in that room."

"I know it's hard," Jesse's voice broke. "So, talk to the foster mom on the phone."

Melissa followed him closely. "Ask her questions about Zach, how he's doing, what he's doing that day, if he's been bad that week, if he's making progress."

"I do! But she just keeps giving me bad reports, and it makes me feel sorry, and I hate hearing 'em." Bobbi's voice went from anger to despair as her gaze fell to the floor. "Because when Zach was with me he never did any of this stuff."

Melissa seized a chance to utilize and redirect Jesse's harsh ultimatum. "Isn't it true, Bobbi, that you need your family very badly 'cause you're in foster care and you need them to help you?" She paused. The girl did not respond. "You don't want them to just pull back and not call you and not come to see you and not show up to therapy."

"I *can't* see him, that's the thing!" she shot back. "I've been working on that too, but nobody wants to work on it. I can't even get a hold of Cassie. I can't get a hold of none of them."

"Okay," Melissa pressed on, unwilling to give into the despair. "I'm asking you a question about your relationship with your folks. Do you need them to show up here, to call you and to be there for you now that you're in this situation?"

"Sometimes . . . " Bobbi managed, with an unmistakable pout, "sometimes I need them."

"Well then, Zach needs you to be there for him," Melissa said. "Just like you need your parents to be there for you." It was a multilayered statement, reminding Bobbi that she was the most important part of her own child's recovery, as well as an important child within her family.

Beth followed, "If you can call me at work, and you can call me at Uncle Jim's, why can't you pick up the phone and talk to your son?"

"I do call him! But every time I call him I never get to talk to him."

"Okay," Beth said with a patient firmness, "you said the other day you got the answering machine when you called, why don't you just leave a message asking how Zach was doing and asking them to call you back?"

"I can't give her the number," Bobbi lied. "My foster dad said I'm not allowed to give the number out, even to foster parents."

Jesse fell for the diversion. "Well, I think I'm gonna have a talk with them, because they're stepping in between you and Zach."

"And that's not right," Beth added.

"I'll take care of calling Bobbi's foster parents." Melissa reflexively put herself in harm's way to protect Jesse and Beth from the sort of anger at CPS or the foster parents that has derailed so many a reunification plan. "It should be my job to call them, because I have nothing to lose if they get mad at me."

Jesse nodded slightly. "I'm just saying they should know this is important for her."

"The problem is that I'm not really sure if that's the problem," Melissa countered. She knew Bobbi's foster parents were of the highest caliber and very supportive.

Caught, Bobbi quickly dodged again. "The problem is that I never get to talk to him! I always have to talk to the foster mom and never get to talk to Zach. I know Zach's in the room because I hear kids in there."

"Well, Bobbi," Melissa said, "I think it's so hard for you to call that you kind of find excuses not to."

"All we're saying is you need to call, even if you are just talking to the foster mom," Beth said. "And document everything you say. You are a mother now, you need to be taking responsibility of Zach."

"How can I take responsibility when I don't even have him?" Bobbi exploded.

"You don't have to have him!" Beth fired back. "Do I have you? *Do I have you?* On the weekends I do, and I had to fight to get that much. *But I'm still your mother.*"

"And I'm fighting to get him on the weekends," Bobbi stormed. "But I can't never get hold of my social worker 'cause she's too stuck up! She don't even care about me. She don't even call me. I almost lost a weekend with you guys 'cause she forgot to call it in."

Melissa saw her chance. "So maybe you feel a little like Zach does when you don't call him?"

The room fell silent as Bobbi's gaze dropped.

"One step at a time, Bobbi," Beth said gently. "I had to fight to get phone calls to talk to you, I had to fight to get your visits. Take one step at a time. You have to do the one thing they ask. Call Zach." It was sound advice from folks who had been there.

"I been doing the one thing they ask," Bobbi retorted, her energy waning. "That's why I don't understand. I been doing everything that they ask."

"You know, Bobbi," said Beth, "even if I fight to get you guys back home and do everything they say, they're still gonna put stumbling blocks up because you're not doing what you're supposed to do, which is making the phone calls. I don't care, call three, four times a day. I don't care, call on your break from school. She can't say that boy is taking a nap during lunch."

"She'll make up some excuse," Bobbi said stubbornly.

"Well, then we better just give up," Melissa offered paradoxically. "Let's just give up."

There was a brief silence.

"Is that what you want?" Beth asked.

The girl shook her head solemnly.

"Then fight," Beth said softly.

"Because right now you're making excuses," Jesse added with a delicate balance of love and anger. "And you're pissin' dad off!"

Beth followed Melissa and Jesse's lead. "So all the fight me and your dad has done to get both of you back home. You're gonna blow it away with the phone calls? I know it's hard. It's hard for me to let you go back every weekend. It's hard for me to make phone calls to *your* house. I'm in the same boat you're in. But, I do it because I want both of you home."

"And you love her," Melissa inserted.

"And because I love you," Beth agreed firmly.

Bobbi wept. "I'm just getting' tired of everybody . . . "

"There's days I get tired of everything too," Beth interrupted. "But I keep fighting because I want both of you home. I want my family back together."

"I don't understand why they can't just leave me the hell alone!" Bobbi erupted again.

"Well, Bobbi, if you're that tired of it, then we need to accept that." Melissa circled back. "You know, it's not gonna get any easier. And when Zach comes home, you're gonna have a lot more responsibility than just a couple of phone calls."

Beth continued, "And we can sit here and put the blame on this person and that person and the system and everything else. . . ."

"I know it's my fault that I'm in custody," Bobbi sobbed. "But why'd they have to take my son? I don't understand that."

"Well, are you gonna give up on him just 'cause you don't understand?" Melissa asked. "I mean, fight to get him back."

"Fight what?" Bobbi erupted. "You can't fight the system!"

"Yes, you can!" Beth said emphatically.

"No, you can't." Bobbi wept with both despair and conviction. "Because they lie their way out of everything. The system is so screwed up it's pitiful. I hate it."

"And so you're just gonna give up on coming home, too?" Beth said.

"You gonna give up on your son and your mom and dad and everybody," Jesse said, tears streaming down his cheeks.

"You know, Bobbi," Melissa said. "We've sent more kids home here than kids who have stayed in the system. And if you want to be the one to stay here, fine. But if you want to go home, then you need to get on the bus and start driving." No one bothered to ask Melissa what bus she was referring to. Everyone knew that the young girl was in charge at this point, and taking us all with her.

"And quit listening to them other girls that live with you, and start listening to us," Beth said. "Because they don't have parents like *us*. They don't have *parents that care*. And I want you home!" Beth paused as her daughter cried, before continuing: "I know one thing. You giving up is not helping. Bobbi, 6 months ago I was 'bout ready to give up. I was tired of fighting. I was tired of listening to Cassie tell me that I'm never gonna have my grandson. I was tired of not being with you, and I was lashing out—and it doesn't work. Matter of fact, it puts you back further. If I wasn't doing all that back then, I probably would've had a lot more right now. I probably would've had you home."

"But I can't beat the system," Bobbi murmured in total resignation. "I just want him to be home, that's all I care about."

"Then push for the phone calls," Beth said quietly, ignoring her daughter's despair, as a lifeguard would ignore a panicked swimmer's protests.

There was a long desperate pause as Bobbi continued to cry, her head now in her hands. It had been a remarkable session, the family showing newfound strength as they pushed Bobbi onward. Yet for all the eyes watching her from both sides of the mirror, we did not realize that she had finally hit the wall. In fact, only her father saw it.

Even as we were planning our next parley safely behind the glass, only Jesse was in tune with his daughter, and he alone knew what to do next. The burly tattooed construction worker rose from his chair and stood silently for a moment, wiping the tears from his eyes. We wondered if he would leave as he had done before when things became too emotional. Instead, he walked across the room and spontaneously fell to his knees in front of Bobbi, clutching her in his huge arms. The girl melted into him like the scared child she really was. After several moments of crying together, he forced himself to pull back and look her in the eye.

"Y'know what?" Jesse wept. "Daddy cares about you." He struggled to get a breath to continue. "Daddy cares about you *and* Zach."

"I care about Zach too. . . ." Bobbi's hand went reflexively to her heart. "But it hurts."

It was astonishing. A teenager's rebellion had been broken, and in its place appeared the will of a mother, wrought by the love of her family—qualities missed by those who came to save a child from them. When I watch this film I still become overwhelmed with the same emotion I felt that night behind the mirror, sharing a very sacred moment in the life of this family.

RISK AND REUNIFICATION

Bobbi never strayed from the plan again. She became a zealous phone-caller, which won her more visits, even as it upset the second foster mother and eventually contributed to the failed placement. Zach was ejected from the second placement as much because of the burden of dealing with reintegration as by Zach's Red Chief status. The foster parents were simply not interested in being put out, so they put Zach out instead.

Shortly into his third foster home, we were ready to upgrade the previous parenting interventions with Bobbi and Zach. We secured an agreement with CPS to have the girl go into the new foster home and work with her son several times a week. We suspected Cassie only agreed to this because she knew the third, well-briefed foster parent would be very critical of Bobbi during her visits, further substantiating the CPS position. We took the risk, however, believing that Bobbi could stand up to such scrutiny. We had coached her parenting in session, and were impressed with her progress with Zach. But the visits never took place. The third foster parent was so biased against Bobbie that she didn't want the girl in her home and found numerous excuses to avoid these visits—including simply not being home when Bobbi arrived as scheduled. Even after Melissa agreed to attend the home-visits, the foster parent remained avoidant. Under pressure from Melissa, Cassie pushed the issue and the foster parent gave notice. Zach went to his fourth placement, reminding us yet again of why CPS was reluctant to give directives to its foster families.

Just before the move, Cassie's supervisor quit, stating privately that she was concerned about the ethical practices of this CPS unit. Upon reviewing the record, the new supervisor was almost as troubled by the case as we had been. Though she remained skeptical of Bobbi, she directed Cassie to share none of her opinions with the fourth foster parent, who was in turn more amenable to the girl's visits in her home. This proved a turning point in getting Zach's behavior under control and assessing areas for improved parenting. It also bought us the time we desperately needed to deal with the larger systems issues. At our next case conference, we argued that the girl, who had not missed a day of school in months, could not be held in custody for truancy any longer. It was simply absurd. Initially, we were surprised at how easily CPS agreed, but then realized they were sending the girl home so that the problems in her family would become more obvious, thus freeing them to force termination on Zach at the 15-month mark. CPS even admitted under scrutiny that they did consider this a test of the larger family unit, and one they did not expect it to pass. We met with the family, made them aware of our concerns, and without hesitation they agreed to take the risk.

Over the next few months, the family beat the skeptics again by continuing their progress in therapy; Bobbi attended school regularly and worked with Zach both in and outside of these supervised environments. Within 90 days of Bobbi's reunification, Zach was returned home. A year later, he was released from legal custody. Shortly thereafter, Cassie resigned. The moral of this story is clear: Our own issues, biases, and experiences too often lead us toward pessimism well before it is warranted and away from the critical optimism necessary to succeed. We must remember that to expect failure is to invite it, and with such expectations we can create nothing better than a system that must be beaten, rather than one that can be utilized to protect the genuine best interests of our child clients.

NOTE

1. We learned nearly 2 years later that Bobbi had been right all along. A child placed in the same home disclosed that she did not want to return to them after a failed adoption attempt. She told the caseworker that although the family had been good to her, they had repeatedly spanked a little boy who was also placed in their home. When she saw them do this on one occasion, they swore her to secrecy saying, "It's the only way we can get him to mind us." Toward the end of her therapy, she saw Zach in our waiting room and mentioned in passing that he was the little boy who had been spanked.

CHAPTER 11

Defending September

ME

I have tried many times to tell people how I am
but no one understands.
No one listens.
I know you'll listen.
I am like a rose.
Inside I'm soft, delicate and easily torn.
These are my many petals.
Yet on the outside my stem has many thorns
letting no one touch the petals.

—A 13-year-old girl

Just 4 weeks after her father Tommy's telephone apology, September lay near death in the local emergency room. Her suicide attempt had been the closest thing to success the teenager had experienced to date. Another 30 minutes and the doctors believed she would have died. This was no doubt her plan for a future she did not care to endure; she had downed 84 lithium and 8 valporic acid tablets while nobody else was home. Only the unexpected arrival of her 12-year-old foster brother started the chain of events ending in her rescue. Worse, September didn't see this as a turn of good fortune. When she awoke to find that she had failed yet another of life's awful tests, she explained to the staff that she would simply lay low, work the program, and await her next opportunity to suicide.

I was quite literally sickened by this turn of events, both the suicide attempt itself and my lack of surprise that she had done it. For 14 months I had been trying desperately to turn September's life into something she'd want to live out. I'd come remarkably close with the unplanned but powerful phone apology. However, since then everything had spiraled downward after an unprecedented intrusion from external forces. Now September had come within a hairsbreadth of death, and I had some very difficult decisions to make.

INTO THE FRAY

I could not have offered a work of fiction more unpredictable and off-balance than the one describing the weeks between the phone session and September's suicide attempt. Yet as I sat at my computer that morning in May, compiling an extensive position paper for the court, I felt I was doing just that. I did not realize it at the time, but this report was about to become *the therapy*. In fact, from this point forward some of the most meaningful aspects of September's treatment would be conducted outside my office, in the larger system via reports, investigations, position papers, and our personal correspondence.[1] I was about to move from an interpersonal and family therapy toward one of advocating for September's best interests.

I prefaced my 13-page report to Judge Honeyman as follows, unwittingly documenting my earliest thinking on a therapy of justice.

> When working with children in custody, our systems of justice, child protection, and mental health face an awesome responsibility. Each day we must act to protect the lives of our child-clients, raising the likelihood that they can grow up with dignity by making careful, thoughtful decisions. Too often, this child protective system collapses into conflict, miscommunication, political wrangling, personality conflict, and power play, rivaling the most dysfunctional families I have seen. In our desperation to deal with the endless flow of families and children, our thinking becomes unclear, our emotions rise, and our best intentions become incongruent with our behavior. The decisions that alter the lives of families and children are made on inadequate information, dialog, theory, or reason. We try to introject a boilerplate solution onto every case, as if one family's situation were remotely similar to any other. We become steeped in one paradigm to the exclusion of new ideas that could offer fresh avenues for change with new and difficult cases. Though I am no stranger to the shortcomings of "the system," I have never seen a case in which a young person's difficulties have interacted so tragically with a flawed system of child protection.

I went on to recount the case from the day I had met September until the telephone apology in late January, the core event now generating an unexpected and astonishingly bitter controversy. I explained that session in detail, as I did in chapter 6, including a complete transcript, and offered to show the film in court. I wrote:

> Regarding September, I was faced in that session with a suicidal girl who needed to hear the truth from her father about her abuse, and knowing that Mr. Dupree would come through, I made the phone call. Mr. Dupree did a nearly perfect job of telling September that he was responsible for his treatment of her and begged her to keep herself alive so he could try to atone for it. He also thanked her for telling the truth and stated that he was glad he was going to get help because of her disclosure. This brief dialog speaks volumes about the power of a contrite offender to account for the pain that he himself caused.

I then explained, as best I could, what I knew about the events leading up to September's near-suicide 1 month later.

> Unfortunately, we completed no other meaningful therapy than this, as our February 8 session became an impromptu termination. Just as we were beginning to have success in giving September a reason to live, therapy was cast asunder by the Assistant State's Attorney [ASA] citing "a conflict of interest," which she errantly assumed favored Mr. Dupree. Most amazing was her claim that "September needed 'her own' therapist," completely ignoring September's contention that she already had a therapist who was deeply cognizant of the problems she faces. By their report, Hanna Winthrow and Connie Dixon made the ASA completely aware of the danger their actions posed and yet both claim that the ASA was wholly unwilling even to discuss the matter. In fact, no one in the ASA's office even bothered to pass on to me that therapy was to be terminated, leaving that painful task to the girl herself.

It had been an ugly, angry, and tearful scene when she came to my office the next day to fire me. I struggled in the days thereafter to figure out how to respond to this bizarre series of events. I contacted Selma Burns, the *guardian ad litem* (GAL), but she had not returned my calls. I'd called the ASA, but she had been just as elusive, returning my call once and giving nothing but a confusing message that she would have to get back to me after considering the facts, which she never did. Ultimately, I had withdrawn from the fray, fearful that too many adults in conflict in the life of a child was itself destructive. The last thing I wanted to do was add to September's problems, so I allowed the forced termination to stand without formal objection. Unfortunately, I had grossly underestimated September's desperation at this moment and her sense of connection to me as the one consistent adult in her life. Nor had I anticipated the sloth-like process the GAL and ASA had for finding her a new therapist. Nothing like this had happened before, and neither attorney knew what they were doing in making a referral, so they simply argued about it for 4 weeks.

Things were much clearer to me the day after September's arrival in the psychiatric emergency room. Pulling back had nearly cost the girl her life. I would not allow the bullying of these attorneys to prevent me from carrying out my obligation to her. I called Hanna to let her know that I would be back on the case whether the ADA or GAL liked it or not and that we could discuss the issue in court if she wished. I also reminded her that, under state law, clients 14 years of age and older could sign themselves into treatment without parental consent. On the advice of the CPS attorney, Hanna backed me completely and directed me to proceed *without* contacting either the GAL or the court. A day later, September was moved to the long-term psychiatric unit and we reinitiated therapy.

In my subsequent report, I explained the dilemma facing the girl and how it had influenced my decision to continue the case in spite of the growing rift with the ASA.

> Since entering custody September has consistently requested visitation with her family and when that has not been offered her, she has acted out to get it. While some view this as strange or dysfunctional "victim behavior," it is quite consistent with my clinical experience in cases of incest and that of my colleagues and consultants. In fact, for a year every other professional in this case has endorsed and permitted properly supervised contact with Mr. Dupree and used it therapeutically to help September get through this difficult circumstance. It is obvious that this girl will remain in foster care at least until she is 18. With a 2-year restraining order on her father, the ASA has condemned September to live the rest of her minority in the system isolated from the one person who can offer her sorrow, repentance, reparation, and to the extent possible, reconciliation. And at every supervised conversation between father and daughter, Mr. Dupree has provided *exactly that message and no other.*
>
> After making a disclosure that she sees as betraying her father and with no other family left, September has now been forced to break with the only consistent adult she has known throughout her year-long ordeal, and as she approaches 16 years of age she has no say in any of these decisions. This is the therapist who assisted in her difficult disclosure, took her father's confession, and promised to stick with her though the trauma that was bound to result. The subtleties of this political debacle are beyond September's comprehension. She simply believes that she has been abandoned once more by adults who were supposed to lessen not increase her trauma, adding to her sense of hopelessness and her desire to simply give up.
>
> Moreover, it is nearly always iatrogenic to suddenly terminate an important therapeutic relationship with a child, especially one who is suicidal. In fact, such action by a therapist is grounds for malpractice and a licensure complaint, and I would refuse to take such a case as a referral. A near-16-

year-old girl forced out of one therapy and into another is not giving informed consent. In fact, both CPS and the foster parent claim that September was actually threatened with *psychiatric commitment* if she did not agree to change therapists. This conduct speaks volumes about the ASA's command of basic psychological principals and simple humanism.

The bottom line in this case is that September has faith in me to do something others refuse to do—heal her family. It is not only a fundamental human right to have a family, but a basic human need. Even as her parents have proven abhorrent in their treatment of this girl, she has the right to participate in their recovery and to have them participate in hers. Even if that recovery fails, and that is always a possibility, September will see that failure first hand and thus move beyond any illusion or culpability in that failing. Isolation is most certainly not the answer for this girl as she has proven quite painfully in last few days.

The accumulation of her anger and hurt has resulted in September's decision to end her life. This was not an idle threat or cry for help. She believes that no one is listening to her cries. She sees her life as wholly determined by forces outside her control and even outside her awareness. People she has never met or met only occasionally are calling the shots, while those who know her best are forced to the sidelines or barred from contact. Faced with a system that has failed her and made her a failure, September Dupree silently surrendered.

Recent contact with the ASA's office provides an even more dismal picture than any of us could have imagined. CPS reports that Hanna Winthrow attempted to mediate an agreement with all parties to get September's therapy back on track. Instead, the ASA referred to Tom Dupree as "a scum" and "a puke" and stated that she will fight "tooth and nail" to maintain the no-contact order. All of us who spend our lives working with victims of abuse are tempted to resort to such a diatribe at one time or another, but I believe the ASA has completely lost sight of the real issue in this case. It is irrelevant how much justifiable contempt *we* feel for Mr. Dupree. His daughter still feels both *love and contempt*—and it is this very tension that forms the core of her troubles. When Hanna Winthrow confronted the ASA on this, noting that our primary concern should be September's mental health, she made the most insensitive reference to a traumatized child I have ever heard, suggesting why this case has become so misguided. The ASA told Winthrow, "She just needs to get over it."

THE LABYRINTH

Over the next 7 months things were consistently remarkable. Judge Honeyman was deeply perplexed by all that was before him. I attended the next hearing with CPS on my side. Stunned by my tenacity and not expecting my presence, the ASA and GAL were beyond livid, displaying courtroom tantrums that would, according to later rumor, draw admonishment in chambers. It was a scene without parallel: The ASA and I stood just a foot from one another across the bar of the courtroom, as she yelled at Hanna about me. She would not even look me in the eye. Hanna was quite shaken before Honeyman summoned both attorneys to the bench.

But upon return to their respective positions, things only became more heated. Realizing her culpability in the matter, Selma Burns, the GAL, began to cover herself. She stated that she didn't really care who September saw in therapy, a total retraction of her agreement with the ASA to fire me. "My concern," she continued, "is that September told me that she thinks if she sees her father in therapy that she will get out of the hospital sooner."

Hanna and I looked at each other and stood up.

"Your honor," I said. "That is absolutely not—"

This time it was Selma who made a sudden turn and engaged me directly and angrily. She knew I was about to remind the judge of her complete failure to protect the girl from self-harm, despite dire warnings. She was desperate to cut me off, and for the moment she was successful. Judge Honeyman demanded we all take our seats.

Before doing so, Selma turned to September, and with a sugary tone asked her to leave the courtroom.

"No!" September said. "I'm no going to leave."

"Judge," Selma said, "Dr. Crenshaw is just upsetting this poor girl."

"No he's not!" September said. "You—"

"Come on, honey," the GAL said in a tone of sweetness and desperation. "Go on right now."

September looked at the judge. He nodded and she turned to exit, with Selma literally pushing her from behind. The girl muttered under her breath the entire way. I was glad none of us could hear what she had to say.

Before anyone could speak, Judge Honeyman issued his decree. I was to continue with September, but for now there would be no conjoint therapy with Tommy. He would assign a court-appointed special advocate (CASA) to investigate the situation and provide her findings to him.

The GAL and ASA stormed out of the courtroom, speaking to no one.

I thought I understood what had happened that day in court, but there was more to it than met the eye. I saw September the next day and learned that the behavior of her GAL had been more purposive than reactive. When Selma claimed that September only wanted to see her father to get out of the hospital, the girl had mouthed the words "that's a lie" to the judge. Apparently, Selma had caught her doing this and knew she needed to get September out of the courtroom before she brought down the entire proceeding on top of both attorneys. From the bench, Judge Honeyman had seen what I had not, and his nod to September had confirmed receipt of her message. It had all been quite bizarre, and to this day I have never seen anything like it again.

Despite Judge Honeyman's favorable ruling, the situation remained very tense, leaving me more than a little apprehensive about the referral to a CASA. I could not imagine how this middle-level manager, wholly untrained in therapy, the law, or investigative procedure, could wade through a complex case and render a meaningful edict. Yet when she appeared on my doorstep a few days later, it was obvious that she was going to try her best. I responded fully to her questions, but suggested that all she really needed to do was watch the videotape and review the transcript. As I set up the VCR, we discussed the case, and I asked her why she thought we had landed in so much hot water. She disclosed that the issue of controversy was actually the letter I had written on behalf of Tommy, which in the estimate of the office of the State's Attorney had wrecked an otherwise easy prosecution. The ASA imagined me to be in Tommy's court and not September's. No amount of persuasion by the girl, CPS, or the foster parent had impacted her, nor had she bothered to contact me for clarification.

After watching the film of the apology session, the CASA left my office in tears, apparently quite clear whose side I was on in this matter of family injustice. "I just feel like everything is riding on what I say," she said as I escorted her to the elevator. "This girl's life . . . it's such a terrible burden."

I gently explained to her that I did understand her position. "It's what we do everyday."

September was aware of all that swept around her and unbeknownst to me she offered up her own report to the court from her hospital room. Now distrusting her own GAL and by extension the CASA, she mailed her letter directly to the courthouse and copied it to the other professionals so it would not be *ex parte*. The idea had come from a charge nurse who helped with the logistics, but it was still the innocent plea of a young girl, devoid of political ramblings and intrigue. It was the world according to September, and it struck a chord in all that saw it.

May 29

Dear Judge Honeyman:

How are you? I am writing you because I need your help with a few things. I know I have court soon. I'm hoping that you will consider thinking about these things before then.

The first thing I need you to know is that I feel that I am being punished for what my dad did. I'm feeling that CPS and the court systems are all blaming me, and I have a problem with that. I feel that because of all of this they are trying to take my therapist away from me as a punishment, because there is no reason he shouldn't be my therapist. He's done

> nothing wrong. I told him stuff that is hard to talk about and I trust him, and he helped me. He stuck with me through thick and thin, even when I didn't want to stick with myself.
>
> I feel Selma Burns should not be my GAL. She never returns my phone calls and when I talk to her in court she is rude. She doesn't care what I think, and I feel that she flips things around and lies. If she would talk to me herself, she'd know what I think. But she doesn't. Would you please consider giving me a new GAL?
>
> Thank you for your time.

The judge questioned Selma about September's wish to have her removed. However, the GAL dismissed the complaint as one of racial conflict. Either the girl's racism had escaped me in our discussion of Selma's conduct or it was an overt attempt to minimize the validity of the girl's claim. In any case, nothing was done, which provoked September even more. When the CASA's report came out 3 weeks later, a copy was furnished to us both. As we reviewed it together, September was pleased to see that the CASA's recommendation did not differ much from hers.[2]

> Our courts require punishment for the offender. However, in this case we are also punishing the victim. September is not asking to live with her dad, and she understands why he is being punished. She merely wants a chance to begin healing her relationship with him. She is conflicted by her love for her father and her guilt for the problems she believes she caused him by disclosing his abuse. Dr. Crenshaw is extremely invested in this case, but he is also genuine in his desire to help September. I believe that victims all share a basic need for apology: To know that they did nothing wrong, that it's not their fault. Dr. Crenshaw is giving September the chance to work through these emotions in a style that may well succeed. Given that she is obviously suicidal, it is *vital* that all professionals involved in this case set aside their differences and personal issues and examine the situation from each other's perspective to find creative ways to be sure this girl survives and thrives. By working together and building a strong foundation, we can give September a chance to heal.

Yet far from creating the sort of cooperation the CASA had demanded in no uncertain terms, the report only served to infuriate both attorneys to the extent that they demanded yet another report from an "independent, professional evaluator." Judge Honeyman accepted the attorneys' demands for reasons that were never made clear, but which appeared to be the product of the deteriorating political climate surrounding the case. Simply put, the attorneys would not stop until they got the answer they wanted, and the judge appeared unwilling to stop them.

In the midst of all this, September was released from the hospital back to her foster mother Connie's home. Under the circumstances, I was quite thankful that Connie had agreed to take her. As I had feared, the evaluator for the attorneys turned out to be Weston Parks, a psychologist considered an expert in sex abuse evaluation. He was also a ringer for CPS, having obtained CPS grant money on more than one occasion for publications on the topic, and he rarely testified against the state. Puzzled at what exactly he was supposed to evaluate, Parks instead approached the matter as a mediator, trying incessantly to get everyone to reach consensus. He even told me in my interview that he was trying to appease the state's attorney and asked where I would be willing to compromise. I stated that I was not September's attorney, that she could share her feelings for herself on that topic, that it was not my proper role to compromise in her treatment, and that I did not think it was his either. Not surprisingly, the only compromise anyone made in the case was one forced upon the girl, which in fact violated every one of the requests she had listed when Parks interviewed her. Worse, this report was kept secret with only Hanna, the judge, and the attorneys being given a copy to review.

With the unrelenting heat of the ASA's office bearing down upon her, Hanna took refuge in her ability to control the one thing she could control—information. She interpreted the report like a work of ancient Greek that only she could fully understand and explicate. Initially, she claimed that Parks had complimented my work but felt September was too dependent on me—a point I had made several times myself. However, rather than suggest the girl get out of the house and get a life, or work to reconcile with her family, Parks inexplicably recommended that she be assigned yet another therapist, this one of the ASA's and GAL's choosing. Even Parks knew this made no sense from a therapeutic standpoint, but it was the compromise demanded by the attorneys and at this point they appeared to be calling the shots. Clearly, they wanted another professional on their side more than they wanted September's situation to improve, and I felt lucky even to have been kept in the game.

None of this was lost on the girl, and she became even more angry and rebellious at the outcome of the Parks report. In this she was not alone. Offended at being given a difficult task and then ignored, the CASA openly agreed with September by stating to all involved that the Parks plan was designed to "meet everyone else's needs and not the child's" and then dropped out of sight, I assume in resignation. After a little coaxing on my part, September agreed to attend the new therapy in order to stem the controversy, a mature response to an increasingly childish process. After all, I coached her, it really couldn't hurt that much.

I could not have been more wrong.

Directed not to call me for any referral information, the new therapist was apparently not well versed in the ways of foster care and outplacement and was even less knowledgeable about September's case. Thus, she brought Connie Dixon into the latter part of their second session and allowed September to describe everything she didn't like about her. It was exactly the wrong strategy for maintaining a foster placement, and it had a horrific and immediate impact. With all she had been through with the girl, Connie was so vexed that she made a direct trip to my office for a crisis debriefing. This was, of course, a ludicrous twist as I found myself asked to help the girl and her foster parent work through their issues with another therapist, but I took time out of my supervision group to do my best to calm things down. In the coming days, therapy became little more than an uphill battle to hold the placement, as things were never the same between Connie and September. As with so many foster parents, Connie preferred to be thanked and not rebuked for her sacrifices, even as gratitude was not something the angry young girl could find within herself at that moment. Even when I sternly and successfully coached September to be contrite for her impoliteness and to take responsibility for her share of the growing conflicts, Connie remained resentful. Moreover, she was increasingly annoyed at the growing bevy of therapies and therapists required by the Parks report. She lived 20 miles from town and was now taking the girl to not 1, but 2 therapy appointments a week plus a medicine check and the full series of evaluation appointments and CPS meetings. Moreover, Connie was a professional parent by design, trained in special education and behavior management. Like the CASA and September, she felt ignored by the ASA, GAL, the judge, Weston Parks, and now CPS. In response to this and September's tirade at the other therapist's office, she became rather bitter. This impacted her treatment of September, who was in turn more skilled at bitterness than she, and the situation quickly spiraled downward. By the end of August, Connie was looking for an excuse to disrupt the placement. I was determined to avoid giving her one for as long as possible and commenced home-based therapy to at least assuage her concerns regarding transportation. In the meantime, September had shut out the second therapist just as she'd threatened to do. We had now achieved the worst possible conditions for therapeutic success—maximum pain and minimum gain.

On August 31, after an individual session at Connie's, I wrote September a letter summarizing the session. I did not know that it would be the first of many such letters, harkening back to one of Milton Erickson's favorite methods of dialogical intervention. We both knew her days at Connie's were numbered. I used the common intervention for professional parent homes, pointing out that it didn't matter how Connie felt about September, she was not her mother and the girl had nothing meaningful to work through with her. But she would not let Connie off so easily, and we argued for an hour about how to transcend the current reality. She took the fatalist perspective that things were already damaged beyond repair, and the placement was not worth the emotional effort. It was better to let the chips fall as they might. I took the position of free will, arguing that she could choose her path regardless of external influence. As usual, I was alone, and losing.

Yet under this pall of deterministic gloom, I had seen something new emerging in the girl. In the latter part of the session, she had allowed herself to be more vulnerable. For the first time, I could see a part of her that genuinely wanted to attach to Connie, to be her disciple. She wanted to offer her most difficult side to this substitute parent and have Connie stand by her through it all, to care about her unconditionally, to take the place in her heart that her parents had abdicated. At the same time there was also a part of her that was frightened to do any of this, a part that knew the risk was too great and the probability of benefit too remote. Sadly, by now this struggle was lost on Connie, who was so busy fishing for validation that she missed how much the girl really wanted to care about her and to be cared for. In my letter I wrote of this pain in the first person to give voice to what I knew September was feeling—hopelessness and shame at yet another impending failure.

> You pushed very hard Monday night, reminding me yet again of how few good answers there are to all the equally lousy questions you face. I wonder if you'll ever come to the realization that pushing doesn't answer those questions—it just puts them off for awhile. It's hard for me not to feel like a failure right now. I know that we've moved forward, making so much progress in the last months despite more obstacles than either of us could have imagined. Yet, with so many hard-fought sessions behind us, we sit once again wondering where you'll be tomorrow. Even as I feel pride in *your* successes, I am disappointed in myself and my inability to get us further.
>
> When you first came to see me I honestly believed I could help shine a light on the path of your future—but I've left you stumbling too many times since then. The one time you trusted me ultimately, and told me your darkest sorrows, the wheels went into motion that are still rolling over you today. I shouldn't wonder why you too often take matters into your own hands. I keep thinking I've earned your good faith—but as I think back I realize that I probably haven't.
>
> So how do we survive this? How do we accept our flaws, forgive ourselves and find a way to create the possibility of life for our mutual friend—you? How do we reconcile the past and plan for tomorrow? How do we find you a place to belong—not only in the physical world of homes and families, but also in the spiritual and emotional world of the heart? Even though the world of foster homes and hospitals seems much more

real at times, in the long run belonging in the world of the heart is more important. It will guide who you love in the future and who loves you, and whether your life will take a turn for the better or stay stuck where it's at. It is also a much harder world to face because it is so personal. It takes more courage and determination than many 16-year-old girls can muster to find the world of the heart.

I know you think *your* heart is broken beyond repair—but it is not. Even as you try so hard to hide it, I can see that heart at times and it beats strong. For 1 hour and 43 minutes on Monday you dropped the anger, yelling, insults, sarcasm, and diversions and let me in for a rare glimpse of your heart. It reminded me of why I stick it out with you. Because under all that armor, we both know who you are—a brave, lonely, desperate, frightened kid who just wants somebody to see her broken heart and spend the time and energy it takes to help her put it back together. I don't know how we're going to get from here to there, but I know it's where we must go. Never give up.

Failure is not an option.

September read the letter several times, and it became for her an important keepsake in a life that had few others. Yet it was to no avail in maintaining her placement. By the first of October, Connie the "therapeutic foster parent" had turned out to be no different than other foster parents in her tolerance for this troublesome girl. After an emotional blow-up in which neither would back down, September was back in a girl's shelter some 300 miles from home. She lasted only a few days there before getting into a scuffle with the staff, kicking a hole in the door to her room, and being arrested on a misdemeanor charge of criminal damage under $50. She was returned to the community and placed in juvenile detention, the same place we'd recently done pretrial assessments on one girl who had killed her mother and another who had sexually assaulted her 7-year-old cousin.

Things went downhill from there.

After months of constant turmoil, Hanna blamed September for the placement collapsing, ignoring Connie's contribution. She also undertook a new exegesis of the Greek in the Parks evaluation. This time she claimed that it recommended my firing. She even showed up in court and testified that "this girl is just manipulating him, and the entire court system for that matter." This seemed a mighty feat for a girl in an orange jumpsuit, locked in juvenile detention. Hanna went on to blame me in absentia for the disruption and stated, "I for one am tired of dealing with this girl and her family and her therapist." With no other data before him Judge Honeyman decided to send September to lockup until her hearing the following month. However, there were significant space limitations at the local detention center and the facility was in no way appropriate for the girl, so she was transferred to a psychiatric group home in another city. This lasted only a few days before September ran away to the home of a local relative where she spent the Christmas holiday somewhat connected to the system, but not quite under its control. The girl contacted Hanna and requested to stay with her own mother until her adjudication in January. The frustrated judge acquiesced.

September's desire to be with her mother for any length of time was as much a surprise as Judge Honeyman's decision to allow it. Mattie Dupree had divorced Tommy when September was only 4 after a violent and abusive marriage. The girl had remained with her for several years, during which time Mattie had been drug and alcohol addicted. She also exposed September to Rick, her live-in boyfriend and September's first offender, which resulted in the girl's first internment in CPS and subsequent sexual abuse by a foster parent. Several years after reintegration when September was 10, her mother's life became so unmanaged that the girl began to go back and forth between her home and Tommy's. At age 12, Mattie had her committed for a brief time for her angry acting-out against her mother's alcoholic conduct, and on release September was placed with her father full time. In addition to all this, September held her mother accountable for leaving her nowhere to turn when stepmother Barbara moved out and Tommy began molesting her. And so, since that first day in my office, we had scarcely discussed her mother, even as I knew Mattie had been in recovery for over a year and might perhaps be a placement option. When I brought this up, even in moments of desperation when there were no other options, September stifled me. Her anger at her mother was too great for her to use Mattie as a form of expediency in her case. Moreover, she shared this view with Hanna Winthrow, who could not stand Mattie and would never have considered a reunification plan with her. Now, for reasons I could not quite explain with my usual conceptualization of family injustice, Mattie was suddenly at the forefront of September's life.

In fact, there were a great many questions I wished to pose to September, but because of her placement and eventual disappearance, I lost touch with her in November and December. While staying with her mother over the holidays she reinitiated contact, but the utter confusion around the Parks report made that tenuous at best. When we did meet, I found her unusually difficult to reach, much as she had been just before the phone apology. It would be several more months before I learned why. This did not stop me from working on her behalf and at her request to advocate for her best interests, even as our poor connection was making it quite difficult to determine what they were.

Before her dispositional hearing in January, we discussed the situation with September's new attorney, who had been appointed when she transferred out of CPS and into the Juvenile Justice Department (JJD). Along with everyone else involved with the case, he was taken aback by the way the system had turned on the girl. He saw Judge Honeyman's movement of the case from CPS to JJD as an effort to avoid an open hearing that might expose some of the worst aspects of the system. He suspected the judge had simply interrupted the entire process in an overt attempt to clean the slate rendering any probe of the larger system a moot point. If this was his intent, it had worked. Our staff was divided between those who favored the new attorney's view, and those who supported my more benign explanation. Honeyman was a respected judge, and we had found him to be fair and impartial in the past. He had rescued this case several times already, going against his own court officers to keep therapy on track. I believed he realized the peril September was in from her own attorney, caseworker, the ASA, and the whole of CPS, and had extricated her through the only means available to him—a rather bizarre transfer to JJD. This clean sweep outcome was the same as in the attorney's hypothesis, but the rationale infinitely more benevolent.

Unfortunate for my theory, Judge Honeyman's next decree was noticeably lacking in benevolence. The following Friday, he remanded September Dupree to the physical custody of the State Girls' Detention Center, rejecting her petition to continue her residency with her mother. Moreover, September would be moved within 24 hours by a direct bench order, even though the facility had a 12-week waiting list for referrals. I will never forget the faces of her family, attorney, and treatment team that day in the courtroom as they considered her situation. This troubled and troublesome girl, a victim of severe sexual abuse and systemic mismanagement, was about to be placed among girls who were murderers, sex offenders, and drug dealers at the highest-level girls' lockup facility in the state.

On an unusually cold day in late January, as we walked out of the courtroom, one of my case managers suggested the most cynical twist of all. September had achieved a most remarkable distinction for a girl of 16: For all intents and purposes she was now a political prisoner.

IN EXILE

September could not have on-site visitation at the detention center, nor would they have credentialed me even if she could. The last act of CPS was to request that I be excluded from the case, even though Judge Honeyman had not ordered me removed. As a forensic facility, they were not covered by the statute that allowed hospitalized patients to have contact with an outside mental health provider. However, 60 days into the placement, with the help of September's JJD worker who had read the reports and saw through the entire debacle, I was granted permission to exchange confidential letters with the girl. I opened with what amounted to a substitute apology. Someone had to take some responsibility for the circumstances in this case, so I personified the shame all the adults should have expressed but never would. On April 2, I wrote,

> As you know, I am quite ashamed of how your case has turned out. When I told you that things would get better after you told the truth about your dad, I genuinely believed it. Instead you have suffered repeatedly for things that are not your fault. A hundred times I have reflected upon what I should have done differently to prevent this turn of events. You have made your mistakes too, but that is no excuse. You are the client and I am the therapist. Your job is to have problems, and my job is to help find solutions. I am afraid I haven't done my job very well.
>
> I understand that you are working with the staff at the Detention Home to stay on Level 3. This is *very important* and I thank you for your effort. The staff is in no way to blame for your predicament, and working with them is vital to bring about your goals. Without that effort, our work here would be a failure. I am sorry I must say it again, but *you must be patient.*
>
> There is a psychiatrist named Viktor Frankl who survived a concentration camp during the Jewish holocaust. His entire family was killed. Had the war not ended, he too would have died. He spent much of the rest of his life trying to understand the same thing you are trying to understand right now. He wanted to know "why." What meaning could there be in the terrible things he had experienced? I want to share with you what he said when I heard him speak in 1990.
>
>> The meaning in life is always there. . . . It may be the deeds that we have done, or the things we have learned, the love we have had for someone else, or the suffering we have overcome with courage and resolution. Each of these things bring meaning to life. Indeed, to bear a terrible fate with dignity is something extraordinary. To master your fate and use your suffering to help others is for me the highest of all meanings.
>
> I want you to read this, every day if you have to, until the day you return. I want you to seek for yourself the meaning in this struggle by bearing your fate with dignity and with courage. If you can, your pain will not be wasted.

Interestingly, our letters crossed in the mail and bore the same postal date, yet her thoughts were so in sync with my own that it seemed as if her letter was actually a response to mine.

> Dear Wes:
>
> Hi, how are you doing? This place doesn't care, but my time here has really gone by fast, it really has. I got here on the 25th of January and on April 25th it will be three months. If I don't leave from court on the 15th, I will be leaving around May 16th. I've wrote you before, but I couldn't give them to you. I really miss being able to talk with you. I wish I would have listened to you and stayed at Connie's. Oh well, I've learned you can't relive the past, you have to learn from it and move on. This place has really taught me a lot. I am shocked. I think people need to stop using this place as a threat. All girls need to go through this place. I'm for real, really I am. Can you believe it, September Dupree is saying this? This is the one place I don't say "well it was better (wherever)." I would rather be at mom's house but this place is going to help me so much when I do get out.

A few days later, I received a second letter that really was reflective of my own.

> Thank you so much for writing me. Your letter touched me. I really thought you gave up on me. No Wes, it's not your fault. It's mine. I chose to leave Connie's. I chose to run away. I chose to tell on my dad. It's not your fault. You are just a person who is trying to make the world fair and a better place and help someone out. I brought myself to this place. I kicked out the door, you didn't.

I was impressed that this angry, oppositional teen could take a stand of personal responsibility. She would need this to get through the detention center and into adulthood. But it was also sad to see the double-edged sword of self-determination cut so deeply both ways. As she had just before the phone apology, September was rejecting the notion that we all shared in the deterioration of her life and was attempting to rescue me as she had her father. By her account, she alone was to blame. She alone should suffer, as much for telling the truth as for disrupting her placement or running away. And in this September joined the chorus of professionals who sought to blame the victim.

She went on to share her successes at the detention center. She was on her way to the highest level, would receive her GED in May, and would go through a graduation-style ceremony. She admitted a few thoughts of self-harm but had weathered them, and she had even been appointed the leader of her anger control group. It was poignant for a girl who had known few successes, no opportunity at leadership, and nary a ceremony thrown on her behalf that she would experience each while incarcerated. She then went on to clarify the several months of her life I had missed after her disruption at Connie's. She had begun using drugs while AWOL, including marijuana,

LSD, and some form of amphetamines. This terrible, if predictable, ordeal explained the strange distance I'd found during our brief December contact. Of this she wrote,

> It was a hard time in my life. Nobody understood me unless I was tweekin' or high. I don't know why I went this route, but I did. I got so bad that I couldn't go to sleep without pot. Or I would be up for 24 hours on speed. My mom didn't understand so I just stayed away and went to get high all the time in my room, at parties, etc. I don't know why I'm telling you this. I just hope you understand. Do you? I read a book called *Go Ask Alice*. You should read it. It's good. There is a part I want you to know about. Here it is:
>
>> A raindrop just splashed on my forehead and it was like a tear from Heaven. Am I really alone in the whole wide gray world? Is it possible that even God is crying for me? Oh no, no, no, I'm losing my mind. Please God help me.[3]
>
> Wes, I would like to know why all this happened to me. I want an explanation for it. I think I deserve that much, don't you? I'm sorry this is so long but there is just so much to say.
>
> What am I supposed to do up here? What else can I do? I've been off my meds for a long time, since last October. I am doing fine. I get depressed a lot but I guess that is normal. Well, I really don't know what is normal anymore. The world is so unfair. It really is.

I wrote and rewrote a response befitting September's thoughtful and heartfelt treatise. At this point, the case was no longer billable in any form, but I could not escape both an ethical and moral obligation to the girl. Moreover, her letter touched me in its coherency and depth. Even as the chips were down, I could now see in her letters the possibility of a future for September. I reflected this in my letter of April 10.

> I was happy to get your letters. I am even happier to see that you are working with the staff and that you are finding it a positive experience. It really takes a load off my mind to know that you are learning from the past as well as the present. Ultimately, I believe that justice will prevail and we will finish the important work we started.
>
> Naturally, I am very disappointed in your drug use. I do expect better from you, but I am very glad that you were brave enough to share this information with me, knowing how I would feel. I am glad to hear that you have moved beyond this stage in your life. This, too, took courage. Keep it up. By the way, I haven't read the book, but I have seen the movie *Go Ask Alice*. Good movie, except I think she dies—not a happy ending.

> I have continued thinking a lot about how people suffer, particularly those who do not deserve it. As you know, I think it is important to study people who have suffered in the past so they may guide us in the future. Your letter inspired me to do more reading on this. The French author Jean-Paul Sartre wrote of his experiences in World War II. I am sending you some of his thoughts on freedom and what is called "determinism," that is the control others have or believe they have over us. Read this carefully and think about it. Although he talks about facing physical death, I think he meant it also as the spiritual or emotional death each of us faces when our lives are shattered.

I shared with her the quote from Sartre asserting the radical belief in free will (chapter 3). I continued the letter with my own exegesis of this piece as it applied to a young girl caught up in a drama beyond explanation, trying to point September toward a future in which all this would fall into a greater context.

A great deal happened in the intervening days between our letters. Mattie continued to step up to the plate, and the JJD worker was taking her seriously as a placement option for September. Despite my usual predilection for such plans, this one left me uneasy. Mattie did not have a good record as a parent, and her recovery from alcoholism was early and fragile. September had never spoken highly of her mother, except as she now found herself without any other escape. I was also concerned as to what would happen if September were finally free to find herself in such an unstructured environment. Would she dedicate her free will to seeking a new life or spiral out of control? Might she and Mattie discover something in each other that could develop into a mother–daughter relationship or would they tear each other to pieces? There were no certain answers, but I knew we had to try. The very belief in free will required us to give this mother and daughter one more chance. Moreover, from a treatment standpoint I needed Mattie right now just as I had needed Tommy. I could not conduct this therapy alone anymore and expect to be successful. Thus, I put myself fully behind Mattie and worked with her to prepare for September's return.

I had not heard much from the girl in the days prior to the court date, and I hoped this was a good sign. But after a 6-hour round trip from the state detention center she began a letter to me, deeply dejected when a continuance was ordered and no action taken. It took her 2 more days to finish her thoughts sufficiently to send them to me.

> I went to court and it was a big disappointment and waste of my time. My JJD social worker is talking about sending me to a foster home instead of going to my mom's, and I want to go home. I've worked hard at this place to try and get there. Now they are giving me no hope for my teenhood. You

know how I wanted to help kids when I get older? Well, what am I going to tell them—that if your dad or somebody hurts you don't tell, because you'll pay more than he will? You'll be taken away from your family and put through all this stuff. I broke a $40 door, but my dad broke me and nothing has happened to him. But with me, I think of it as I'm not even worth a $40 hollow piece of wood. Sometimes I get really depressed because I am locked up in a place with people who killed other people. And they think I'm that bad. I don't understand it. . . . I really don't. There is a girl here who raped her little brother. Do you know how mad that makes me? She tells you what she did and thinks nothing of it. Am I not the victim? Am I not the one who got taken away from my family? So why should they put me here?

I've been thinking a lot and I don't know why I'm going on with my life. It's not that I want to die. I'm just trying to figure out why I should go on. The other night I dreamed that I was into some kind of trouble that I couldn't get out of, and then I looked out of my window and I seen a bunch of people including you, just reaching out to try and save me. But it was too late and I was dead. I can't remember anything after that. Wes, I am really thankful that you stuck with me through all this. You have done your job. I am just so hardheaded.

Do you ever see my dad? If you do, would you please tell him "hi" for me? I really do love him. I haven't seen him for a long time. I wrote Barb three times but she didn't write back, so I guess that they all want me out of their lives, including Bobby and Billy. I am very sad and hate my life. I really do. Well, I have to go. Thanks for always being there. You will never know how much it has, and is helping me.

This was as dense a letter as I could have imagined, but I was determined in my response to try to address her raw despair and give her a bit of hope to cling to, which was of course not easy via this medium. On April 24, I wrote,

I understand your disappointment with court—however, I think your return to the Detention Center and the chance for you to finish your GED is too good to pass up. I think you should consider the stay until May 16th as a blessing in disguise. I think your dream is self-explanatory. We'll talk about it someday. It should tell you that (a) there are people who care; and (b) without your help, we aren't powerful enough to get the job done.

Yes you are hardheaded. I hope that when we work together again, you will please pay me some heed. Being hardheaded is not in and of itself a bad thing. It is just desperately important that we pick our battles wisely. Being angry about sexual abuse or the injustices of our world is righteous and important anger. Being mad because you don't always get your way is not. There were many problems at Connie's and not all of them were yours. I saw that and I understood it. However, your anger became too petty at times and not reflective of the real pain you felt. Admittedly, the system didn't let you deal with that pain very well. If it had, I believe you would not have felt the need to throw the tantrums you threw.

As for the feeling that your life is not worth much—have you not been reading my letters? I hope you are thinking about what I wrote, and about the work of Frankl and Sartre. If you look hard enough, you will see that they are right. If you need some more obvious examples, I should let you know that people are asking the same questions you are asking yourself. Why did any of this have to happen? Why is the system so stuck that it can't deal fairly with difficult cases? What will it take to change it? We believe there is some hope that your case could bring about change.

In the long run, these predictions would prove true, but before she could read them her daily existence became even less tolerable to her. The detention center was in no way a psychiatric facility, and they offered little more than behavioral counseling to September, aimed solely at social control. Designed to confront young clients into accepting personal responsibility for their crimes, this tack was a terrible mismatch for a girl who was infinitely more victim than offender, and it pressed her deeper into despair and self-loathing. When they were not confronting her, they were pressing September to discuss her sexual abuse in an institutional environment that was as far from safe and secure as one could imagine. Thus, she began to turn her letters into a diary of her experiences, struggles, and innermost feelings, writing page after page and then mailing them all to me at once. Sometimes they were rambling and disjointed, and at other times quite cogent, but they were always from her heart—a place where she was becoming more aware and, at the same time, afraid.

April 26, 7 P.M. I've hit rock bottom. I'm in an emotional stage. I can't stop crying. I really need to talk with you, really soon. I am going crazy. I lost 2 weeks. I am thinking a lot about my dad. I miss him. I haven't seen Bobby or Billy for a year. I am sad. The therapist here just kept digging and digging about my dad. I hate my life. Everyone keeps telling me that my life will get better soon. My birthday is coming up, so now I've been waiting 17 years of hell, waiting for my life to get better and it isn't and I am losing hope for the future and all I'm living on is a "what if." That's all. Do you understand? I hope so. I hope you don't mind me talking to you about this. But it's the way I feel, that if I were dead, I wouldn't hurt anymore. And it would be great not to hurt anymore. But on the other hand what if it does get better soon, then my life will get better, but what if it don't? You see? What do you think? Please write me back soon. Please.

April 27, 6 A.M. I just reread "Grounded Angel" and it's like they already took my wings and I will never find the stars. I look around me and I think that I'm living in Hell and I am walking through it and I know what I need to do. But what if they don't let me go home? I don't want to go to any more placements. No more. I told them over my dead body I'll go to another placement and I mean that—every letter of it.

May 1, 4:30 P.M. Well for the past 2 days I have been so depressed I don't know what to do. Today is my birthday and my mom was supposed to come and didn't. I am so sad. I didn't even get any mail. Sometimes I wonder if I am loved. I don't mean to complain but it's the way I feel. I've been trying to deal with my inside feelings by myself, but it doesn't work. It just makes me feel even more upset. Do you know where I am coming from? Will write more later.

May 5, 7 P.M. I got your letter yesterday dated April 24, and I am sorry for having the attitude that I didn't care. I talked to my dad. He called me. He sent me a birthday card. I really need to talk to you. I told him that I really messed up my life. He said, "Well, I helped." I really need to talk to you. My mom came up. It was very touching. It was a very emotional day for me. Then my counselor told me about 10 A.M. that my dad was going to call at 1 P.M. It felt like somebody kicked me in the stomach really hard. And he gave me a card that my dad sent me. He wrote "I Love You, love dad." At 1 P.M. he came and got me and I got on the phone. I wouldn't say anything until I felt comfortable.

May 6, 7 P.M. I wrote a poem about my life. I wanted you to read it. It's called "Who"

September who is afraid of loneliness,
Who feels left alone in this world,
Who needs companionship,
Who fears herself,
Who would like to change.

September, a child-like adult,
Who feels immature,
Who needs to grow,
Who gives what she wants,
Who fears adulthood,
Who would like to be grown.

I read all this, and quite a bit more that I lack the space to share. It was becoming increasingly difficult to keep her spirits up. Things really were improving—she just wasn't in a position to see them. In fact, after a May 5 briefing from the attorney and JJD worker, I began preparing for her imminent placement with Mattie and return to face-to-face therapy. It had been comparatively easy to fight for September's rights and best interests. Actually, treating her many problems had always presented a more complex problem, and this could only increase in the tense and untested context of her mother's home. As a start, we exchanged letters regarding the ground rules for continuing therapy and community placement. But on May 30, before we could finish that dialog September left the state detention center to the custody of Mattie, with whom she had not lived in nearly 4 years.

I would like very much to say that the story ended here, that Mattie and her daughter found one another, that the system ultimately allowed her father to perform a complete apology and then offered one of its own, that September's progress over the next few months astounded those who had made her course so difficult, that Mattie proved wrong those who had denigrated her and rendered moot my own fears about her parenting, and that the case's tragic twists and turns raised the consciousness of the system, making it a better place for kids. It would have been a just and meaningful ending to a story desperately short on either.

But none of this happened.

DEAD ENDS AND DEADBEATS

It is the ultimate shortcoming of total institutions that any good they do happens outside the client's natural context and without influence on it, and thus their interventions rarely generalize well. As I had expected, any progress September made in the state detention center began to ebb within weeks of her release. She did not return to drugs or overt misconduct. She broke no doors and did not run away. But neither did she make any headway in forming the critical relationship with a mother who was ill prepared to deal with September, who was smarter and far more controlling than she. Within days of her return, September became bitterly critical of her mother for numerous reasons dating back to the time of her first sexual abuse by Rick. In response, I began a crash course on apology with September and Mattie, but when asked to state the injustices done to her, September's withering list was more than her mother could withstand, particularly as Mattie found no disagreement with any of it. September seemed bent on defying the very ambivalence toward her mother that had been so key in her relationship with her father. For her, Mattie's pitiable condition was cause for overt contempt beyond anything I'd seen before. As a barely recovering alcoholic, Mattie was highly susceptible to such critique and thus easy prey for the girl's scorn. September found a way to fail with her mother at every turn, driving Mattie into whimpering regression in nearly every session. Try as I might, I could find no quick way to empower Mattie to transcend these poundings and win her daughter back. With September, only the strong survived and Mattie was quite weak.

Then, in early August, September did something as shocking as it was predictable. The barely 17-year-old took up with a 34-year-old convict she had met at an AA meeting. Before I even realized what was happening, she had scheduled an appointment with the family planning clinic, not for birth control but for a pregnancy test. We were all horrified at this turn of events, but no one was sure what to do. Mattie offered some feeble pontification about the dangers of older men. Her JJD caseworker complained to me but admitted that there was nothing we could do, as the girl was above the age of consent. When I asked if there might not be a prior offense for which this fellow could be barred from contacting September, the JJD officer offered a long list including armed assault against his ex-wife. Unfortunately, he was not violating his parole by sleeping with September. While she *was* violating her probation by consorting with him, the JJD officer had no legal sanction except a return to detention, which she was loath to enforce for what was clearly a treatment issue.

Everyone agreed that it fell to me to try to correct her course through therapy. But when I confronted her, September was not only uncertain of her own reproductive status, she didn't much care. Both sensitive and disturbed, the girl desperately sought something or someone to connect to. If those in her life would not give it to her, she would produce it for herself. The 34-year-old felon was little more than window-dressing. His selection was not wholly incidental, however. September's experience of contrition was painfully incomplete, as she was still barred from a full apology and reconciliation 2½ years after her disclosure, leaving her in a state of perpetual fascination with her offenders. When given the chance, she recapitulated her own victimization, hoping this time to achieve mastery over it. Needless to say, the entire plan begged failure.

I felt like Dante in the lowest level of therapy hell. There could be no worse turn than this for September's life. Having survived betrayal by her father and the state, she now faced the saddest cut of all—betrayal of herself by herself. She had gone from being literally suicidal to being sexually and emotionally so, a most insidious form of self-harm because it did not occur in a discrete place and time. This form of suicide would not only bring her down now, it would introduce an innocent child into her unstable and disconnected world, becoming the next domino in a series of tragedies that would replicate itself for generations to come.

The entire situation was intolerable, a point I argued with the stubborn girl for nearly an hour before offering a silent Hail Mary, and lobbing my last pass at the end zone.

"I'm sorry, September," I said. "I think this is where I get off."

Not the least bit ready to end our discourse on the matter, the girl looked at me as if I had spoken my position in Aramaic.

"What are you talking about?" she asked. "What do you mean get off?"

"I'm through."

She continued to stare at me in disbelief.

"It's been nearly 3 years and I've fought with you, beside you, and for you. I've written one report after another saying that you were a good kid who just needed a break. Well guess what? You got one. And this is what you did with it."

"You don't even know him," she snapped.

"Oh, really?" I said. "What happened to this guy's last wife, September?"

"They got divorced," she said, assuming I was bluffing.

"Uh huh," I said. "How?"

She smirked. "I dunno."

"Really?" I said more than asked.

"No," she said, "I know what happened."

"I'm sure you do. He was involved in a police stand-off for 3 hours while he held her hostage," I said. "At gunpoint."

"He was drunk," she retorted. "That's why he's in AA."

"No, that's why he's court-ordered into drug and alcohol treatment," I said. "AA is just a part of that treatment. He served 3 years for kidnapping his ex-wife and he's on 6-years' probation. Look it up yourself. It's a matter of public record."

September shrugged.

"Before that he was on probation for domestic violence. Hm. I wonder who that was against?"

"He's never done anything to me."

"No, and you've known him all of 2 weeks now."

"It's been a month," she said sheepishly.

Even as it was unfolding, I noticed something odd about this debate when compared with all those that had preceded it. Normally, September would have been on an all-out campaign to defend her position. Yet I got the distinct impression that for once *she didn't want to win*, that she actually wanted me to be right. I decided to take this to the bank.

"Ah, a month," I said sardonically. "And he hasn't even hit you yet? Well, that is a record for this guy, from what I hear. He broke three of her ribs, September."

"She beat him up more than he did her," she argued weakly.

"Really," I said. "Well, he must be a real wimpy guy then. 'Cause I used to run a battering men's group and every one of them tried to pull that one on me and I said, 'oh can I come over and knock the crap out of you now? 'Cause I outweigh your wife by about 100 pounds.' And you know what? Not one of them was willing to say they were scared of me. So do you think this guy was so scared of her that he had to beat her and hold her at gunpoint? Not a chance."

September lowered her gaze.

"You know what you're doing, September." I said with all the intensity I could muster. *"And I will not be a party to it. I will not condone it."*

She looked up and we stared straight into each other's eyes. I could see the tears leaking out, defying her every attempt to contain them. The tension was palpable as we connected at a level well beyond the verbal. And then quite suddenly the girl stood up and exited the room. In nearly 3 years, regardless of the rancor, pain, or confrontation, she had never walked out of a session, and I was a bit unsure of what to do now that she had. She was too unpredictable to risk a prolonged absence, so I followed her out the door and through the lobby. The elevator doors closed behind her before I could push my way in. I saw she was going down. I shot down the stairwell and caught her in the confines of a glass-enclosed entryway. It was not the main exit, and fortunately there was no one there to witness her breakdown. For some reason she had stopped there and sunk to the floor, her head between her knees.

I sat down cross-legged next to her. "Listen to me," I said firmly and desperately.

"No," she shot back, tears rolling down her cheeks. "I'm not going to listen. How can you do this to me?"

"I can do it because all this is completely out of control, and I can't make you see it any other way. You've found just the perfect man, a 34-year-old violent criminal, to reenact your sexual abuse by your father and Rick. It's sick, September, and I'm not going to sit here and watch you hurt somebody that I care about. It's your body and your life. Do what you have to do, but don't expect me to support you and to try and help you work through it and make it seem like it's all okay."

"You don't know him!" she reiterated weakly. "He's changed."

"I'm not even going to discuss it with you," I said as emphatically, but with a more gentle tone. "You know you're wrong, and you're too proud and scared to admit it. That's your choice. You can follow my advice, your mother's advice, and that of this treatment team and your JJD worker or you can go find another therapist who will go along with this because I won't. I didn't support your suicide before, and I'm not gonna support it now."

"I'm not going to kill myself!" she stormed. "You should know that by now." I thought I did, but it was a relief to hear her say it.

"I believe you," I said. "But to do this is to kill your spirit. I am here for you if you want to work at this and I always will be. But if this is what you want to work on, then I'm not the right therapist. I can't do it." As I stood to go, she looked up and caught my gaze, attempting a retort but realizing she had nothing to say. "You know something, September?" I said. "For 17 years people have screwed up your life in every way imaginable. And today, you just became one of them."

And with that, I went back to my office and alerted her mother, her JJD worker, and the rest of the team that September was in crisis.

But as I reflected on the case, I was not very happy with myself. Neither was the treatment team. In fact, I contacted Cloé Madanes in Washington, D.C., for a consult. She too felt that I had overshot the mark with September and come down too hard on her. She reminded me that this fellow was a dangerous man, and September a smart girl, and I needed to utilize both attributes. Rather than bludgeon the girl with obvious truth, Madanes suggested I let him prove himself. I was to call September, apologize for getting after her, and ask her to bring the 34-year-old man to therapy. "Look at how she responded when you got upset with her," Madanes said. "*She wants you to do this.* She'll come back."

Although this was excellent consultation and my apology and reversal of position quite genuine, it did not hit the mark. September did accept my invitation to come in the next day, but she would not bring the man in question. In session she was quiet and distant, more I felt from embarrassment than retribution for my harshness. In the coming days and a few more sessions, I realized I had been right on target in my Hail Mary confrontation and September knew it. She actually began to distance herself from the relationship and scheduled an appointment for contraception at the local health clinic after learning, to her relief, that she was not pregnant.

But even as the situation seemed to be improving, Madanes's words proved true. The depth of the confrontation had left an indelible mark on the state of our therapeutic alliance. I had used up my influence with the girl in stemming the tide of her own self-destruction and in doing so I had hurt her deeply. In response she began to disconnect from therapy into a very sad and lonely place, and in subsequent sessions we could not find a way to turn things around. Mattie called to let me know that the girl had become even more detached from her. A few days later, September appeared at the steps of the psychiatric hospital and checked herself in. At discharge, a week later, she offered herself to her JJD worker for placement anywhere in the state. She did not stop to say goodbye. My desperate Hail Mary seemed to have won the battle, only to lose the war.

But September's story was not yet over.

TODAY WELL LIVED

I heard nothing from the girl for over 5 months, but she maintained contact with Mattie, who dropped by occasionally to let me know how she was doing. As her mother's reports improved, I became more hopeful and more welcoming of the news of September. She had been moved to a family placement with a young couple in a rural part of the state where she had done something unheard of in her case—she had maintained a placement without incident for nearly 4 months. Even more surprising was her impromptu reconciliation with Connie Dixon over the Christmas holidays, after which Connie appeared unannounced at my office. We had not spoken since September had left her home.

"She really wants to talk to you," Connie said. "But she's afraid that you're angry at her."

"I can see how she might think that," I said. "It has bothered me since she split. Would you please tell her I'm not. I was just . . . very, very worried for her."

"She told me what happened and that the guy is out of her life," Connie said. "I don't know that I'll see her again, but I already told her that I knew you were just trying to help and that you weren't angry with her. But I think she wants *you* to tell her." Connie also mentioned that she had met September's new love, a fellow about 5 years older than she, who September reported to be responsible, a homeowner and a hard worker with a good-paying job in his father's ranching operation. Connie thought him a good influence on the girl. Mattie stopped by a day later to reiterate all this and more. She was clearly proud of her daughter's progress. I asked her to tell September that I was very sorry about the events of August and that I hoped she would contact me. Not wanting to overstep my bounds, I felt it more appropriate that she make the active decision to seek me out rather than the other way around, and I assured Mattie I would respond appropriately.

Three weeks later, on February 3, two years since the controversial phone session and over three years since our first session, I received a letter from September. I assumed it was reflective of contact with Mattie or Connie, but it was not. In fact, Mattie had lost her phone to an unpaid bill and had not spoken with her daughter since seeing me, and September had not called Connie. The girl had taken the risk of contacting me without any expectation of my response.

Dear Wes:

This has been a long, hard road. Now that I can see the end of the road and it's so close that I can taste it, I'm scared shitless. But I'm also looking at it in a good way. I get to start my life.

I know that I really messed you over. And I am sorry. I really am. You are a great person and if you weren't there for me all through those hard times in my life, I would have been dead. You know it and I know it.

I've been in this same foster home since August. I found this great guy. His name is Sonny and he is 22. He is nice and sweet and I love him. He comes from a good home and his parents are great. I never knew a guy could be so nice. You will have to meet him someday. He knows everything about my life. I trust him. Come May 1, I am going to move in with him. By then, we will have been dating for eight months. And we've never even had a fight. I know you think living together is a mistake, but we want to do it before we get married. I got to go. I will mail this tomorrow. You won't get it til Monday. I hope to hear from you soon. Remember:

> "Today well lived, makes every yesterday a dream of happiness and every tomorrow a vision of hope."

Thanks for saving my life.
Always

September

I was impressed with her wise and articulate perspective and deeply moved by her words of kindness and attempt to set things right between us. As usual, she was not the one who owed an apology. I wrote back at once offering support and encouragement for her already successful course and my own apology for our last encounter. And as I did so, I reached a bit of an epiphany. That flawed but powerful moment had set the stage for me to become a more authentic substitute apologist to the girl than when I had attempted this intervention during her internment in detention. I was now a figure who really had hurt her and, in doing so, inadvertently had become part of her contrition process. Right or wrong—and the jury remains out to this day—the confrontation offered a precious opportunity to raise the completeness of that process and I took full advantage of it.

Dear September:

As you can imagine, I have been very concerned about you since your August disappearance. I was very unhappy with the way you and I parted company. I have gone over those weeks and still don't know how I feel about the situation. I was genuinely scared for your well-being, particularly around that 34-year-old fellow you were seeing and I think I had good reason. I assume, as things transpired, you realized that too. On the other hand, I've never felt that "putting my foot down" was a very smart thing to do. While there is no turning back or redoing the past, I want you to know that in the present, I am sorry that I hurt you so deeply.

I was so proud of you when I read that closing quote ("Today well lived . . ."). That is how to live your life with dignity and grace. I know there is so much left undone—so much that we tried to do and seemed always to fail at. I don't know what you will ask of me in the future, but know that the door is always open to continuing therapy when and if you wish. I was never mad at you in August, only worried for your safety and your happiness. It seems you have found both, and I am much less worried now.

Congratulations on getting your life together. I cannot find words to adequately commend you for the courage, strength, and self-love it has taken to walk out of the darkness and into the light.

Wes

NOTES

1. To deepen the disguise in this case, I have heavily edited these reports even as they have been released by September for publication. While paraphrasing the wording, I have carefully preserved the original content so as not to detract from the case. Our personal correspondence is only edited to exclude extraneous commentary.
2. I have again paraphrased this document for disguise, but the content is absolutely true to the original. It is a remarkable treatise on family injustice written from the stance of a reasonable person observing the process of healing in this family and understanding it intuitively to be right.
3. The book *Go Ask Alice* (Anonymous, 1971), about a teenager who becomes caught up in the drug culture, was later filmed as a made-for-TV movie (Isenberg, Korty, Sparks, & Violett, 1973).

CHAPTER 12

Ringing the Bell

Integrating Contrition into an Existing Program of Treatment for Offenders and Victims of Abuse

WES CRENSHAW, DAVID BARNUM, AND BRUCE LAFLEN

> I still quote Eugene Debs . . . in every speech [I make]:
> "While there is a lower class I am in it, while there is a criminal element, I am of it; while there is a soul in prison, I am not free."
> In recent years, I've found it prudent to say before quoting Debs that he is to be taken *seriously*. Otherwise many in the audience will laugh. They are being nice not mean, knowing that I like to be funny. But it is also a sign of these times that such a moving echo of the Sermon on the Mount can be perceived as outdated, wholly discredited horsecrap.
> Which it is not.
>
> —Kurt Vonnegut, *Timequake* (1997)

THE KANSAS CITY PROJECT

If we accept Madanes's supposition that we must find an echo of ourselves even in treating an offender, then the idea that we each have an innate capacity for such behavior is uncomfortably close behind. And if we have a capacity for malevolence as well as beneficence, this must also be true for the offender, calling into question not whether he can respond to this higher ideal, but whether we can make that invitation heard and answered. This is the view from our trenches, that as long as people commit family injustice we are bound to treat them in this spirit. This chapter discusses a program of treatment for the most insidious family injustice, sexual abuse. However, it is quite applicable to any organized program for abusive or neglectful families. The Kansas City project began when Bruce Laflen attended a program presented by Cloé Madanes in conjunction with our institute in 1996 and then contacted me for consultation thereafter. His goal was to integrate Madanes's apology process into his program in Kansas City, which at the time was the largest outpatient sex offender treatment program in a four-state region, with hundreds of cases and 26 full-time professional staff. It was also nationally known for its innovation with this very difficult population. Moreover, it was comprehensive, offering treatment even for the most severe sex offenders as well as their victims. As an offender therapist, Bruce approached Madanes's model as a true skeptic. However, the training was for him as it had been for me 6 years earlier, a paradigm shift that would ultimately turn the program into the largest implementation of the contrition model to date.

At the beginning Bruce found the model a tough sell to his veteran staff. As the consultant hired to train them, I found myself in the fray between Bruce's vision and enthusiasm and the staff's affinity for stasis, which rested in large part on their family-phobic resistance to the idea of contextual change. It was an uncomfortable position indeed, and late in the second of four day-long training sessions I knew I was losing my audience. I had been considering an illustrative example that I thought might generate a breakthrough and set the group on their own paradigm shift. Feeling I had little to lose, I decided to go ahead and show the closing scene from the movie *Witness* (Feldman et al., 1985) in which corrupt police officers are about to kill their colleague John Book (played by Harrison Ford), who has been hiding among the Pennsylvania Amish. As they storm the house, Book sends the little Amish boy he has been protecting away to safety while he distracts two of the officers. But as the boy escapes across the field, he realizes he cannot leave his family in peril. He runs back to the house to find the corrupt police chief holding his grandfather and mother at gunpoint in a stand-off with Book. The grandfather sees him, and out of sight of the chief, signals with a strange gesture. He reaches into the air and twice pulls an imaginary rope. The boy understands what the audience does not and runs to a bell hanging in the yard, pulling its cord again and again, yielding a remarkable turn of events. From over the hill in all directions, Amish men, women, and children pour in response to the bell. Before the scene is over, the chief, armed, desperate, and dangerous is rendered powerless by a crowd of neighbors having no defense but their presence. Untouched by anyone and yet overpowered by their *witness*, he drops his gun and falls to his knees before the crowd in an act of ultimate surrender.

As the film ended and the lights came up, I was surprised to see tears among some of the hardened therapists, and many more seemed deeply moved. They sat without comment, question, or critique, which was certainly a first in nearly 16 hours spent together.

"This is what you have to do," I said. "You have to ring the bell. The system will be gone one day . . . you, the courts, and social services. You have to strengthen what will always remain—the natural community of the victim. You can't leave until you do, or all your work will dissipate, because no one will be there to say again what you have said or be a witness for the victims. You have to ring the bell."

This was the turning point in training, and the group began to speak regularly about "ringing the bell" as their common metaphor for involving families in treatment. They became a good deal more enthusiastic about Bruce's vision thereafter. In fact, I continued with Bruce's staff for over a year, which proved an evolutionary experience in my own conceptualization and refinement of the approach. It was therefore a natural inclusion in this book, which seeks to make a practical contribution regarding how our approach does work, not just how it should. In 2000 I asked David Barnum to interview Bruce specifically because David was uninvolved with the original training, and had been out of state when it was conducted.

OVERVIEW

BARNUM: Who are you serving in the program?

LAFLEN: In addition to the many cases we already had in process at the time we started collecting data in 1998, we have admitted 55 adolescent offenders, and 60 adult offenders into the program, and 150 child victims and about 50 more clients or collaterals that are neither victims nor offenders themselves.

BARNUM: Do you get your referrals mainly from the court system or do you get self-referrals also?

LAFLEN: About 99% of our sex offenders are court referred.

BARNUM: What was the program like in '96 before you implemented the new protocol?

LAFLEN: It was pretty standard sex offender and victim treatment. We saw victims for a number of years and we saw the perpetrators for like 2 years. The perpetrators did have to do an apology at that time, usually through a letter to the victim. Generally those were given during offender/victim dyad sessions. Sometimes the nonoffending spouse or parent would be a part of that, sometimes not. The apologies often happened about a year into the process, but sometimes up to 2 years. Victims and offenders were kept apart throughout the treatment for at least a year to a year and a half.

BARNUM: Were they given separate therapists?

LAFLEN: It could have been a combination, but sometimes we'd have four or five therapists on a case if it was a large family, and sometimes just one or two. It would just kind of depend. But the whole philosophy here, and in the sex offender treatment world at large, was the emphasis on separation of victim and offender, rather than trying to work on that relationship and unifying the victim and the offender if that's what they choose to do. Of course, that is still the prevailing view among most programs.

BARNUM: Coming to this as a sex offender expert, why is the notion of separation such an important key to the traditional approach?

LAFLEN: Well, honestly, I think there's a lot of these assumptions that are being challenged in the field right now. We're one of the programs leading that challenge. These assumptions have been in there for a long time. One is that sexual offenders are compulsive and that they can't help themselves. But at the same time the literature says that you *can* teach them to help themselves. The other assumption was "once a sex offender, always a sex offender," that once you did it, you would do it again and again if given the right opportunity, the right chances. So they were seen as essentially hopeless. But we've changed our philosophy about this, especially for the adolescents. If you look at the politics of this issue back into the '80s and early '90s when I got involved in sex offender treatment, you had two factions—the offender therapists and the victim therapists. The victim therapists tended to believe the worst thing in the world that could happen to a child was sexual abuse. So the idea of separation was very much out of a need to protect that victim from further trauma and they saw any reminder of the offense or offender as very traumatic. They assumed that the child could not take that kind of trauma. I think, also, that there was a lot of unmitigated anger toward offenders in the way professionals and other people treated them. When I first started treating offenders I worked in the prison and the style was very much that you got in their face and you really broke them down so that they would comply with treatment. Today and in this program, we look at that much differently and the entire field is looking at that much differently. It's no more tearing down and making them comply, but trying to connect with them and to get them to listen and to maybe change some of their philosophies about how they treat others. Back then, I think there was just a big schism between victim and offender therapists, and you didn't have a lot of people doing the same kind of work with both.

BARNUM: What was the impetus for implementing the new approach in 1997?

LAFLEN: We had managed health care and we still do, but then it was just looming on the horizon. We had the privatization of foster care that was also looming. Then, clinically, the apologies we were doing just did not feel appropriate. They felt canned, they felt staged, and they felt like the message just didn't get through to the victim—that it wasn't your fault, you did a good job in telling, and I'm working to not do it again. It just seemed to get lost. And also it felt weird that we would do this with the victim and the offender, and we didn't have anybody else other than the therapist in the room. And sometimes we'd have a mom or nonoffending spouse in there and sometimes we wouldn't. So it just started to not feel very good in the sessions. I had also worked with victims and a lot of them would ask, "Can I see my dad?" "Can I see my brother?" People would say, "No, you're not ready" or "He's not ready" and they'd want to know why. There were a lot of problems with that model.

BARNUM: So among other things the needs of the victim really began to emerge in your thinking.

LAFLEN: Absolutely, and also with some of those political forces like with managed care, they would say, "Why are you doing what you're doing? Can you justify what you're doing?" And back then we really had no justification for what we were doing. As a field, the research was starting but we were not where we are today. Today we know a lot about what can predict recidivism. So the quality of the research was a lot different then, and this was one family model that had been researched (Madanes, 1990; Madanes, Keim, & Smelser, 1995). Of course it was limited, but it had more research behind it than what we were doing. So I think that helped me move from the traditional approach where the client says, "I'm gonna write this letter, the group's gonna go over it, everybody's gonna scrutinize it before I give it to the victim" and only then after 1 or 2 years we're going to bring them together in therapy. Also in the sex offender treatment literature and in the victim literature they always *talked* about family therapy, but they never gave you a model to go by. I guess they assumed people would just come up with it on their own.

TOWARD A PARADIGM SHIFT

BARNUM: So what was the initial reaction of your staff?

LAFLEN: Shocked, then excited, then they were resistant. In talking with them about the model, they were kind of shocked that we were moving into more family therapy because we really weren't a family therapy unit. We did some family therapy, but we never had a model. So, I think they were a little shocked that this was the model that we were going to use. I also think they became scared at the idea of going through the training and consultation because it really challenged our thinking about how we work with a population that we had been working with for a long time. A lot of us came from the prisons and were trained in that model. The other therapists who didn't come from the prisons, but who had worked with victims here or at another agency, didn't have that experience of confrontation and they were very uncomfortable with getting the victim and the offender together so soon into the treatment process.

Some resistance came when we started training, especially with the offenders getting on their knees in front of the family and then asking other family members to get on their knees. Some felt it represented Judeo-Christianity. Some saw it as shame-based. Some said it just didn't feel right and some saw it as more an exercise in grandstanding for the therapist than a meaningful intervention for the offender or victim. Others thought the whole intervention was more for the offender than for the victim. But really, I think the big thing was that they knew it was a change for them—a true paradigm shift.

BARNUM: What was the excitement for them?

LAFLEN: To do something new and to learn a new skill. I think they were very excited about that and it challenged them a lot. And also that we were, as a program, going to stick our necks out and lead this field a little farther toward family therapy, while hanging on to our base which is sex offender and victim treatment. It was very interesting and it took the whole year of consultation, I think. It took us, the managers, myself, the therapists, the case managers, a long time to figure out how this model was going to work with our population and with us as a team.

BARNUM: How did you cope with the shock and resistance?

LAFLEN: Well, I had very good administration that helped in that process, helped support this as the direction things must go. It also helped to have a consultant to help temper some of the anger, some of the resistance. Part of the coping was just being real clear with them that this is a change in paradigm, it's a change that I believed was a good change, and that the administration believed was a good change, and it was what we were going to do. At the same time, it was important to be able to listen to their concerns, while guiding or sometimes pushing them down this path.

BARNUM: What did you see as the initial turning point in the training?

LAFLEN: Well, I think it was when we got to the point of actually watching some of the videotapes of it actually happening. It increased people's anxiety, but it also helped a bit. Another big turning point was when we were able to go into live supervision, which frightened most of the therapists. But once we got there, and we were able to see the process happening and unfolding in front of us, and we were able to see the results of a family coming together—I think that really turned a lot of them. It turned their thinking to a more positive view about this approach. But it took awhile; it just didn't happen overnight. They had to understand when we did live supervision that we weren't critiquing them. We were going to help them, and we were going to teach them this process. Once we were able to see someone do it successfully, then he or she was more apt to get on board. And they got feedback from the other therapists and from the consultant and supervisors about how *well* they did, that seemed to boost their confidence to go back in and do more sessions. Nowadays we have conflicts about whose turn it is to get time in the live supervision room. A lot of the therapists now want that live supervision, because they want that extra person helping them work with this family.

BARNUM: We've found that the apology is actually a natural process and there are a variety of world traditions from which the idea comes into the clinical arena. I'm wondering if your staff began to see that most resistance is from us as therapists and not from the family?

LAFLEN: Oh, I think they saw the resistance and really any problems we had with this model as mainly coming from our lack of being able to implement it at first. I think this is a highly skilled therapy. I don't think you can just come out of graduate school with no supervision, read a book and do this approach. I don't think it would work. It takes a lot of time and a lot of energy and a lot of thought to do this therapy. Rarely did the resistance come from the families not wanting to participate, because, frankly, if you ask a family to come in they're going to come in. It doesn't matter the circumstances. It's how you ask them. It's how you *invite* them. We very rarely have families that won't come in for the apology.

BARNUM: What accounts for the long-term acceptance of the approach by your staff?

LAFLEN: I think the reason it stuck so long and is really ingrained in our work is because we see results when we do it. We see results whenever we're sitting in, when we're doing live supervision and an offender is not taking responsibility, and we go in with a more utilization-based intervention rather than a real confrontational approach. We do that in a more indirect, roundabout way and we get results. When you see that, the therapists are more apt to respond.

INTEGRATING AND EVOLVING THE CONTRITION MODEL

BARNUM: What immediate changes did you see once the program was implemented?

LAFLEN: With the staff I started seeing that they were gaining confidence. At first I think they were intimidated by the model and by some of the thinking in the model. But once they got into it and were successful, that really helped. We don't have any data to support this yet but just from clinical observation we've had fewer complaints from families about their child or their husband or wife getting "picked on" by the therapist. There's more of an atmosphere of cooperation and utilization between the therapist and the family, and the offender and the victim, to help this family come together. When we do experience resistance, we always go back to the family and say, "We're here for the same reason you are, we want your family to get back together if you so choose, and we want the person in the family who has caused the pain to not cause pain to anybody anymore," and then the family works with us more than ever. They see us as much more helpful than they did in the past.

I also think in the past they saw us as quasi-court service officers, quasi-attorney, quasi-judge, and so on. With this model we've taken ourselves out of that. I think it's just made us more open for clients to do the changes that they need to do. The current state-of-the-art literature says that you have to connect with that client, and that client must trust you enough to listen to what you say, and then must change their thoughts and feelings. You can't beat therapy into them, you can't trick them into it, you have to help guide them down this path and this approach does that through its emphasis on personal influence and utilization, whether you do it individually or you use the whole family. And when you have success or you see cases closing appropriately instead of people dropping out of therapy, then the therapists feel better about what they do, and then the clients feel better too. And if they come up with problems in the future, they're more apt to give us a call or to give somebody a call and go back into therapy.

BARNUM: What has been the long-term impact of this approach on your program?

LAFLEN: We now use this model with people who physically abuse their children and have been referred to us through criminal court. Also, with anybody we get here we are very attentive to contextual change. We're always going to say, "where's the family," whatever the problem is, whether it's a violent offender case or not. And we bring the whole family in and we ask for their help and we bring in the father and so on. We actively seek non-participating parents. That's been a really huge change for us. And we'll have an involved parent tell us that the other parent is not available, and we'll say "thank you very much, but we really want to call them and see if they'll at least come in and talk to us." The idea of not having them come in is kind of funny now. I can't stress that enough. I think that, in and of itself, is so healing for these people, for the offender and the victims, because what was once a secret is no longer secret and no longer *allowed* to be secret in that family. I think that's very helpful. I think whenever you have the parents of an offender apologize it is very helpful to the victim and to the offender. Now we don't always get the non-offending parents on their knees, and I know Madanes and your group wouldn't like that, but we just sometimes don't do that. We've learned in consultation and with 3 1/2 years of experience that it's very much a call by that supervisor at that moment. But even with the parent apologizing to the victim in front of that offender, in any form, it is helpful. The idea of reparation is also very helpful, because it gives the offender that bigger picture that he has harmed other people, has harmed his community, and that now he has to pay back, to repair what he has done. I think those are the curative things that we've seen.

BARNUM: One area we've found to be of key importance in developing the model is having the involvement and support of the community. You've already mentioned that in terms of the natural community. But how did you get the court, CPS, and other agencies behind this project, especially when it was such a radical departure from what they were familiar with?

LAFLEN: First of all, this program has been here for 20 some years so there's a connection to the court, and they trust us. So that relationship was already there. When we started this project, we invited a court service worker to come to the initial training. That was sometimes helpful and sometimes not helpful, but we started with that. But what has really worked is including them in the process. Whenever we have an apology session, we ask the family if its okay if their probation officer or court services officer sits behind the mirror and watches the process. Then they're able to watch that process and they're able to see how that has been helpful to their client. They see it first hand. Moreover, they're able to see how the client is held responsible by that process. So the live supervision has been very helpful in allowing them to watch the therapy as it is evolving. To be honest with you, that's been our biggest asset and the fact that our court system does trust us. At this point, there's really no question from the courts or CPS about what we're doing with the family.

BARNUM: That's an interesting modification to not only involve more people in the session, but to involve observers like the court or CPS, who also have a stake in the process.

LAFLEN: Yeah. It's like the live supervision room is an intervention in and of itself. Of course, if there is a third party like an attorney or something we have to tell them, so that actually becomes part of the process. And it has been very helpful in getting the offenders to go along with this process if we've had resistance from them in the session.

Another of the changes we've done here is that we go for more of a team perspective. If we have an offender who is having a problem in treatment, they come and visit with their whole treatment team. And the offender knows that those folks are probably sitting behind that mirror and at any time if he doesn't cooperate with treatment, we can refer him back to court services. And so that mirror has been very helpful to get some of them to go along with this process. I think it is just working one on one with the community people and explaining what we're doing and letting them see what we're doing.

BARNUM: Has this made it easier to bring victims and offenders together for apology and reparation?

LAFLEN: Yes, definitely. Because we don't have the problems some places do. When I go out and do training, a lot of those people are asking, "What if you can't get that probation officer to release the no-contact order?" It's actually written into our probation contracts here, that the PO will respect the therapist's opinion about supervised contact with the victim. So really that has been transferred more to the therapists than the probation officers. They don't question us. Now we just let them know that we are going to have an apology session and we don't have that resistance of "no you can't do that, it's against the rules."

BARNUM: So the court has accepted the model.

LAFLEN: Oh very much so. Very much so.

BARNUM: As you mentioned, it's commonly talked about as a paradigm shift, from a retributive form of justice to a restorative form, the idea that maybe somehow the system can give something back rather than just take things away.

LAFLEN: Yeah, absolutely.

BARNUM: What other modifications have emerged and how did they come about?

LAFLEN: We also used the approach when we don't even have a victim. We bring in the offender's family and he apologizes to the family for shaming them, for bringing the family name into the court system. And we have it down now so we get through the entire apology in about two sessions. Generally, we get to the issue of reparation in the first session. Then they come back. Before, it took us three sessions to get through the whole apology—or 2 hours a session. I think we've become a little more efficient with the model.

One of the interesting things that we did, that I don't think we would have done without this model in place, is ask an offender to tape record his apology process and then sign releases so we can share it with the nonoffending parents of children who've been sexually abused by someone else and also to train people. That was part of his reparation. Without this model, we would have never done that. In another case, the family came up with the reparation of having the teenager make a videotape for us on the topic of why he stayed in denial so long and what it took for him to get out of denial. He basically said, "I've been there, here it is. You may want to make a different decision at this point in treatment because I ended up in a correctional facility where hopefully you won't, because you'll make a different decision than I did." And that was the family's idea, and they released it to show to kids and families who come for treatment.

BARNUM: From our experience, everyone will want to know how soon you attempt to do the apology?

LAFLEN: Three to 6 months after they've started treatment here. The sooner the better, but only when everybody is ready. If they go past 6 months, we begin to question the therapists about why we haven't had the apology yet. So it is really 3 to 6 months into the treatment.

BARNUM: One of the things we've borrowed from you is that you have the offender tell the victim that there are certain times and situations in which the offender can't be trusted.

LAFLEN: Oh yeah, absolutely. I forgot to mention that. That's a major one. We have them tell the victim that there are times and situations in which she can never trust the offender again.

BARNUM: How did that evolve? It makes a lot of sense, but how did it emerge?

LAFLEN: That is actually part of the old apology process that we used to do with the letters. In the letters it was very clear that the offender says to the victim "don't trust me any more, because I may do this in some situation." That is how that came about. Also, we're really big on how they kneel. They have to be on their knees, and they have to have a straight back and so on.

BARNUM: You've done quite a bit of innovative work with substitute apologies, even having substitute victims for the offender to apologize to when you can't include the actual victim. We've never dared to try this. How has it worked out?

LAFLEN: They seem to work fine. Especially with an offender, if you can get a family member to come in and take the victim's place. We still get the same emotion and we still get the same closure for the offender and family member. If you were to see the videotapes of one where we did it that way and one where we had an actual victim sitting in, you wouldn't be able to tell by the affect. It works very well because what they are doing is apologizing for what they did and on behalf of the substitute victim's offender. And the substitute is hearing it as a victim herself, and she's hearing her own offender apologizing to her. Yeah, I think it works. That is one thing I like about this model, it works really well in a lot of different situations. It is also very culturally sensitive and I like that, too.

BARNUM: Yes, and there is the flexibility in using it to bring in anyone from the community who needs to be there, especially the inclusion of whatever religious leaders are important to the family. What a profound image that is to have all those influences there in one setting. Sometimes it's the great-great-grandma that just needs to be present to be an influence.

LAFLEN: Absolutely, and what we find is that there are certain people that get invited that are the ones that the offender most needs to do the apology to in order for it to be most meaningful. They are often the last to be invited or folks you wouldn't expect. This summer we had a mom and dad with an adolescent offender, and we brought in grandma and an aunt and uncle. He wanted them to be there. This was a case with an outside victim, and she wasn't there because we couldn't get her to come in. Well, he did his apology to mom first and then to dad and to grandma. Then he went to the aunt and uncle and he apologized to them as a unit—and that was the hardest apology for him to do. And we predicted that it would be this way, because when we watched the family the aunt and uncle brought up the issue of shame saying, "You really disappointed us. We're angry with you but we still love you." They were the ones who really said that to the kid. And so when he got to their apology that's where he was able to get more into his affect and to show some really soft feelings about what he had done. So it's interesting that those family members we wouldn't have invited in the old model are the ones that are sometimes the most important to come in because they really represent that community. It's harder sometimes for the offender to apologize to them.

BARNUM: It's interesting. More than anyone else that we know of you even work with fixated offenders using acts of reparation. That's been very innovative in this approach and revolutionary in the larger offender-therapy world. Could you describe some of these interventions?

LAFLEN: Absolutely. My caseload always had those kinds of guys on it, because I like those really tough cases. I like working with pedophiles. I had a guy with literally a thousand victims and had been through tons of therapy and such, and a part of his reparation was to go down and to ring the bell for the Salvation Army. Of course, he had to do it in an area and at a time where there were no kids. There was a specific area we had here that we knew was safe. He had to do it out in the cold. He couldn't do it inside. But we always try to make sure the reparations are not retributive in any way to anybody. With this guy I said, "When you ring the bell you should ring it at least a thousand times for every victim that you had and when you do you need to think about that. That these are the people that you've harmed and caused pain for."

Another one we actually had to take to the administration to get approval for. The offender would landscape for the agency. We're a nonprofit, but I was a little concerned about a dual relationship here. But the administration felt that it was fine because really the offender felt like he was paying back to the center for what he had gotten here and also to the victims who come to the center, that they would have a nice place to come to and feel comfortable. Of course, we were careful in timing this and supervising it so no children were exposed to him. So that's been one of the closest ones to the line, just because of the dual relationship. But we went through channels and everyone felt it was fine.

BARNUM: With fixated offenders or pedophiles, it sounds like you're doing more global reparation to the community at large, paying back to the spiritual system as a whole.

LAFLEN: Yes, absolutely. And we love using churches for that, also. We've had some where if the clients can't come up with a reparation themselves, we can always find a church and communicate with that church and let the offender come in and clean or paint, doing something to give back to the community. It works really well with some of our guys who are spiritually connected, and it helps them in giving something back. We are always careful when we set up these "outside" reparations. We have releases signed, we bring the recipients into a session, we explain to them what this person has done and the dangers of having this person around children, the whole 9 yards. Then we talk with the offender about it. We say, "This is in the spirit of repairing for this community and for you building your relationship back into the community as a whole." It's not like community services in which you say, "Okay, you're going to go clean someone's yard and you're going to be done with your reparations." We want to connect it to their spiritual being. I have one who we decided had to take special time with his grandmother whom he had neglected for years and had caused pain to her. I think he had to do 3 hours a week sitting and visiting with her and helping her around the house.

BARNUM: And it's different in this situation than with a related child-victim in which the offender produces something to enhance her future, like a college fund or something. It's about behaving in a more community-conscious manner.

LAFLEN: Absolutely. Absolutely. And the other rule when we talk with the recipients, we ask that they not thank the offender for the act. Because that's not why you do it, for a "thank you." You do that because it is the right thing to do.

BARNUM: What do you see as curative in the act of reparation?

LAFLEN: Connecting them. Well, if they are able to do the reparation to their victim, it is honoring that victim and actually helping that victim in a way that gives back what the offender has taken. And also for the victim it is a way of getting some . . . relief in some way for the stress that has been caused them. For the victim, I think this reparation is happening for them, and also it lets the other family members know that this offender truly is sorry for what he did to them, and is willing to act on that sorrow. Of course, there is a balance we have to weigh out. We have to be clear that they aren't making that victim special anymore, as they did when abusing her. It's because of the damage that was done that we have to start repairing this relationship.

To be frank, most of our reparations are geared toward the family if we have the victim and offender in the same family. We really try not to single the victim out. I know that's not consistent with some of the earlier thinking. Like a year ago we had a father who molested his daughter. He was out of the home and she had been outplaced, but then reintegrated. There were siblings in the family. The family hadn't been on a vacation. We couldn't think of reparation, and the daughter really didn't want anything. So the offender sent the whole family on vacation as a way of saying "well I'm going to start repairing this." He didn't go, of course. But he sent them on vacation to get away from the stress of what they had been through and to help build that unit together. So that's one example.

BARNUM: So there is a piece of it that would be reparation to the individual girl in that you are giving her back her family through this process.

LAFLEN: Yeah. Exactly. We use a lot of metaphor in our reparations. Because, you know, that was one of the big resistances to some of the therapists, that this not be a pay-off to the victim. We had another father/daughter incest case where she was a very religious young person, and she wanted an opportunity to go to church camp. They couldn't in the past, and so he made that possible for her and it was done in the spirit of reparation. We thought that was very appropriate, because that connected her back even more strongly to her religious beliefs. It also gave her an opportunity to use that time to reflect upon her own healing and growth. We don't accept just anything as reparation. We try to be really careful and think them through.

BARNUM: There is elegance in finding a symbol that carries meaning. Sometimes the traditional college fund doesn't quite do that.

LAFLEN: Absolutely. Actually, we stay away from that money thing. And that is also a political thing for us, too. Our court does not look as kindly upon reparation that is monetary as one that is experiential.

CASE EXAMPLES

BARNUM: What sorts of cases have been the most difficult for you to treat with this model?

LAFLEN: I can tell you that easily. The biggest problems we have faced with this model is when we waited too long for the apology. You may have for some reason a therapist that is too connected with that offender, and he just can't get him to get that apology done. We just had an example of that where it was a victim outside the family. The therapist waited until 3 months before discharge for him to do an apology to his wife and daughter, and we did it and it was very strained. Because what happened was that the family had already done their own apology without us and we were asking them to bring it all up again. The daughter and mother were very angry about having to come in for that session. And they took out their anger on the therapist. Of course, the offender was about to leave therapy so he was very appropriate in the whole thing, but that is one case where it just didn't work. It's in the timing. If you wait too long you have problems. Now if you go too early, I've found that it doesn't stick. So it is really timing it with that victim's treatment and that offender's treatment.

BARNUM: Describe some of your greatest successes with the model.

LAFLEN: It's hard to find one success because we've had so many, in that we've brought the families together. And we've had the apology session and then the family was able to make better decisions about whether they were going to stay together or not. So those are easy to come up with. I'm trying to think of just one good one to talk about.

There was a fairly recent case that is interesting because the family sought treatment before the court forced them to and they are still in the process of trying to get some resolution in court, even as we've had them for over a year now. It is a very good case to talk about because a year ago we had the offender in treatment here and the mom and the victims at another agency that took a Christian-based approach to therapy, which they saw as fitting their values.

So we do the polygraph and plethysmograph, the standard protocol on this offender, and his spouse, who was the mother of the victims, comes in and says, "You're mistreating my husband, etc. etc. How dare you, how dare you." So, we tried to explain to her why we have all these rules and such and really what our mission is here, but she was very resistant and would not participate. So we invited her anyhow and asked her to at least allow her children to be a part of the apology and the reparation process, and we even offered to work with the therapists at the other agency. We just really didn't get into an argument with her but were just more reflective about her feelings and utilized them in our responses. We were telling her that we understood and we wanted to help her family get back together if that is what she chose. She still left, saying, "You all are crazy and I don't want anything to do with you."

So she went back to her therapist, and at that time I don't think she even signed releases for us to visit with that agency, but pretty soon we got a call back from her and she says, "I'd like to maybe try that mom's group you mentioned. Is it okay if I try that mom's group, but I stay with my therapist here?" We were fine with that and invited her to come over, whereas 4 years ago we would have said, "No you have to have your therapist here or we won't let you in the group."

So she came to mom's group and stayed with her therapist and pretty soon in mom's group she said, "I'd like to have my therapy over here now." We said, "It's okay if you stay with your therapist, we don't want to interrupt that." But she insists. So we begin apology work and to make a long story short, the victims' therapist came over with them to do the session, and we had the whole family here and so she was able to come to see that we were helping her husband and wanting to help her family resolve their relationship with her husband. And eventually she moved the entire family over here for therapy, because she saw the way we did family therapy here was moving this process along. Over there they didn't know how to deal with the offender, how to incorporate him into a family therapy model, just as we didn't in past years. That's one of our better success stories of helping a family who has chosen to remain together safely through this process of apology and reparation. It is also an example of a family that is ahead of the legal system with this.

One that wasn't successful in the beginning but has a good ending is an adolescent offender with young victims outside the family. He was in denial, said he didn't do it. We brought dad and mom in and did live supervision and tried to do utilization with them to come along in this model and to think about helping him own up. But they stayed stuck. And they did not respond to anything, absolutely nothing. They were in complete denial as a family. The child ended up in a correctional facility and did his work up there and came back and owned up to what he did. Then the family reinvolved themselves in the process, and we did the apology. So we have a mother who, 2 years ago, was saying we were crazy and how could we accuse her son of this, later facing her son who was now admitting what he'd done but refusing to get on his knees. So she gets on her knees of her own choice, and says, "This is how you do it. If I can do this, you can do this." And he did and the apology went very well. The kid is in a group home right now, but is going home very soon because now we have supportive parents.

BARNUM: What about failures?

LAFLEN: I remember one apology that was not very successful at all. We had stepparents and it was an adolescent offending small children in the family. Part of the family lived something like 10 hours from here. And they all came down, and we were going to do this session, and we really didn't time it right, nor did we spend enough time with the family members who came from far away or working with the two separate families beforehand. And we started the session and before we were done one mother almost punched the other one, literally. And the therapist had to get in the middle of it. We learned we should have spent more time understanding the jealousy that was still in the family between the ex-spouses. We rushed the kids out, and we did some work with the two families, and they came in the next day and went though the apology process. So even that turned out okay, but we had to rethink the whole situation and adjust in a hurry.

CONCLUSION: A PROGRAM CHANGED

BARNUM: You've mentioned that you've undertaken research on this approach as a part of a larger project examining the entire program. Can you describe that research?

LAFLEN: That's an interesting project. What the researchers have done is to come in and look at historical cases from before 1997 when we started this approach. And they've collected this data on several dimensions of the victim's functioning, the offender's functioning, the nonoffending parent's functioning, and all the family members. What we're doing now is that they are coming back to review charts that have been closed since we started this process. They are going to compare the two groups on these different dimensions. So, like on victim functioning, I think it is education level attained, trauma level, etc., and they'll compare the old model and new model for differences.

Preliminarily, we've seen some differences in dealing with the denial process. We just got the data from the old cases (pre-1997) and we actually had some clients finishing the program in denial. With this model, after 8 weeks of treatment we have about 93% of our clients owning up to the offense they've been charged with. Now if we just examine those who enter in complete denial despite legal charges and we look at them in 8 weeks, even 80% of them are owning up. Overall, I think we've found that we're moving people through this process a lot faster, and we're also able to better look at who we can treat and who we can't treat.

BARNUM: What would you have done differently in implementing this program?

LAFLEN: I think I would have tried to do a little more process with the staff around the issue of where we want to go. I'd have asked, "What do you all think?" "What's good about it, what's not good?" "What are your fears?" Maybe spend a little more time preparing rather than saying "This is what we're going to do, and we're going to order the books, and you're going to have something to read." So probably now, I'd be a little more strategic myself in how to get them involved in the process.

BARNUM: It is really exciting to see how you've done this, implementing a whole different idea of how to think and do therapy. I'm doing that now, and the only reason I felt I could do it was because I have a group of young, new therapists who were looking for a mentor. To hear you tell a story about having to do that successfully with existing staff and bring about good outcomes, good connections in the community, and a sense of creating a stable program that responds well to that community's needs and works, that is exciting and all too rare.

CHAPTER 13

Epilogue

> A man was walking along the beach after a tropical storm. He came upon a native who was feverishly picking starfish up off the sand and pitching them back into the sea.
>
> "Why are you doing this?" asked the man.
>
> "The starfish cannot live without the sea," said the native.
>
> "But there must be a thousand starfish along this beach, and there must be a thousand beaches like this one, each with a thousand starfish. You are just one man. How can you expect to make a difference?"
>
> The native did not break his rhythm as he reached down, picked up another starfish, and pitched it back into the sea.
>
> "Made a difference to that one," he said.
>
> —Adapted from Loren C. Eiseley (1978)

Three years, 5 months, and 16 days from the date of our first session, September aged out of the child protective system and moved in with her boyfriend, Sonny—the typical independent living plan for the majority of girls leaving custody. Atypically, however, was the fact that this scheme actually worked as a tentative step into adulthood. The state offered little else, and what they did have for 18-year-olds, September neither wanted nor trusted. At some point Hanna had applied for and received Social Security disability reimbursement for September, based on her psychiatric hospital diagnosis. A few weeks after her 18th birthday September she was called to report to the Social Security office to have her Social Security check made out to her instead of the state.

September declined. "I don't think I'll be needing that," she told the stunned agent.

The young woman took me up on my invitation to continue her therapeutic journey, and consistent with the *Good Will Hunting* approach discussed earlier, I have continued to see her over the years as needed in therapy. Sometimes we have gone months between sessions, at times I see her weekly. However, we have never returned to the dark days of her adolescence, and aside from occasional bouts of recurrent depression and insomnia, little has emerged that could be considered a serious emotional or psychological problem, quite a state of affairs for a girl deemed by her psychiatrists a few years earlier as "manipulative," "hopelessly borderline," "chronically manic-depressive," and a willing recipient of her father's sexual advances. Condemned to a prognosis of heavily medicated mental illness, September has taken great delight in proving them wrong.

Desperate for freedom, September nevertheless struggled a great deal with independence. In fact, Sonny spent a fair amount of time in conference with me expressing just how much he felt oppressed by September's dependency. Working together, we were able to get her through her driving test, into a good factory job, and later into a position at a daycare center, which was more to her liking. Though the relationship with Sonny ultimately ended, as do most relationships in late adolescence, he was a very nice young man and was irreplaceable in helping September get on her feet. We speak highly of him now that she no longer grieves his loss.

The following year, she became involved with Jeff, a man in a neighboring city. They moved in together a bit too soon and over the next 3 years had 2 children together. The second of these had a severe and debilitating medical condition, which nearly broke September's well-worn heart. Jeff called me to the hospital in the middle of the night explaining as best he could what was going on. When I arrived, September tearfully explained the seriousness of the baby's condition before asking me the question I had been dreading all the way into the city.

"After all I've been through," she wept. "With everything that happened to me in the system and with my family . . . why did this have to happen to me? Why me?"

I had been working on an adequate answer to that question for the entire commute but it was not until I looked into September's swollen eyes and saw the pain in Jeff's face that I knew the answer. "Because," I said gently, "with everything you've been through, you are the only person I know who could handle it."

This proved far more than an encouraging reframe in the years hence and quite an accurate prediction of how September would parent a disabled child. Despite all the odds against her, she has not only been a good mother to both children, she has found a job helping other children, just as she had said she would. Ultimately, she has also reached a healthy accord with her father and Barb, and I am pleased to say that Tommy has done an exceptional job of providing reparation, even though his treatment program made no such requirement of him nor did it even suggest he apologize. Fortunately, the phone session that stirred so much unnecessary controversy appears to have been sufficient for September in this regard. That point is underscored by the fact that she and I watched the tape over and over again in therapy for many months before she was exiled to the detention home and after she returned. It became a symbol of Tommy's sorrow and love for his daughter, and when she turned 18 I presented her with a copy, which she keeps safe and available if she should need it. Her relationship with Mattie has been on and off again, based largely on her mother's concomitant state of sobriety.

As for the other cases in this book, Bobbi and her sisters struggled with school but they avoided further pregnancies—a concern we all shared with CPS. We lost track of the family about a year after the case was reunified, but they were doing well at the time, working as a team to raise Zach. I met up with Cassie's supervisor at court a few days after the case closed, and she expressed great appreciation for the work we had done with the family. It was both pleasing and a bit of a surprise.

Justin worked with Greg for several years after the apology and was doing well when his case finally ended. A pleasant surprise to everyone, Gwen remained substance free throughout her second recovery phase. In an interesting aside, Justin offered tremendous help in providing "co-therapy" with Greg in the later treatment of his younger brother, who was even more intelligent than Justin and a bit feistier.

Because I left the agency about 6 months after the Larson family's apology, I have very little follow-up on Leia's family. Laird remained out of the picture, and Debbie never reunited with him.

Bruce Laflen left the Kansas City sex offender treatment program shortly after the interview and moved to Florida where he worked with offenders and the mentally ill in a climate more to his liking. While they met with some resistance from their colleagues in the field, his staff supported the contrition model before and after he left. In fact, in 2001 the agency contacted me for a refresher course, including four staff from the original core group. They were uniform in the view that the model had made them better therapists and their program more effective and efficient. During the training, they offered numerous case examples to prove it. Unfortunately, as with so many innovative success stories, this one does not end on a happy note. Due to budget cuts and a change of agency priorities toward case management of the mentally ill, the nationally recognized program was first downsized and eventually was eliminated.

By far the most striking trend my colleagues and I have faced, in the years since these cases were compiled, is the systemic changes suggested by Wexler (1995) and others and enacted in the late 1990s in various jurisdictions including our own. For years, we and other family advocates argued that a percentage of children were being taken without sufficient cause and being held in the system too long. In 2000, our own state government admitted there were in fact 1,200 children who simply didn't belong in custody. With budget cutbacks, welfare reform, and distrust of government winning elections, many states "discovered" foster care to be an expensive and inefficient proposition.

Two remedies for this predicament have emerged, both of which were at the top of Wexler's (1995) list of recommended improvements to the system. The more widely adopted trend was the movement of funding from foster care to family preservation, which when *correctly applied* did safely reduce the number of children entering custody. I consulted for a year with a private family preservation provider and learned a great deal in the process. The second trend, which is still edging onto the foster care scene, is a shift in incentive schemes to encourage efficient reunification and discourage long-term custody. This typically includes privatizing the foster care system. Because each initiative greatly mitigated the central and at times oppressive power of CPS, we generally supported both strategies in theory and have been living with them in our own state of practice for 7 years now. However, though the data are far from complete, both family preservation and privatization of foster care have created their own problems when taken off paper and put in practice. As with most responses to social injustice, the pendulum at times swings a bit far in the opposite direction.

First of all, most of these changes were adopted by legislatures in the erroneous belief that they could cut costs by privatizing or downsizing services for children. Like managed care companies these lawmakers became concerned about cost effectiveness for all the wrong reasons. Where we saw injustice to families and children in a stagnant system, legislatures saw vast expenditures with poor outcomes. Where we saw systemic determinism, they saw big tax-and-spend government intruding on the private lives of the citizenry. Where we saw the need for CPS to reform itself in obligation to its wards, they saw an opportunity to shift the entire burden onto private charities, causing them to subsidize the state through private contributions. The entire process was never about enhancing families any more than the deinstitutionalization of the mentally ill was about helping them live more fully in the community. In each case, reform came into being in an attempt to save money, which is rarely in the purview of justice.

This point has been underscored over the last 7 years as we find our practice in a position I would never have imagined when working the cases in this book. Not infrequently, contingency reversal has caused us to advocate under oath that a child be taken into custody or kept there, even as we are opposed tooth and nail by a private foster care provider or family preservationist. This astounding reversal of fortune occurs because the contractor has a financial incentive for fulfilling a line item of its contract with the state. Just as Wexler urged, the state reinforces these agencies for getting children out of the system rather than encouraging a state bureaucracy to maintain itself by keeping them in. Though both family preservation and privatization have demonstrably lowered the number of children in foster care (from 220 to 80 in our home county alone), it is extremely important to note the problems this profit-based revision creates.

Simply put, neither the state bureaucracy nor the privatized one is motivated by beneficence, but instead acts out of self-preservation. And regardless of the individual staff, who may be quite benevolent themselves, a system that is designed around profit cannot reinforce anything else. Of course, the reunification of families and the enactment of justice is more cost-efficient than perpetual foster care; *however, efficiency and profit should never become any sort of motivating factor behind reunification.* When this happens, we simply trade the contamination of countertransference and state bureaucratic hegemony for that of profit and corporate hegemony. In doing so, we introduce a dangerous financial bias into a complex clinical process.

Some of these problems were mitigated in our state when the legislature ended the managed care contingency model in the third year of privatization, after it had produced ridiculous goals, disastrous outcomes, public backlash, the bankruptcy of one charity, the near bankruptcy and closure of another, and an expensive financial bailout. Without the profit motive at its core, the system has to some extent begun to work, largely because the private contractors are more responsive to concerns and changes essential to remain efficient and retain its contracts. These agencies are also more liable to civil action than was CPS.

In working in other jurisdictions and gaining knowledge about different systems and their idiosyncrasies, we have been afforded some diversity from what we have presented herein. In our favorite of these environments, we have found a cohesive team of like-minded professionals, particularly at the level of the court system. While that experience is a bit too contemporaneous to discuss comfortably in this book, we have for some time been involved with a skilled and venerable judge who runs a tight ship, a child-focused and humanistic state's attorney determined to see that children are properly served, a well-managed CASA system, and a professional and respected review board. Most important, we have allies in the private foster care system who have unusual skill at balancing child welfare and the bottom line. In fact, most players in this system have a family-friendly focus alongside a state mandate to reduce the number of children ill served in foster care. This leaves us practicing in a radically different world than the one described in these pages and one more in concert with our model. Even so, like the Kansas City project, our success in this jurisdiction has had more to do with the personalities and buy-in of key players and less with official rubric. Not infrequently, these allies have purchased our genuine cohesion at a significant price from the larger system by advocating for positions consistent with our model, even when that was professionally and politically difficult. I cannot tell how solid a foundation we have to continue this work before we become blacklisted by less tolerant forces. Despite our success at moving children to permanency over the course of our contract, we have worked with such systems long enough to know that any era of good feelings will pass like Camelot and well before we are ready to see it go.

In looking back over the cases in this book and in learning through teaching and consultation how much they parallel a great many across the country, I am both encouraged by our successes and disturbed at our difficulties in achieving them. Each victory seems like a small island in a surrounding riptide of chaos. So often we find ourselves swimming against that tide, hoping that our conceptualizations, interventions, and client families will prove stronger. Sometimes they do. Sometimes they don't. In consideration of this imprecise state of affairs, reflection and insight often fail and understanding becomes moot, leaving us to grapple with the same "why" and "who" questions that so preoccupy our clients. In the end, one can only go so far in understanding the inexplicable nature of family injustice, much less the injustices of the system intended to protect afflicted children. Beyond this, it has been more useful to consider Arendt's (1976) writings on the "banality of evil," as she made her own search for these same answers in a very different context.[1] Rather than spend their lives pursuing an understanding of something the essence of which is stupid and incomprehensible, we must help victims direct their energy toward reconciliation of injustice, thereby becoming ever more free of its bonds.

As self-utilization with more than one client at this crossroad of life I have recounted a conversation between my father and me early in my doctoral program and late in his final stages of leukemia. In my early studies of the children of abuse and neglect, I asked him a question that people of conscience have asked the wise for thousands of years: "Why do you suppose it is that that people who need each other as much as we do in this world hurt each other so badly?"

"I don't know," said the 35-year veteran of the ministry. "I guess that's the reason you are becoming a psychologist, so you can learn why. Then you can explain it to me."

In the years since his death, I have certainly learned a great deal about the injustice of families, systems, and societies. I have earned my Ph.D., studied with some of the masters of therapy, and lectured and consulted in several regions of the country. I have visited the former Soviet Union as a member of a medical ethics delegation, learning how psychiatry may become a formal method of social control, and I have toured the dungeons of the KGB. I have published papers on psychiatric seclusion and restraint, the treatment of abusive families, and the process and implications of mandatory child abuse reporting. I have watched the terror of 9-11 with my then 4-year-old, and visited the World Trade Center site with her 4 months later, transfixed by her need for closure. And of course I have spent many years in struggle with September and a few hundred cases like hers, hearing and seeing things so heart-rending that they leave me haunted, imaging I could never hear things worse. And yet I always do.

From all this and more I have learned just how badly we can hurt each other.

But I still don't know why.

NOTE

1. I am indebted to Cloé Madanes for this conceptualization.

References

Alighieri, D. (1971). *The divine comedy of Dante Alighieri. I: Inferno* (J. D Sinclair, Trans.). Rev. ed. London: Oxford University Press. (Original work published 1948).

Allison, D. (1992). *Bastard out of Carolina.* New York: Dutton.

American Heritage Dictionary of the English Language (2000), Fourth Edition. Boston: Houghton Mifflin.

American Psychiatric Association. (1994). *Diagnostic and statistical manual of mental disorders: DSM-IV.* 4th ed. Washington, DC: Author.

American Psychiatric Association. (2000). *Diagnostic and statistical manual of mental disorders: DSM-IV-TR.* 4th ed, text revision. Washington, DC: Author.

American Psychological Association. (2003, June 1). Ethical principles of psychologists and code of practice. Retrieved October 1, 2003, from http://www.apa.org/ethics/code2002.html

Anonymous. (1971). *Go ask Alice.* Englewood Cliffs, NJ: Prentice-Hall.

Anonymous, Connors, M., Fribourg, A., Gries, L., & Gonzales, M. (1998). Mental health services for children in out-of-home care. *Child Welfare 77,* 29–40.

Aponte, H. (1994). *Bread and spirit: Therapy with the new poor: Diversity of race, culture, and values.* New York: Norton.

Arendt, H. (1976). *Eichmann in Jerusalem: A report on the banality of evil.* Rev. ed. New York: Penguin.

Barth, R., & Blackwell, D. (1998). Death rates among California's foster care and former care populations. *Children and Youth Services Review, 20,* 577–604.

Bateson, M. C. (1991). *Our Own Metaphor.* Washington, D.C: Smithsonian Institution Press.

Bender, L. (Producer), Van Sant, G. (Director), Damon, M., & Affleck, B. (Writers) (1997). *Good Will Hunting* [Motion picture]. United States: Miramax.

Benedict, M., Zuravin, S., Brandt, D., & Abbey, H. (1994). Types and frequency of child maltreatment by family foster care providers in an urban population. *Child Abuse and Neglect, 18,* 577–585.

Birmaher, B. (1998). Should we use antidepressants for children and adolescents with depressive disorders? *Psychopharmacology Bulletin, 34,* 35–39.

Blome, W. (1997). What happens to foster kids: Educational experiences of a random sample of foster care youth and a matched group of non-foster care youth. *Child and Adolescent Social Work Journal, 14,* 41–53.

Boszormenyi-Nagi, I., & Spark, G. M. (1984). *Invisible loyalties: reciprocity in intergenerational therapy.* New York: Brunner/Mazel.

Bowen, M. (1978). *Family therapy in clinical practice.* Northvale, NJ: Jason Aronson.

Cook-Fong, S. (2000). The adult well-being of individuals reared in family foster care placements. *Child and Youth Care Forum, 29,* 7–25.

Crenshaw, W., & Barnum, D. (1996). *Apology and repentance: A general strategic model.* A workshop presented at the National Conference on Forgiveness in Clinical Practice, Baltimore, MD.

Crenshaw, W., & Cain, K. (1998). A couple's ordeal of sorrow. In L. Hecker & S. Deacon (Eds.), *The therapist's notebook: Homework, handouts, and activities for use in psychotherapy.* New York: Hayworth Press, pp. 113–118.

Crenshaw, W., & Tangari, G. (1998). The apology: Creating a bridge between remorse and forgiveness. *Family Therapy Newsletter* (November–December).

Cummings, R. (1966). *The philosophy of Jean-Paul Sartre.* New York: Vintage.

Darden, C. (1996). *In contempt.* New York: ReganBooks/Harper Collins.

Davis, N. Custer, K. Marcey, M., & Solarz, V. (1996). *Once upon a time: therapeutic stories that teach and heal.* Oxon Hill, MD: N. Davis.

Davis, N., Custer, K., & Solarz, V. (1990). *Once upon a time: the therapeutic stories to heal abused children.* Rev. ed. Oxon Hill, MD: Psychological Associates of Oxon Hill.

DeShazer, S., & Berg, I. (1988, September/October). Constructivism: What's in it for you? *Family Therapy Networker, 12,* 27–35.

DiGiulo, A. (Producer), Huston, A. (Director), Meredith, A. (Screenwriter) *Bastard Out of Carolina* [motion picture]. United States: Showtime and Gary Hoffman Productions.

Eiseley, L. C. (1978). *The star thrower.* New York: Harvest Books.

Emslie, G., Rush, A. J., Weinberg, A. W., Kowatch, R. A., Hughes, C. W., Carmody. T., & Rintelman, J. A double-blind, randomized placebo-controlled trial of fluoxetine in children and adolescents with depression. *Archives of General Psychiatry, 54,* 1031–1037.

Erickson, M. (1980). *The collected papers of Milton H. Erickson, Vol III: Hypnotic investigation of psychodymanic processes.* E. L. Rossi (Ed.) New York: Irvington.

Feldman, E. S. (Producer), Weir, P. (Director), Kelley, W., Wallace, E. W., & Wallace P. (Writers). (1985). *Witness* [Motion picture]. United States: Paramount.

Fish, V. (1993, July). Poststructuralism in family therapy: Interrogating the narrative/conversational mode. *Journal of Marital and Family Therapy, 19,* 223–232.

Frank, A. (1952). *The diary of a young girl.* Garden City, NY: Doubleday.

Frank, J. (1961). *Persuasion and healing: A comparative study of psychotherapy.* Baltimore: Johns Hopkins University Press.

Frankl, V. (1990). *Man's search for meaning.* Keynote address at the Evolution of Psychotherapy Conference, Anaheim, CA.

Freire, P. (1970). *Pedagogy of the oppressed* (M. B. Ramos, Trans.). New York: Seabury Press.

Freire, P. (1974). *Education for critical consciousness.* New York: Seabury Press.

Freire, P. (1998). *Pedagogy of freedom: Ethics, democracy, and civic courage.* Lanham, MD: Rowman & Littlefield.

Gardner, R. (1991). *Sex abuse hysteria: Salem witch trials revisited.* Cresskill, NJ: Creative Therapeutics.

Gillespie, J., Byrne, B., & Workman, L. (1995). An intensive reunification program for children in foster care. *Child and Adolescent Social Work Journal, 12,* 213–228.

Haley, J. (1984). *Ordeal therapy.* San Francisco: Jossey-Bass.

Haley, J. (1996). *Learning and teaching therapy.* New York: Guilford.

Haley, J. (1998). *Unbalancing a couple* [Video]. LaJolla, CA: Triangle Productions.

Henry, O. (1996). *The ransom of Red Chief and other stories.* New York: Gramercy Books.

Herman, D., Susser, E., & Struening, E. (1994). Childhood out-of-home care and current depressive symptoms among homeless adults. *American Journal of Public Health, 84,* 1849–1851.

Hubble, M., Duncan, B., & Miller, S. (1999). *The heart and soul of change.* Washington D.C.: American Psychological Association.

Isenberg, G. I. (Producer), Korty, K. (Director), Sparks, B., & Wiolett, E. M. (Writers). (1973). *Go ask Alice* [Motion picture]. United States: Metromedia Productions/ABC.

Irving, J. (1985). *The cider house rules: a novel.* New York: Morrow.

Kemp, C. H., Silverman, F. N., Steele, B. F., Droegemueller, W., & Silver, H. K. (1962). The battered child syndrome. *Journal of the American Medical Association, 17* (181), 17–24.

Kinney, J., Haapala, D., & Booth, C. (1991). *Keeping families together: The homebuilders model.* New York: deGruyter.

Lewis, R., Walton, E., & Fraser, M. (1995). Examining family reunification services: A process analysis of a successful experiment. *Research on Social Work Practice, 5,* 259–282.

The Lion King (1993). Walt Disney Home Video.

Lowry., L. (1993). *The giver.* Boston: Houghton Mifflin.

Madanes, C. (1991). *Strategic family therapy.* In A. Gutman & D. Kniskern (Eds.), *Handbook of family therapy, volume II* (pp. 396–416). New York: Brunner/Mazel.

Madanes, C. (1990). *Sex, love and violence: Strategies of transformation.* New York: Norton.

Madanes, C. (1993a). Strategic humanism. *Journal of Systemic Therapies, 12,* 69–76.

Madanes, C. (1993b). *Strategic/structural integration conference.* Bethesda, MD.

Madanes, C. (2000). *Evolution of psychotherapy.* Anaheim, CA.

Madanes, C., Keim, J. P., & Smelser, D. (1995). *The violence of men: New techniques for working with abusive families: A therapy of social action.* San Francisco: Jossey-Bass.

Mangine, S., Royse, D., Wiehe, V., & Nietzel, M. (1990). Homelessness among adults raised as foster children: A survey of drop-in center users. *Psychological Reports, 67,* 739–745.

McDonald, R., Allen, R., Westerfelt, A., & Piliavin, I. (1996). *Assessing the long-term effects of foster care: A research synthesis.* Washington, DC: Child Welfare League of America Press.

Memmi, A. (1965). *The colonizer and the colonized.* Boston: Beacon Press.

Microsoft Corporation. (1999). *Microsoft Encarta world English dictionary.* Author.

Millon, T. (1999) *Assessing adolescents with the MACI: Using the Millon adolescent clinical inventory.* New York: Wiley.

Miller, S., Duncan, B., & Hubble, M. (1997). *Escape from Babel: Toward a unifying language for psychotherapy practice.* New York: Norton.

Minuchin, P., Colapinto, J., & Minuchin, S, (1998). *Working with families of the poor.* New York: Guilford.

Nichols, M. (1984). *Family therapy: Concepts and methods.* Needham Heights, MA: Allyn and Bacon.

Nichols, M., & Schwartz, R. (1998). *Family therapy: Concepts and method.* Boston: Allyn and Bacon.

Polansky, N. (1978). Assessing adequacy of childcare: An urban scale. *Child Welfare,* 57, 443–448.

Pelzer, D. J. (1995). *A child called "it": One child's courage to survive.* Deerfield Beach, FL: Health Communications.

Pelzer, D. J. (1997). *A man called Dave: A story of triumph and forgiveness.* New York: Dutton/Plume.

Pelzer, D. J. (1999). *The lost boy: A foster child's search for the love of a family.* Deerfield Beach, FL: Health Communications.

Pilowsky, D. (1995). Psychopathology among children placed in family foster care. *Psychiatric Services, 46,* 906–910.

Price, J. A., & Keim, J. (1993). Introduction to Special Edition on Strategic Humanism. *Journal of Systemic Therapies, 12,* 1A–1B.

Random House Webster's unabridged dictionary (2nd ed.). (1998). New York: Random House.

Scott, B. (1994). *Out of control: Who's watching our child protection agencies?* Lafayette, LA: Huntington House.

Shaw, G. B. (1999). *Pygmalion.* New York: Bartleby.com. http://www.bartleby.com/138/ (Original work published 1916).

Simeon, J. G., Dinicola, V. F., Ferguson, H. B., & Copping, W. (1990). Adolescent depression: A placebo-controlled fluoxetine treatment study and follow-up. *Progress in Neuro-psychopharmacology and Biological Psychiatry, 14,* 791–795.

Smucker, K., Kauffman. J., & Ball, D. (1996). School-related problems of special education foster-care students with emotional or behavioral disorders: A comparison to other groups. *Journal of Emotional and Behavioral Disorders, 4,* 30–39.

Spencer, J., & Knudsen, D. (1992). Out-of-home maltreatment: An analysis of risk in various settings for children. *Children and Youth Services Review, 14*, 485–492.

Susser, E., Lin, S., Conover, S., & Struening, E. (1991). Childhood antecedents of homelessness in psychiatric patients. *American Journal of Psychiatry*, 148, 1026–1030.

Toth, J. (1997). *Orphans of the living: Stories of America's children in foster care.* New York: Simon & Schuster.

Truax, C. B. (1966). Reinforcement and nonreinforcement in Rogerian psychotherapy. *Journal of Abnormal Psychology*, 71, 1–9.

Vonnegut, K. (1966). *Mother night.* New York: Harper & Row.

Vonnegut, K. (1997). *Timequake.* New York: Putnam's.

Wexler, R. (1995). *Wounded innocents: The real victims of the war against child abuse.* Buffalo, NY: Prometheus.

Zehr, H., & Mika, H. (1997). *Fundamental concepts of restorative justice.* In *Restorative Justice On-Line Notebook.* Retrieved October 1, 2003, from U.S. Department of Justice Web site: http://www.ojp.usdoj.gov/nij/rest-just/ch1/fundamental.html

Zeig, J. K. (1992). *The evolution of psychotherapy: The second conference.* New York: Brunner/Mazel.

Index